ITALY

A Cultural Guide

ITALY

A Cultural Guide

ERNEST O. HAUSER

NEW YORK

Atheneum

MCMLXXXI

Maps By Cartografia Riccardi, Rome

*Several of the entries in this book first appeared,
in different form, in* Reader's Digest.

Library of Congress Cataloging in Publication Data

Hauser, Ernest O., 1910–
   Italy, a cultural guide.

   Bibliography: p.
   Includes index.
    1. Italy—Civilization. I. Title.
DG441.H38   945   81-65998
ISBN 0-689-11175-4   AACR2
ISBN 0-689-11233-5 (pbk.)

TO CARMEN

PREFATORY NOTE

———◆———

THE ITEMS I selected for this book range from early history to Italy's emergence as a modern nation. My choice was dominated by two considerations. There were the musts without which no such potpourri would have sufficient substance—the Divine Comedy, Humanism, Michelangelo, Bernini, Opera, the Etruscans, among others. But there were also non-obligatory subjects, some of which have fascinated me since my childhood, and which I now collected for sheer pleasure. Full of passion, blood, and treachery, such as the Cenci murder case and the adventures of Casanova, they make "good stories," and in their own way, they shed some light on Italy. This is no inventory of Italian culture. I am not a scholar, but a journalist. My purpose was both to enlighten and to entertain. The traveler, no matter how intelligent and curious, can hardly be expected to spend his time in Italy poring over learned books. This little guide, I hope, will make his visit more rewarding. If there is a strong emphasis on personalities—and even most of the "impersonal" entries lead to people—it is because of my belief that it is the individual that moves the world.

CONTENTS

vii

CONTENTS

Museums Mentioned in the Text

———————⋖◆⋗———————

Berlin West: Staatliche Museen Preussischer Kulturbesitz (Dahlem).
Boston, Massachusetts: Isabella Stewart Gardner Museum.
Chantilly: Musée Condé.
Detroit, Michigan: Institute of Art.
Dresden: Staatliche Kunstsammlungen, Gemäldegalerie.
Edinburgh: National Gallery of Scotland.
Ferrara: Palazzo di Schifanoia.
Florence: Galleria dell' Accademia.
    Galleria Palatina (Palazzo Pitti).
    Galleria degli Uffizi.
    Museo dell'Angelico (Convento di San Marco).
    Museo Mediceo (Palazzo Medici Riccardi).
    Musco Nazionale (Bargello).
    Museo dell'Opera del Duomo.
    Palazzo Vecchio (Palazzo della Signoria).
London (and surroundings): British Museum.
    Hampton Court Palace.
    National Gallery.
    Victoria and Albert Museum.
Mantua: Palazzo Ducale.
Madrid: Museo del Prado.
Modena: Palazzo dei Musei.
Milan: Castello Sforzesco.
    Pinacoteca di Brera.
Munich: Alte Pinakothek.
New York: Frick Collection.
    Metropolitan Museum of Art.
Naples: Galleria Nazionale di Capodimonte.
Oxford: Ashmolean Museum.
Palermo: Galleria Nazionale della Sicilia.
Paris: Musée du Louvre.
Rome: Accademia di San Luca.
    Galleria Colonna (Palazzo Colonna).
    Galleria Doria Pamphili (Palazzo Doria).

Museo e Galleria Borghese.
Museo Capitolino.
Museo Nazionale di Villa Giulia.
Musei e Gallerie Pontificie del Vaticano.
San Diego, California: San Diego Museum of Art.
Sansepolcro: Palazzo Comunale.
Siena: Museo dell'Opera Metropolitana.
Palazzo Pubblico.
Tarquinia: Museo Nazionale.
Urbino: Galleria Nazionale delle Marche (Palazzo Ducale).
Vienna: Kunsthistorisches Museum.
Venice: Galleria dell'Accademia.
Palazzo Ducale.
Palazzo Rezzonico, Museo del Settecento Veneziano
(Cà Rezzonico).
Washington, D.C.: National Gallery of Art.
Worcester, Massachusetts: Worcester Art Museum.

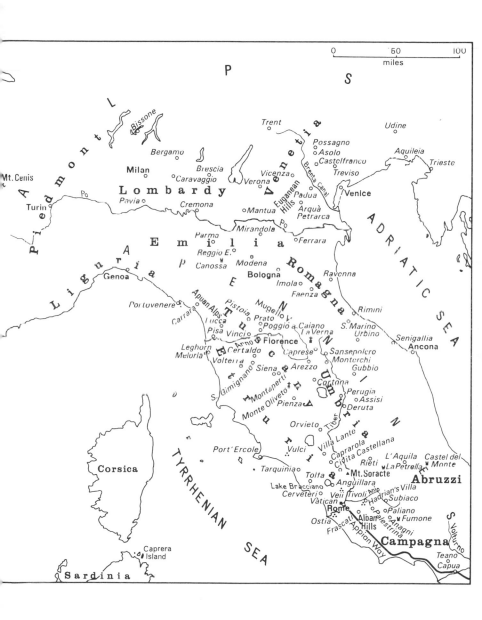

Rome

APENNINES

Troia

Volturno

Teano

Capua

Canosa

Trani

Bitonto

Bari

Ruvo

Apulia

Cumae

Naples

Vesuvius

Melfi

Appian Way

Brindisi

Herculaneum

Pompeii

Salerno

Taranto

Capri

Amalfi

Paestum

Calabria

Sybaris

Crathis

TYRRHENIAN   SEA

Croton

Messina

IONIAN

Segesta

Palermo

Cefalù

Aspromonte Mts.

Marsala

Calatafimi

Mt. Etna

SEA

Selinunte

Sicily

Agrigento

Gela

Syracuse

0   50   100

miles

ITALY

A Cultural Guide

ALBERTI, Leon Battista (1404–72). Architect, writer, sculptor, urbanist, playwright, poet, musician—the first of the great universal figures of the Renaissance. He was born in Genoa, the illegitimate son of a Florentine exile, and studied law and physics. His athletic exploits were remarkable. He could ride the wildest horse and toss a coin up to the vaulting of Florence cathedral. At Rome, in 1432, he worked on drafts of papal documents. Later he returned to the papal court to help Pope Nicholas V (1447–55) modernize the Eternal City by restoring ancient monuments, embellishing the Trevi Fountain, as it then was, and devising an urban plan that would accommodate the increased flow of traffic and provide a worthy setting for new buildings. He constantly enlarged his field of knowledge by questioning all kinds of people, including cobblers, about the secrets of their craft. He composed music, played the organ, drew portraits from memory, and wrote a Latin comedy that passed for a lost classical original. Among his writings are an essay on the ideal family. His treatises on painting—*Della pittura* (1436)—and architecture—*De re aedificatoria* (1452) —make him the chief theoretician of the Renaissance. He argued that simple geometric forms, like circle, square, and cube, are intrinsically beautiful, and that the proportions of a building should be based on mathematics to be perfect. As an architect, he limited himself to the design, letting others execute his projects. He probably produced no more than half-a-dozen structures (his connection with Rome's Palazzo Venezia, begun in 1455, is doubtful) and only two of them entirely; no more than three were completed in his lifetime. Yet, Alberti's influence is paramount. His own stylistic evolution over some three decades indicates his progress from the faithful use of classical elements —which he had studied in Rome—to the eclectic freedom of the Renaissance. Among the works he undertook for the Rucellai family in Florence are the portal and the upper part of the façade of S. Maria Novella, which masks the disproportion between the high central nave and the low side-aisles by way of two large marble scrolls—an ingenious innovation that quickly became commonplace. The palace he designed for the same family— which still inhabits it—was to become the model of the aristocratic town house; its elegant, subtly articulated street front shows Alberti's preference for pilasters over columns, whose roundness, he felt, clashed with the flatness of façades. Alberti's fame as a designer took him to Rimini, the Adriatic fief of Sigismondo Malatesta (1417–68), the hot-blooded descendant of a house immortalized by Dante. A man of humanistic culture, and a brilliant condottiere who had won his first victory at the age of thirteen, adventurous and utterly amoral (he once was sentenced in absentia by a papal court to death for heresy and murder, and burnt in effigy), Sigismondo was turning his small court into a center of the arts. He charged Alberti, in whom he saw, no doubt, a fellow-superman, with the ambitious project of designing a marble shell for Rimini's old Church of S. Francesco. The Veronese Matteo de' Pasti, best known for his portrait medallions, was responsible for the interior. Sigismondo had been married successively to an Este and a Sforza. When the latter, daughter of the great Francesco, was found strangled in 1448, he was already the lover of the beautiful Isotta degli Atti, whom he eventually married. Alberti's church was to enshrine their love. And though, as a result of Sigismondo's changing fortunes, it was never finished, the Tempio Malatestiano (Malatesta Temple) stands today a fitting memorial to Malatesta—and Albertian genius. Its front, Italy's first true Renaissance façade, is an imaginative variation on the theme of a Roman triumphal arch. The interior contains the tombs of Sigismondo and Isotta; and, everywhere there are their initials, an S pierced by an I. The cupola Alberti planned for it was never built. In 1459, he went to Mantua, ruled by the Gonzaga dynasty, where he designed the churches of S. Sebastiano and S. Andrea. The proportions governing the latter's airy, single-nave interior are repeated in its monumental front where tall pilasters recall the rigor of a Roman temple; the central arch stamps it as unmistakably Albertian. The ripest fruit of his maturity, designed shortly before his death, S. Andrea is a showpiece of the Renaissance. With Filippo Brunelleschi, his senior by twenty-seven years, Alberti set the pace for an age of furious building. But while the former was a doer, whose message is written in stone, Alberti was a thinker, whose structures, with their measured beauty, seem but illustrations of his theories. Ideas taking form behind his lofty forehead that topped a long, lean, classic countenance, were to guide the aesthetics of humanism.

———————⟨◆⟩———————

A M E R I C A . A continent named, in a roundabout way, after Amerigo (Lat. *Americus*) Vespucci (1451–1512), Florentine merchant and navigator, long a controversial figure. Scion of a distinguished line of public servants, he received a humanistic education, and entered the banking house of the Medici family. Late in 1491 or in 1492, the Medici sent him to join their ship-chandler's establishment in Seville, Spain, run by one Giannotto Berardi, who helped in the preparation of the first trans-Atlantic expedition of his Genoese compatriot, Christopher Columbus. Vespucci and Berardi later assisted Columbus in outfitting ships for his two subsequent journeys. That Vespucci knew Columbus is proved by a letter written by the latter to his son Diego in 1505, expressing friendly feelings toward Amerigo. After Berardi's death, Vespucci managed the Seville business. Having been granted Spanish citizenship in 1505, he became an officer in the powerful Casa de Contratación de las Indias, the govern-ment-run commercial agency for the West Indies. Three years later he was appointed *piloto mayor* ("chief navigator"), a job he held until his death. In this capacity he examined pilots, inter-viewed returning sea captains, and drew up the official maps of trans-Atlantic sea-lanes and of Spain's new territories. Vespucci himself shipped out on journeys of discovery. The most impor-tant and best documented of these journeys is an expedition of four ships commanded by Alonso de Ojeda in 1499. Leaving the flotilla on the American side of the Atlantic, Vespucci sailed southward and may have been the first to become cognizant of the mouth of the Amazon River. During his next expedition, made with Portuguese backing in 1501, he reached the River Plate. Doubts about his character stem from the existence of two different sets of his letters, both purporting to describe his expedi-tions, and full of inexplicable contradictions. One series lists two journeys; the other, four—the two additional ones describing discoveries as important as those made by Christopher Columbus. Did these two extra voyages actually take place, historians asked, or did Vespucci manipulate the facts in an attempt to steal Columbus's thunder? Ralph Waldo Emerson, in 1856, wrote: "Strange that broad America must wear the name of a thief! Amerigo Vespucci, the pickle dealer at Seville, who went out in 1499 . . . in an expedition that never sailed, managed in this lying world to supplant Columbus, and baptize half the earth with his own dishonest name!" Modern scholars tend to rehabilitate Vespucci, considering him an audacious navigator and explorer. Although the shadow of a doubt still mars his credibility, he certainly took part in expeditions that did sail, discovered the River Plate, and was greatly honored by the Spanish government. The crucial fact is that he was the first to realize that the new lands across the ocean were not, as Columbus thought, far shores of Asia, but a New World. It is for this reason that the German humanist, Martin Waldseemüller, in a set of maps published in 1507, bestowed the name "America" on the new continent. Though he limited the term to South America, others soon extended it to the entire hemisphere.

FRA ANGELICO, also known as *Beato* ("Blessed") Angelico (c. 1400–55). On the family tree of Florentine painters, the "Angelic Brother" has a branch all to himself. A Dominican friar, originally named Guido di Pietro, he painted in a sweet, devotional style, which earned him his gentle epithets. When, in 1436, his order received the Convent of S. Marco in Florence from Cosimo the Elder de' Medici, Angelico moved from his hillside convent to the house in town, which he proceeded to embellish with his paintings. S. Marco—where Savonarola later served as prior until his execution in 1498—is now the Angelico Museum. The one hundred-odd works by the master it contains range from the simple meditative frescoes in the friars' cells to complex altarpieces, including the poetic *Linaiuoli Triptych* (named for the linen-drapers who commissioned it), and a large *Crucifixion*. Among his masterpieces outside Italy are an *Annunciation* in the Prado and a *Coronation of the Virgin* in the Louvre. In 1447 he was called to Rome to decorate a tiny papal chapel with frescoes of St. Stephen and St. Lawrence. Far from being naive, as he may seem at first sight, Angelico was in full command of Renaissance sophistication, and had absorbed much of Masaccio's plastic force. But he was not a humanist. The wellspring of his art was faith—a faith that makes his angels seem messengers of God; his Virgins, blessed among women. His blues are the most transcendental colors ever summoned up by a mere mortal hand. Angelico could have no true followers. Still, one of his disciples, Benozzo Gozzoli (1420–97), disarms us with sheer beauty. His frescoes of the *Journey of the Magi* in Florence's Medici–Riccardi Palace, depicting a rich pageant of gentlemen and young ladies moving through an ideal Tuscan landscape, rank with the most delightful in the city.

AQUEDUCTS. "If anyone will consider the abundance of [Rome's] public supply of water," writes Pliny the Elder (A.D. 23–79) in his *Natural History*, "for baths, cisterns, ditches, houses, gardens, villas; and take into account the distance over which it travels, the arches reared, the mountains pierced, the valleys spanned—he will admit that there never was anything more marvelous in the whole world." Today, the sight of ruined aqueducts—rows of ivy-clad arches marching across the dry Campagna (the countryside verging on Rome), perhaps with browsing sheep added for picturesqueness—sends the romantic traveler into raptures. And though he sees only a few time-battered remnants of a once living system, they do convey the majesty of what was there. The aqueducts supplying ancient Rome with spring water from the surrounding mountains were miracles of engineering. Whether flowing through cement-lined, gently sloping tunnels, or lifted across plains and valleys on bridges of tall, stone-built arches, the water was protected from sun, dust, and insects, arriving at its destination as pure as it had sprung from the far hillside. Earliest Rome had depended for its water on the unsanitary Tiber and some local springs. The first aqueduct, no trace of which remains, was built in 312 B.C. by the censor Appius Claudius, who also built the Appian Way. Its length, nearly all of it underground, was 10.3 miles. The second, Anio Vetus (from the source of the small river, Anio), built forty years later, proved disappointing, its water being often murky. But the third, Aqua Marcia, built by the praetor Quintus Marcius in 144 B.C., proved a "gift of the gods," providing Rome with its coolest, most refreshing, drinking water. Of its fifty-six-mile course, a six-mile stretch rested on arches high enough to carry water to the top of the Capitoline Hill. The Aqua Virgo, so called because a little girl (*virgo*) had pointed out the hidden source to thirsty soldiers, was built in 19 B.C. by Augustus's son-in-law, Marcus Agrippa, to feed the baths he had presented to the people. Its water was the most agreeable for bathing, finicky Romans said. The noblest aqueducts, however, were the Aqua Claudia and the Anio Novus, both built by the mad emperor Caligula and finished by his successor Claudius in A.D. 52. Frontinus, the inspector of waterworks (c. A.D. 30–104) to whom we owe the basic book on aqueducts, calls the two structures "most magnificently made." Their drinking water was the best after that of the Marcia. The Claudia had as many as nine miles of arches, whose beautiful remains can still be seen a few miles south of Rome. The Novus, with a length of fifty-nine miles and a short stretch of 109-foot-high arches, was Rome's longest and highest aqueduct. Just outside the gates, the two grand fabrics merged to form a single bridge with two superimposed conduits. By A.D. 100, Rome's nine aqueducts (five more were added in the next two centuries) supplied the city and its suburbs with a daily flow of 58 million gallons: equal to the amount of water, it has been calculated, carried by a thirty-foot-wide, six-foot-deep river, moving at a speed of 1.7 miles per hour. Rome did require a huge quantity of water, not only for its citizens, but for its crowded public baths, its fountains, and its mock naval battles staged in flooded circuses. The waters coming in were caught in cisterns whence they were piped, via intermediate stations, to tanks installed in almost every house—

thought to be the first such service ever. History has not been kind to aqueducts. Whenever Rome was besieged, the enemy destroyed them to force a quick surrender. Polluted Tiber water was hawked in the streets during the Middle Ages. Some of the popes restored the ancient conduits, using portions of tracks that had remained in good repair. Nicholas V (1447–55) rebuilt the Aqua Virgo which was, for centuries to come, to feed the Trevi Fountain. Sixtus V (1585–90), whose given name was Felice, built the Aqua Felice, another reconstruction. Paul V (1605–21) combined old conduits into the Aqua Paola, for which he created the fountain, built in the form of a triumphal arch, on the wooded slope of the Janiculum. And Pope Pius IX (1846–78) revived the Aqua Marcia, whose waters once again delighted Romans with their freshness. None of the aqueducts now functioning make use of the old arches, but run entirely below the surface. One-half of Rome's daily supply of 400 million gallons is now brought in, by a modern conduit system, from the forest-covered mountains near Rieti, north of the capital. Any part of the total inflow may be channeled to any quarter of the city according to its need, so that the connoisseur no longer can be sure of tasting his or her favorite brand. And Rome's famous fountains, so long fed and identified with this or that renowned old aqueduct, are now recirculating their own water.

A R E T I N O , Pietro (1492–1556). Self-styled "Scourge of Princes," blackmailer, satirist, playwright, a dominant figure in Renaissance Italy. A gifted, often devastating writer, he mixed threats of exposure with flattery to secure the patronage of the high and mighty. Among his sponsors were the Medici popes, Leo X and Clement VII. The emperor Charles V, whom he had publicly slandered, paid him a handsome pension to keep him from doing it again, and, on passing through Verona province, invited him to ride on his right side, engaging him in amiable conversation. Charles's enemy, Francis I of France, paid Aretino double the emperor's pension and presented him with a heavy gold chain. "Truly, I am a terrible man," Aretino once confessed, "because kings and emperors give to me out of fear." His letters, of which six volumes are preserved, are journalistic in tone and frequently touch on politics. Enjoying wide circulation, they enabled him to spread insinuating rumors about those who wouldn't play. For years, he pestered Michelangelo, whom he called "Prince of Sculptors," for some rough sketches, "fit to be thrown into the fire," and, on receiving finally just that, revenged himself for being taken at his word by charging Michelangelo with "impiety"—a fearsome accusation. Having been stabbed in Rome after publishing some particularly caustic pasquinades, he settled in Venice, whose intellectual freedom served him well. There, from his comfortable house overlooking the Grand Canal, he watched the waterborne traffic—the fruit and vegetable boats, the boatmen hurling raw invective at one another, the fancy gondolas carrying richly dressed ladies. His ear for the broad language of the common folk helped him lard his writings with their speech and create robust characters. His five comedies (he also wrote one tragedy) and his best-known work, *Ragionamenti* ("Reasonings"), abound with crude phrases and obscenities. There is ample evidence that he respected humble poverty and had an open hand. Bursting with vitality, he lived a hedonistic, licentious life, savoring rich food and embracing a succession of easy ladies. He had two daughters, Adria and Austria, and doted on the pleasures of fatherhood. In Venice, he was much sought after for his charm and witty conversation. Titian, whose fame he constantly promoted, was his intimate friend. A brief message is preserved in which he invites the painter to dinner at his house—there'll be two pheasants, and his current mistress will do the honors. Titian portrayed his broad-chested, thicklipped, bearded friend in a defiant stance, regally dressed and wearing his gold chain (Florence, Pitti; there is another portrait by Titian of Aretino in the Frick Collection, New York). Not everyone treated him with respect. Tintoretto once pulled a pistol on him—"to measure him for a portrait." The English ambassador, whom he had charged with theft, had him beaten up. But Aretino was more loved than despised, and the Venetians called him *divino*. His unfulfilled ambition was to be named a cardinal. He died of apoplexy in a tavern, laughing, it is said, at an indecent joke.

BAROQUE ARCHITECTURE. The dramatic style spanning a period of some two hundred years—c. 1570–c. 1770—but finding its full expression in seventeenth-century Italy under the three-star constellation of Gian Lorenzo Bernini, Pietro da Cortona, and Francesco Borromini. The term, baroque, applied also to sculpture, painting, furniture, and music, is thought to be derived from the Portuguese *barroco,* an irregularly-shaped pearl. It appeared in English, via France, during the nineteenth century. Its original meaning was, on the whole, pejorative, suggesting something irregular, degenerate, absurd, bizarre—a product of bad taste. Baroque was admitted to respectability and recognized as an individual style succeeding the Renaissance (to whose classical discipline it may have been an emotional reaction), by the Swiss art historian, Heinrich Wölfflin (1864–1945), in his *Renaissance und Barock* (1888). Today, Baroque denotes an idiom based on classical conventions but striving for spectacular effects. Dynamic concepts edge out static forms. Curves are preferred to straights. Movement is beauty. Color and light conspire to create a scenic whole. Many baroque works—churches, palaces, fountains, even tombs—convey an impression of exuberance, giving free rein to fantasy and imagination. The Rome of the great seventeenth-century popes is its chief arena, reflecting, as it does, the genius and the virtuosity of Gian Lorenzo Bernini (1598–1680), whose extravagant creations, especially in the apse and crossing of St. Peter's, are the quintessence of the style. His performance is complemented by that of Pietro da Cortona (Pietro Berrettini, 1596–1669)—architect, painter, decorator—whose most eye-catching works in Rome are the façade and portico of S. Maria della Pace, a little jewel of baroque scenography; the elegant, convex façade of Ss. Luca e

Martina; and the cupola of S. Carlo al Corso. Cortona's festive gold-and-white stucco decorations in the grand-ducal apartments of the Medici in the Pitti Palace, Florence—a startling contrast to the general sobriety of that city—anticipate the hyperbolic style of France's "Sun King," Louis XIV. (Cortona submitted a project for the transformation of the Louvre in Paris, which, like Bernini's, was not executed.) The counterpoise to the sensuous side of the Baroque is represented by Bernini's sometime associate, Francesco Borromini (1599–1667), whose structures, such as the Church of the Four Fountains (S. Carlo alle Quattro Fontane) in Rome, are products of a reasoning mind. This "intellectual" Baroque is carried to extremes by Guarino Guarini (1624–83), a member of the Theatine Order and author of a treatise on geometry and mathematics, whose Chapel of the Holy Shroud (Capella della S. Sindone), Church of S. Lorenzo, and Palazzo Carignano, all in Turin, are masterpieces of calculated brio. Guarini and the Sicilian latecomer, Filippo Juvarra (1678–1736)—architect of the mountain sanctuary of Superga, the hunting lodge of Stupinigi, and the grand staircase and façade of the Palazzo Madama—turned Turin and its immediate surroundings into the north-Italian capital of the Baroque. Southern Italy and Sicily were highly receptive to the Baroque. Venice, which, like Florence, had resisted the style, nevertheless possesses one of its most famous monuments—the huge, octagonal, domed Church of S. Maria della Salute, built by Baldassare Longhena (1598–1682) to commemorate the city's delivery from a plague. Rising at the broad entrance to the Grand Canal, it welcomes the arriving sailor with a white splash of seaborne grandeur.

BASILICA. The word derives from the Greek, *basileus* ("king"); specifically from the Basilike Stoa, a public hall in ancient Athens, wherein the meaning of "royal" had changed to "public." In pagan Rome, from the second century B.C. onward, the term denoted a public building, such as a law court or commodity exchange, affording ample room for milling citizens. According to Richard Krautheimer, in his *Early Christian and Byzantine Architecture,* the shape of the structure varied, the most common type being an oblong, with or without aisles. An apse, or recess, which might be placed on any of the basilica's four sides, contained the seat of the magistrate or tribunal judging law suits or validating commercial contracts. Under the Empire, the interior of the hall was often richly decorated with gilt and marble. Ruined examples are Julius Caesar's Basilica Julia in Rome's Forum and, nearby, the three eighty-foot-high arches of the magnificently vaulted fourth-century Basilica of the emperor Maxentius. They stand as the last monuments of pagan splendor. Christians, who in earlier times had worshiped in private houses or modest community centers, began to rear basilicas after Constantine had granted their religion full legal status by the so-called Edict of Milan of 313. Most of these commodious churches were rectangular, timber-roofed halls, many of them with aisles divided from the nave by columns, and with an apse and altar at the far end, opposite the entrance. (Christian churches, as a rule, are "oriented," with the altar in the east and the main entrance in the west.) A typical example of an Early Christian basilica is S. Sabina on Rome's Aventine Hill, built between 422 and 432 (restored), which is illuminated by thirty-four large windows, and whose aisles are divided from the high nave by twenty-four columns of exquisite gray-streaked white marble from the island of Proconnesus in the Sea of Marmara. This standard form of the basilica (later equipped with a transept giving it the shape of a T or a cross) was used for Christian churches, off and on, for many centuries. "Basilica," however, is also an honorific title, bestowed by the pope upon a church regardless of its shape. A major basilica (none outside Rome) has a papal throne and altar, reserved for the pontiff or his delegate. Minor basilicas, scattered throughout Italy, take precedence over all other churches in the diocese, save the cathedral. Rome has four major basilicas—S. Pietro, S. Giovanni in Laterano, S. Paolo fuori le Mura, and S. Maria Maggiore; and three minor ones—S. Lorenzo fuori le Mura, S. Sebastiano, and S. Croce in Gerusalemme. Some of them were founded by the emperor Constantine, and all date back (not always in their present form) to the fourth and fifth centuries. Together, they constitute the "seven churches" normally visited by pilgrims.

BEMBO, Pietro (1470–1547). Venetian-born classicist, cardinal, and author—one of the dominant spirits of Italian humanism. His father, Bernardo—aristocrat, senator, statesman, collector of rare books—was known, among other things, for his fine penmanship. Young Pietro accompanied him on several diplomatic missions, and his first published work was a Latin dialogue between himself and his father. Greatly concerned with the development of the Italian language, Pietro actively promoted a Tuscan vernacular constructed along classical lines but purged of needless Latinisms. He based his own Italian prose on Dante, Petrarch, and Boccaccio. His discourse on Love, *Gli Asolani*—held among three ladies and three gentlemen in the luxuriant garden of Caterina Cornaro, queen of Cyprus, at Asolo near Venice—is dedicated to Lucrezia Borgia, whom Bembo is said to have courted. Having studied Greek in Messina under Constantine Lascaris, refugee scholar from Turkish-held Constantinople, he brought the manuscript of his teacher's Greek grammar back to Venice, where it became the first dated book (1495) printed by Aldo Manuzio. Aldo also published the *Asolani,* and Bembo edited Petrarch and Dante for him. As secretary to Pope Leo X, Bembo was known for the polished style of his official letters. In 1530, he was named historian of the Republic of Venice. His travels took him to many parts of Italy, and he was on friendly terms with virtually all the leading figures—scholars, artists, princes—of his age. His three portraits by Titian (Washington, D.C., National Gallery; San Diego, California, San Diego Museum of Art; Naples, Capodimonte) show a thinker's noble face, with deep-set, burning eyes, and a high forehead. By his common-law wife, Morosina, who died in 1535, Bembo had three children. In 1539, Paul III made him a cardinal. He died in Rome and was buried in S. Maria sopra

Minerva. His monument in S. Antonio at Padua is decorated
with his bust, distinguished by an extravagantly long beard.

BERNINI, Giovanni (Gian) Lorenzo (1598–1680).
Architect, sculptor, painter, theatrical producer. Known in his
time as the "greatest European," he almost single-handedly
created the Baroque, which dominated much of Europe's taste for
nearly two centuries. The son of a Florentine sculptor and a
Neapolitan mother, he was born in Naples, but grew up in
Rome, where his father worked for Pope Paul V (1605–21).
Rome is a storehouse of his works. Among them are the colon-
naded piazza in front of St. Peter's and, within, the Baldachin,
the Cathedra (St. Peter's Chair encased in ornamental decor),
and papal tombs; the recumbent statue of *St. Teresa*, showing
the Spanish mystic in religious ecstasy (S. Maria della Vittoria);
the Vatican's equestrian statue of *Constantine*, Rome's first Christian emperor, churches and palaces; and fountains that form
islands of enchantment in the city. In temperament, he was the
opposite of brooding Michelangelo. "When I start a new work,"
he said, "I feel as if I were entering a pleasure garden." His his-
trionics startled foreigners. He talked with his whole body,
laughed and wept, and, angered, poured forth market-place insults. His coal-black eyes, known to us from his self-portraits,
missed nothing. He sported a well-twirled mustache; sometimes,
a trim goatee. His charm was irresistible—both men and women
fell in love with him. A prodigy of nine, he was asked by Paul V
to draw the head of the Apostle Paul. Pleased with its quality,
the pontiff offered him as many gold pieces as his hands could
hold; they held a dozen. The pope then turned to Cardinal Maf-
feo Barberini—the future Pope Urban VIII (1623–44)—a
Florentine of taste, and asked him to look after the artistic training of this "new Michelangelo." For the next three years the boy
spent his time sketching the antique marbles of the papal collections, laying the solid classical foundation without which his

15

own lifework, and the whole of the Baroque, would make no sense. Paul's nephew, Scipio Borghese, gave him his first major assignment—a series of marble sculptures for his villa (Villa Borghese), among which are a young *David,* taking aim at an invisible Goliath; and a screaming *Daphne,* metamorphosing into a laurel tree to escape the embraces of Apollo. All of the figures are caught in rapid action, their muscles quivering—one more touch of the chisel, one feels, would have sent them bounding into space. Knighted by Pope Gregory XV (1621–23), he was known as "Chevalier Bernini." When Urban VIII ascended the papal throne, he told him, "We're fortunate in that Bernini lives in our papacy." Urban's first aim was to make St. Peter's the emblem of the Church Triumphant. Bernini labored for three years on the eighty-three-foot-high bronze Baldachin, with its four twisted columns, over the presumed tomb of the apostle. For all its hugeness, it looked graceful in the cavernous interior of the church. Pure chance, Bernini said; he had hit on the right size by guesswork. As architect of St. Peter's, a job in which Bramante, Raphael, and Michelangelo had preceded him, Bernini was cock of the walk in papal Rome. He had free access to the pope's private quarters, and often was the last to leave the dinner table, tiptoeing out when Urban had dozed off. After an ardent affair with a lady called Costanza, Bernini, forty, upon Urban's urging married Caterina Tezio, "prettiest girl in Rome." Of his eleven children, nine lived to grow up, among them a sculptor, a poet, and two nuns. Though he had an army of assistants, many of them foreigners, he planned every work himself and put the finishing touches on every sculpture. Profoundly religious, he practiced the Spiritual Exercises of St. Ignatius Loyola, read some pages of Thomas à Kempis's *Imitation of Christ* every night, and looked upon art as the flow of divine inspiration. He often worked for seven hours at a stretch, admired by apprentices for "never making a wrong stroke," and moving about the scaffolding in an apparent trance, with a studio hand standing by to keep him from stepping off the boards. He gained the favor of Urban's less colorful successor, Innocent X (1644–55), when he took him into the fenced-off area in Piazza Navona where he was finishing the Four Rivers Fountain, with its pierced rock, its armadillo, lion, horse, and palmtree. "You've just added ten years to my life," exclaimed the pontiff.

Bernini composed music, and produced his own plays in a small theater near his house. Fond of pranks, he once sent waves rolling toward the audience, which was about to panic when a sluice gate stopped the flood. When he had carved a bust of England's Charles I from a portrait by Van Dyck, Charles took a diamond ring from his finger and gave it to the sculptor's envoy "to adorn the hand that made this masterpiece." Louis XIV of France, jealous of Rome's splendor, wrote, "Signor Chevalier, my high regard for your merit makes me desire very much to see you, and know more closely a personage so illustrious . . ." Heading north by coach and litter, the artist drew such crowds at wayside stops that he compared himself to a traveling elephant. During his five-month stay in Paris, the sixty-seven-year-old visitor, from whom his host expected much, was treated like a head of state. He kept ministers waiting while he took his siesta. His comments made the rounds: French wines—too dear; French women—milk runs in their veins. The king practiced his poor Italian in meetings with his guest. Yet, in the end, the French adventure proved a failure. Unlike Austria, Germany, Poland, which welcomed the Baroque, France rejected it. Bernini's project to transform the Louvre into Europe's most sumptuous baroque palazzo, which had Louis's blessing, came to nothing, ostensibly because the court moved to Versailles. Bernini's marvelous equestrian statue of the king, changed by the French into the Roman hero Marcus Curtius, languishes in a forgotten corner of the Versailles gardens. Only Bernini's bust of Louis, cut directly from a block of marble in no more than thirteen sittings, and presenting him as the epitome of absolute power, has found a worthy niche in the Palace of Versailles. Bernini, back in Rome, wielded the chisel until he was eighty. The oval Piazza of St. Peter's, nearly 800 feet across, was his crowning achievement. He personally supervised the shaping of each of the 284 Doric travertine columns of the portico. The piazza is designed for crowds convened for papal blessings; and the two curving colonnades, Bernini said, "maternally embrace" both Christians and non-believers. Widowed, the master lived among his children and disciples. He credited his Neapolitan fare—a bit of meat, a glass of wine, and fruit—with his good health. Asked by a priest whether he was troubled by his sins, he smilingly replied that he was off to settle his account with Somebody who did not count in pennies. No artist after him was to enjoy the princely stature the world accorded to the chevalier Bernini.

BLUE. We live under blue skies, surrounded by blue seas. Yet, try to catch the blueness in your hand, and it is gone. The bulk of our planet is made up of browns, grays, yellows, reds, and greens. Perhaps because it is so evanescent, popular lore has long endowed the color blue with magic qualities. Blue stands for truth, chastity, divinity. Druidic priests wore blue. So did the Jewish high priest. And so did Odin, the one-eyed Nordic god of war and wisdom. The Virgin Mary (the "Blue Lady") is clothed in heavenly blue. How to get blue onto a paint brush was long a problem. Although antiquity knew a blue pigment, "Egyptian Blue," obtained by fusing copper silicates under great heat, the formula was lost during the Middle Ages, and painters had to work largely in "earth" colors—reds, yellows, browns, and greens. After the year 1000, when contacts between West and East increased, rumors—and, no doubt, specimens—of a blue stone mined in the depths of Asia arrived in Italy. Marco Polo (c. 1254–1324), on his way east, detoured to see the legendary mines in the snowbound headlands of the Kokcha River in Afghanistan, which then possessed a world monopoly of lapis lazuli ("azure stone") production. Soon, chunks of the "blue gold" were carried west along the ancient Silk Route by camel caravan, and shipped from Middle-Eastern ports to Venice. There, specially skilled craftsmen crushed the stone, removed the whitish streaks and specks of fool's gold (pyrites), and ground the pure blue particles into a fine powder called ultramarine ("from overseas") which sold at prices in excess of the then current gold price. Mixed with binding media, such as oil, it was used in fresco painting and on panels, canvases, and parchment. Some eighteen qualities of it were on the market during the Renaissance, and even the most prominent painters used the top grades almost exclusively for the Madonna's mantle, filling in less important areas with a diluted pigment, or with cheap azurite—a mineral paint that frequently turns green. The fifteenth-century painter Domenico Veneziano wrote to his patron, Piero de' Medici—father of Lorenzo the Magnificent—asking for an advance as he had an opportunity to buy some gold and lapis lazuli at reasonable prices. Vasari tells a story about Pietro Perugino (c. 1446–1523), the teacher of Raphael, who was commissioned to paint frescoes (lost) in the Convent of the Gesuati in Florence. Its prior was so niggardly with his ultramarine that he stood over the painter while he worked, clutching a little bag of the expensive powder and doling it out in minute quantities. "Oh, how much blue that wall is eating!" Perugino, saying nothing, frequently cleaned his brush in a bowl of water, then drained the bowl, and shamed the stingy prior by handing him the pure blue pigment remaining at the bottom. "This is yours, Father. And please learn to trust an honest man." Today, though lapis lazuli is also mined in Chile and Siberia, the top grades are still found in the same Asiatic mines that Marco Polo visited. Ultramarine finally priced itself out of the market. An open competition held in France in 1828 for a cheap substitute was won by a Lyons chemist, Jean-Baptiste Guimet, who had observed a strange blue residue at the mouths of soda furnaces in glass works. Compounded of soda, china clay, and sulphur, this cheap industrial ultramarine is indistinguishable from the real article except under a microscope. It is the blue of Pablo Picasso's Blue Period (c. 1900 to 1904) and, prosaically, goes into laundry bluing and hair rinse.

BOCCACCIO, Giovanni (1313–75). Writer and poet. In 1348, three galleys coming from the Crimea put into Genoa, their home port, where they discharged a lethal cargo, the "Black Death," which was to kill in less than three years some 25,000,000 people, or one-third of Europe's population. The worst epidemic in historic times, it was a combination of the

common (or bubonic) plague, passed on to humans by fleas that
have fed on infected rats, and of its pneumonic form, transmitted
like the common cold. It is this catastrophe, in which Boccaccio
lost his father, his stepmother, and an uncle, that looms behind
his best known work, the *Decameron* (Greek, "of ten days"), a
collection of 100 tales told by an imaginary party of seven
women and three men who have fled stricken Florence for the
country, where they sing, dance, and invent stories. The author
liked to boast about himself. Scholars discount his claim to birth
in Paris and a mother of French royal blood. He was a native of
Certaldo, a hill town twenty-seven miles southwest of Florence.
His father was employed by the Bardi, Florentine bankers, and
young Giovanni was sent to Naples to clerk for that rich family
which was financing Naples's French king, Robert of Anjou.
Unsuited for the job, he switched to studying canon law, and
finally to writing. Soon, he associated with the leading scholars,
gained access to the court where the refinements of French
chivalry were still alive, and fell in love with the nebulous
Fiammetta ("little flame"), who was to dominate his early
works as the embodiment of an ennobling passion. His first
fruits include romances and poems in the French medieval manner, enlivened by his knowledge of the crowd and by an ear at-
tuned to minstrel lays. His poem, *Filostrato,* inspired his contemporary, Geoffrey Chaucer (c. 1340–1400), whom he may
have met during one of the English poet's trips to Italy, and
ended up as Shakespeare's *Troilus and Cressida;* his epic, *Teseida,*
became Chaucer's *Knight's Tale.* The Naples idyll was rudely
interrupted by the Bardi bankruptcy, entailing the collapse of
the Boccaccio family fortune. Giovanni returned to Florence and
to poverty, to devote himself entirely to his art. The *Decameron,*
written between 1349 and 1351, reveals him as one of the
world's great prose writers and storytellers. A poem ends each
"day." Full of humanity, humor, and sadness, it mirrors the
mores of the rising urban middle class, the clergy, and the
peasantry. Composed in freshly-minted Florentine, sprightly and
occasionally ribald, it established him as a man of letters and a
personality. Florence made him a municipal councilor and sent
him on official missions to the papal court of Avignon, to Rome,
and to Ravenna—where Dante had died in 1321, and where
Boccaccio was to hand ten gold pieces to the great exile's daugh-

ter, Beatrice, a nun. The turning point in his life was his meeting, in 1350, with Petrarch, Italy's poet laureate, his senior by nine years, whom he had long admired. According to tradition, Petrarch, then living in Padua, was passing through Florence on a pilgrimage to Rome during that Holy Year, and Boccaccio humbly walked a stretch of road to welcome him outside the gates. Their friendship, in which Boccaccio remained the junior partner, was to last until death. For nearly twenty-five years, they were in intimate touch, exchanging manuscripts and letters, and sounding each other out on new ideas. During Petrarch's stay in Venice, Boccaccio visited the master to present him with a Latin translation of Homer, fulfilling Petrarch's dearest literary wish. With a small group of other thinkers, they refined Italy's new national language—a process set in motion by Dante and his "first friend," Guido Cavalcanti (c. 1250–1300)—salvaged Latin classics, and helped initiate the study of Greek. In his late years, Boccaccio lived the life of an ascetic scholar—Petrarch once kept him from burning his own works—earning a pittance as a copyist, and lecturing on Dante. Petrarch's death, in 1374, prompted one of his most moving sonnets, addressed to the dead friend in Heaven, reunited with his Laura, while his own dead Fiammetta was still waiting for her lover.

> s'a grado ti fui nel mondo errante,
> tirami drieto a te, dove gioioso
> veggia colei che pria d'amor m'accese.
> (If I was dear to you in this errant world,
>   Lift me up after you, so that I with joy
>   May see her who first set me aflame with love.)

Boccaccio died eighteen months later in Certaldo, mourned by the best, who felt that poetry had vanished with him.

BORGIA (Borja). A name evoking daggers, poison, incest, and corpses floating in the Tiber. Though modern scholarship discounts some crimes attributed to this papal family, there still is enough evidence to justify its disrepute. Upstarts from southern Spain, they rocketed to power in the fifteenth century. Of the two Borgia popes, the first, Calixtus III (1455–58), who spent most of his reign trying to contain the Turks, opened a Pandora's box of ills by making his nephew, Rodrigo (c. 1430–1503), a cardinal. Tall, handsome, and robust, Rodrigo only had to look at women, it was said, to possess them. From about 1470 onward, he lived openly with his mistress, Vannozza Catanei, who bore him four children—Giovanni, Cesare, Lucrezia, and Goffredo. Six more children by other mistresses (among them the beautiful Giulia Farnese, sister of the future Pope Paul III) are known. During the Conclave of 1492, he bought the papacy with bribes drawn from the revenues of his three Spanish bishoprics and took the name Alexander VI. Romans believed that he was granted the papacy by Satan in exchange for his soul. His concern was power, and his goal was the foundation of a kingdom which would be ruled by his descendants. With this in mind, he gave much thought to the advancement of Cesare, his second son. In the luxurious apartment which today forms part of the Vatican Museums, he ruled over a worldly court. In Pinturicchio's frescoes embellishing the rooms, Alexander is portrayed, no longer handsome, kneeling in prayer, his beak-nosed, jowly countenance marked by greed and lust. There was a constant to-and-fro of mistresses, children, and Spanish hangers-on. Among the entertainments, it is said, was a ballet performed by fifty naked prostitutes. On one occasion, the pope let Lucrezia preside over a consistory of cardinals. Cesare (c. 1476–1507), a brutal, unscrupulous adventurer of noble bearing, was made a cardinal while still in his teens, but he soon quit the clerical career to become his father's sword arm. Having obtained the Duchy of Valentinois, in southeastern France, from King Louis XII as a price for the papal annulment of the latter's marriage, he was known as "Valentino." Later, he became captain-general of the papal forces and, finally, duke of Romagna, the populous, fertile region in northeastern Italy marked out as the future Borgia kingdom. His (only partially successful) war of conquest was financed from Rome by the sale of cardinals' hats, the seizure of baronial estates, and the murder of rich prelates whose property reverted to the Holy See. In his campaigns, Cesare spread terror through northern and central Italy. Castles and towns were

taken by treachery or force and given up to plunder. Venice and
Florence feared for their safety as Cesare, in 1502, took flourishing Urbino, whose palace, with its art treasures, was sacked,
while Duke Guidobaldo went into exile. In December of that
year, sensing a conspiracy among his top lieutenants, Cesare invited four presumed ringleaders to a New Year's Eve banquet at
Senigallia, on the Adriatic coast, and had two of them strangled
then and there, holding two others for subsequent assassination.
Early on New Year's morning, he told Florence's envoy, Machiavelli, "with the brightest face in the world," what had happened.
(Cesare is the hero of his *Prince.*) In Rome, one night, Cesare's
elder brother, Giovanni, duke of Gandia, disappeared on his way
home from dining with his mother; his body was fished out of
the Tiber three days later, and heavy suspicion fell on Cesare,
who may have seen in Duke Giovanni an obstacle to his ambitions. When his brother-in-law, Alfonso of Aragon, the duke of
Bisceglie, was set upon and wounded, but not killed, by Cesare's
men, Cesare observed, "What wasn't done at lunch can still be
done at dinner." Five weeks later, accompanied by his executioner,
Michelotto, he walked into the convalescent's room and watched
his strangulation. He readily admitted the deed, whose motive is
not clear. The pope forgave him. Meanwhile, Lucrezia (1480–
1519), pretty, blond, and blue-eyed, served as a valuable pawn
in Alexander's game of power politics. Highly romanticized,
she is the heroine of a play by Victor Hugo and of an opera by
Gaetano Donizetti. Aged eleven, she was betrothed to a Spanish
noble; the engagement, and a subsequent one, were dissolved.
At thirteen, she married a member of the Sforza family, which
ruled Milan; four years later, when Alexander had no further
need of Milanese support, he annulled the marriage on the
grounds of nonconsummation. (Lucrezia, who swore to her virginity, is thought to have been delivered of a boy by an unknown
father three months after the decree. The oft-repeated charge
of incest with her elder brothers and her father has never been
substantiated.) She next became the wife of the unfortunate Alfonso, duke of Bisceglie, an illegitimate son of the king of
Naples, by whom she had a son, Rodrigo. Having loved her husband, she went into deep mourning on his murder. At last, aged
twenty-two, the singularly passive and obedient lady was married to Alfonso d'Este, soon to become duke of Ferrara, whose

powerful assistance would prove useful in the Borgias' struggle for Romagna. Eyed from the peaks of Este arrogance, the twice-married daughter of the reigning pope could hardly be considered a prize; but a rich dowry and the implicit threat of papal conquest made her acceptable. For her wedding, Lucrezia wore red velvet trimmed with ermine, and a pearl necklace. Her trousseau was sent northward on the backs of 150 mules. She rode into Ferrara wearing a cape of gold brocade, under a canopy carried by university professors. And, strange as it may seem, they lived happily ever after. She bore Alfonso several children, made friends with her proud in-laws, and devoted the rest of her life to her domestic duties. No doubt, the reason for this unexpected bliss was the death, in 1503, of her father. Cesare and Alexander fell sick at the same time, perhaps of malaria, though it was rumored that they had inadvertently nibbled some poisoned candy they had intended for a rich cardinal. Alexander's body swelled to monstrous size, foam bubbled from his mouth, and his attendants were sure they had seen seven devils hovering about the corpse. During his twelve-year tenure of the papacy, he had dragged it down to its most dismal depths. Cesare was imprisoned for five months by Pope Julius II (1503–13). He later spent two years in a Spanish dungeon, but escaped—only to fall in battle in the service of the king of Navarre, whose sister he had married in 1499. In what seems an ironic epilogue, the family produced a saint—the grandson of the murdered Giovanni, Cesare and Lucrezia's older brother— St. Francis Borgia (1510–72), fourth duke of Gandia, viceroy of Catalonia, and third general of the Jesuits.

BORROMINI (Francesco Castelli, 1599–1667). One of the leading architects of the Baroque. Almost all of his work is to be found in Rome. Born in Bissone, Switzerland, in the foothills of the Alps—a region that had sent stonemasons south for centuries —he was trained as a stonecutter when still a child and prob-

ably was employed in the cathedral workshop at Milan before
arriving in Rome in his late twenties. His burly physique
housed a too-finely-honed, self-lacerating mind. In constant,
anxious search of the extreme and the unusual, he was to leave
behind a group of structures so purely cerebral that they speak
to our intellect before appealing to our eye. His surviving architectural drawings, with their relentless corrections, betray the
agony of the creative act. Borromini spent some twenty years at
St. Peter's, working under his relative, Carlo Maderno (1556–
1629), sculpting decorative elements such as coats of arms and
putti. After Maderno's death, Bernini hired him as an assistant,
and he designed some of the details of the bronze Baldachin at
St. Peter's. But his morbid introversion was incompatible with
Bernini's exuberance, and they soon clashed; we do not know
exactly why. Still, Borromini learned from Bernini much of
what he knew, and the latter was aware of his great talent. Borromini's individual style is documented by his sensitive stuccoes
at St. John Lateran, his work at the Spada and Falconieri palaces, and a large portion of S. Agnese on Piazza Navona. His
first major commission, the church-and-monastery complex of
S. Carlo alle Quattro Fontane, proves him an anticlassicist ready
to jettison, at his convenience, the Renaissance canon that made
the human body the model of all architectural proportions—a
canon still respected by Bernini. The complex was to keep him
busy, intermittently, for thirty-three years. Even while it was
taking shape, the Trinitarian brothers quartered there were
swamped with requests by foreign tourists for drawings of the
architecture. The church itself, *San Carlino* ("little St. Charles")
to Romans, is so small that it would fit into one of the four central piers of St. Peter's. Its interior design is based on interlocking geometric forms—ellipses, lozenges, triangles, semicircles; a
fancifully coffered oval cupola serves as ceiling. Nothing like
this had ever been seen before. Even more unconventional is the
Church of S. Ivo (St. Ives), built by Borromini for the Sapienza,
precursor of the University of Rome. The floor plan is a six-
pointed star—or, conceivably, a bee, emblem of the ruling pope,
Urban VIII. But it's the vertical that triumphs in this structure.
The inner space rises to a startling, almost Gothic, height. Gain-
ing in stature by its situation at the end of a long, narrow courtyard, the church is crowned by a spiraling top, suggested per-

haps by a specimen from Borromini's shell collection, or by the helicoid minaret of the Great Mosque at Samarra, northwest of Baghdad, of which he may have seen a drawing. No doubt as strange an object as ever rose upon the Roman skyline, it bears the stamp of an incredibly inventive genius. Among Borromini's other major works in Rome are a wing of the Palace of the Propagation of the Faith, distinguished by extravagantly deep-cut, superbaroque windows; the Oratory complex of St. Philip Neri, the Counter Reformation order of and for the common man; the Church of S. Maria dei Sette Dolori; and the belfry of S. Andrea delle Fratte, a pile of such incongruous components as winged herms, a circular Corinthian temple, torches with simulated flames, and the arms of the sponsoring Del Bufalo family—a huge four-handled urn topped by a spiky iron crown. Borromini's façades, with their concave-convex rhythm, seem molded by a thumb, and many of them are—he made wax or clay models of all his works-in-progress. His white interiors lack the heavy decor that was the fashion of the time; their splendor lies in their undulating movement. Viewed as a whole, his life-work carries the Baroque to its most intricate refinement. His influence on the next generation, which was to export the Baroque to Piedmont, Sicily, and Austria, was overwhelming. In his own house, he lived surrounded by 1000 books, most of them architectural treatises annotated in his hand. Among his possessions were innumerable paintings; a collection of small curios, including rock crystals; bronze medallions; an old halberd; a gold crucifix; and busts of Seneca (the Stoic councilor of Nero, who died by his own hand) and Michelangelo, the artist he valued above all. But Borromini's curves and calculations haunted him even when he was absent from his drafting board, and he eventually fell into a state of profound melancholia. According to his biographer, Filippo Baldinucci (1624–96), the wild look in his eyes terrified people, and he withdrew from human company, letting himself be comforted only by his parish priest, whom he received with courtesy. The doctor prescribed plenty of sleep. But Thought, his fearful enemy, kept him awake. One stifling Roman summer night, he called his servant and asked for writing pad and lamp. The man politely reminded him of the physician's orders—sleep. When the request was repeated several times, always eliciting the same reply, Borromini, with an anguished cry

—"I can't sleep and they won't let me write!"—grabbed the short sword he kept at the head of his bed and ran it through his chest. The timing was spontaneous, to be sure; the deed itself may well have been premeditated. Only a few days before, he had burned a stack of architectural drawings, many of them of elaborate palaces and churches done for his own gratification, which he had got together for publication as a book. And it is likely that what he wished to write that night was his last will and testament. He drew it up now, during the twenty-four hours it took him to die, leaving the bulk of his estate to a nephew, and handsome legacies to his obstinate servant, and to the brothers of S. Giovanni dei Fiorentini—the church whose russet jasper altar he had built, and where he wanted to be buried next to his master, Carlo Maderno—"so they might increase their daily wine ration."

BOTTICELLI, Sandro (c. 1445–1510). Florentine painter. His name was Alessandro Filipepi; the nickname *botticello* ("little barrel"), given originally to an elder brother, was handed down to the lean Sandro like an outsized coat. Despite his linear style, relying on hard contour rather than on pliant volume, he is one of the most lyrical of Italian painters (Bernard Berenson speaks of "linear symphony") and the favorite of visitors to Florence, where reproductions of his work outsell those of the works of any other painter. Often imitated and as often forged, his paintings, with their elongated, graceful bodies, cast a seductive spell. The son of a tanner, he was apprenticed to Filippo Lippi (c. 1406–69) and was influenced by Antonio Pollaiuolo (1431–98). Soon recognized as an exceptionally endowed artist, he obtained the patronage of the Medici, several of whom, among them Lorenzo the Magnificent, appear in his *Adoration of the Magi* (Florence, Uffizi). The same picture contains his self-portrait, showing a long, tense, earnest face, with heavy-lidded eyes under brown, wavy hair. A superb head of

Lorenzo's brother, Giuliano, attesting to his talent as a portraitist, is in Washington, D.C. (National Gallery). Little is known about his life. Vasari tells a story about a weaver who set up his workshop next door to Botticelli, tormenting him with the din and clatter of eight looms. Sandro retaliated by hoisting an enormous rock onto his roof, which overhung the neighbor's, balancing it so delicately that the slightest tremor would send it crashing down onto the weaver's house, demolishing it, looms and all. The neighbor, writes Vasari, "came to reasonable terms." Asked by a friend why he was still a bachelor, Sandro explained that he once dreamt he was married and woke up so frightened that he rushed from his room and walked the streets till dawn. Yet, it is largely as a painter of women that he made his reputation. His Madonnas, with their wistful expression and their delicate white hands, are among the comeliest of the early Renaissance. The same beauty shines from his three celebrated pagan allegories (Florence, Uffizi), reflections of the humanistic thinking of the age, that were commissioned by members of the House of Medici: the *Birth of Venus;* the *Primavera;* and *Pallas Subduing a Centaur,* thought to be a glorification of the civilizing influence of the Magnificent Lorenzo. In 1481, his growing fame brought him an invitation from Pope Sixtus IV (1471–84) to Rome; during his brief stay, he added three religious frescoes to the wall decoration of the Sistine Chapel, then still lacking Michelangelo's ceiling. Among his later works are drawings for Dante's *Divine Comedy,* another Medici commission. It was under the influence of Savonarola's doomsday sermons that Sandro painted his late, mystical compositions. His final years were spent in the shadow of Leonardo, Michelangelo, and Raphael, all younger than himself—whose heroic style made his own dainty elegance look old-fashioned. He spent his last years on his small farm, tending his vines and fruit trees, and was buried in the graveyard of Ognissanti (All Saints), church of the Florentine tanners.

BRAMANTE, Donato d'Agnolo (1444–1514). One of Italy's major architects; perfected the creation of Renaissance space begun by Brunelleschi and Alberti; fathered the Grand Manner of High Renaissance architecture. Born of a farming family in Fermignano near Urbino, a center of humanism and the arts under its Montefeltro rulers, he is believed to have received his artistic education at that court, working at first as a painter. The influence of Alberti, Piero della Francesca, and, later, of Mantegna is discernible in his few surviving paintings. Little is known about his youth. In Milan, he rebuilt the Basilica of S. Maria presso S. Satiro, whose original structure dated back to before 900, creating an interior testifying to his flair for rhythm and proportion. His chief Milan accomplishment is the eastern section of the Dominican Church of S. Maria delle Grazie, which he built for Ludovico Sforza ("il Moro"—the Moor), duke of Milan. The domed crossing and deep apse are among the noblest Renaissance creations in all Italy. Circles or discs, Bramante's trademark, are the chief decoration. At the ducal court, Bramante met Leonardo da Vinci, whose *Last Supper* fresco is in the refectory next to the church. Both artists left Milan after the Moor's fall, in 1499. Bramante headed for Rome, where, living on his savings, he spent his time examining and measuring antique buildings, including those of Hadrian's Villa outside Rome. Presumably, it was his passion for antiquity that brought him into contact wtih the rich and influential cardinal Oliviero Carafa (or Caraffa), a cultured Neapolitan, uncle of the future Pope Paul IV, who sponsored his first Roman work, the Cloister of S. Maria della Pace. Carafa looked after the interests of royal Spain in Rome and probably obtained for him the commission from Spain's "Catholic kings," Ferdinand and Isabel, for the decoration of the courtyard of S. Pietro in Montorio on the Janiculum Hill. His circular Tempietto ("little temple"), standing in the center of the court, remains one of the truest expressions of the spirit of the Renaissance. Consisting of a domed, cylindrical body ringed by sixteen slender Tuscan columns, it is at once a monument to the Apostle Peter—who, according to a local legend, was crucified here—and a pagan temple, inspired by round structures of antiquity, such as the Temple of the Vestal Virgins in the Forum. Its purpose is to please. A circular portico Bramante had planned as a frame for it was never built. Bramante was, by now, the leading architect in Rome, called in on almost every major building project. The (long-since-vanished) house he built, either for himself or for Raphael, his fellow Urbinate, friend, protégé, and, perhaps, distant kinsman, was widely imitated in Rome. When Giuliano della Rovere was elected pope in 1503, taking the name Julius II, he made Bramante his architect, charging him with the transformation of papal Rome into the *caput mundi* ("summit of the world") it had been under the Caesars. Rising to the challenge, Bramante, then aged sixty, began by welding the disconnected, far-flung structures of the Vatican into a single urban unit. By way of two parallel galleries linking the Belvedere Villa high on Vatican Hill with the cluster of papal palaces on lower ground, he devised a 1000-foot-long, 300-foot-wide enclosure, containing all the buildings as well as an enormous oblong courtyard ending in an open-air theater. Though his ingenious design was modified after his death (the courtyard is now subdivided by two cross-arms), the complex, with its endless corridors, is basically his creation. Pope Julius next entrusted him with his most cherished enterprise, the rearing of a new St. Peter's to replace the decaying basilica built by the emperor Constantine in the fourth century. Neither Bramante nor the impatient Julius were to live to see the task completed. Bramante produced the first of many projects for what was to be Christendom's premier church, symbolic of the pontiffs' majesty: a "Greek cross" structure of colossal size, formed by four equally long arms with four terminal apses, crowned by a central dome. Its walls and vaults were to be made of brick-faced concrete (a compound of cement and rubble), a virtually lost technique that had enabled Roman engineers to "shape" such tough, resilient structures as the Pantheon and the Imperial baths. In demolishing the old basilica, Bramante proceeded, with typical Renaissance nonchalance, without regard for its rich tombs and monuments, acquiring the nickname *Ruin*ante. At one point, he proposed to move the presumed tomb of St. Peter! Before he died, he had built the four mammoth piers that were to carry the central cupola and joined them with strong vaults. It was to take another one hundred years or so to finish the basilica, during which Raphael, Peruzzi, Michelangelo, and others succeeded him, each following his own design, thereby contributing to the architectural hodgepodge St. Peter's is today. Bramante was a man of cheerful disposition. He wrote fair poetry and liked to improvise —like Leonardo—on the lyre. His reported mischief-making for Michelangelo notwithstanding, he was on friendly terms with leading humanists and artists of his time. His influence on his successors, painters as well as architects, is fundamental. The architect Sebastiano Serlio (1475–c. 1554) called him "the inventor and the light of good, true architecture."

BRUNELLESCHI, Filippo (1377–1446). Florentine architect, engineer, sculptor; originator of the Renaissance style in architecture; inventor of perspective construction in painting; best known as the creator of the cupola of S. Maria del Fiore, Florence's cathedral. The son of a prominent Florentine notary, he was educated in the liberal arts and joined the goldsmiths' guild at the age of twenty-one. Finishing a close second to Ghiberti in the competition (1401) for the bronze doors of the Florence baptistery, he emerged from his defeat as an artist to be watched. The story later told about Christopher Columbus was originally told about him: challenged to stand an egg on its end, he did so by smashing its bottom. Fascinated by the achievements of antiquity, he went to Rome as a young man, perhaps first with his close friend Donatello, and several times thereafter, to measure classical buildings and investigate their structure. Brunelleschi's portico of the Florence Foundlings' Home (Ospedale degli Innocenti), completed in 1424, is the direct result of these investigations and the first triumph of the

Renaissance in architecture; it shows to great advantage his life-long specialty, the unfluted column. His two basilican churches, S. Lorenzo and S. Spirito, are marvels of articulation and unity of plan; while his more intimate buildings—the Old Sacristy of S. Lorenzo, the Pazzi Chapel (parts of which may not be his), and the unfinished Rotonda of S. Maria degli Angeli—shine with crystalline perfection. So truly revolutionary are these structures that they alone would make Filippo ("Pippo" to his friends) one of the world's great architects. Yet, his reputation is predominantly tied to his most celebrated work, the cupola of S. Maria del Fiore. The church had a long, checkered history. Originally built in the seventh century as S. Reparata, it had been slated in the thirteenth century to become a cathedral of unprecedented size and splendor, a symbol of the city's wealth. A project by Arnolfo di Cambio (c. 1245–1302) existed, but no sure record of its details has survived. Meanwhile, the rich cloth manufacturers' guild, which financed the cathedral works, had started building a tall, roughly 1650-foot-long, marble-clad Gothic church, leaving a gaping hole over its crossing to be closed by a cupola. What kind of cupola, and how to build it, was subject to much animated speculation, and the unfinished temple was a conundrum and an eyesore. During the consultations carried on among the authorities, the public, and the guilds, it is likely that Filippo was among those approached, and that he opted for an octagonal dome of overwhelming majesty, floating above the rooftops. A tall, solidly built octagonal drum was raised, on whose fourteen-foot-wide rim the cupola would rest. Filippo—at first assisted by Ghiberti—was given the commission and submitted a work plan. Aesthetically the most pleasing, and technically the most difficult, means of spanning a central void, cupolas had long been known as problem children. The ancient Greeks did not build them. The Romans did, drawing on their familiarity with the keystone arch and the use of cement. (A cupola may be envisaged as an arch twirled around its perpendicular axis.) Italy had before its eyes the world's largest and most perfect specimen, the cupola of the Pantheon in Rome, built by the emperor Hadrian in 110–125. A relatively shallow concrete shell with a diameter of about 143 feet, poured in sections and elegantly coffered on the inside, with brick ribs hidden in its mass, and with a round hole at the summit as the building's only source of light, it obviously was a miracle of engineering. But no one knew how it was made, and just what kept it up. (The equally famous dome of S. Sophia in Constantinople, with a diameter of one-hundred-odd feet, built some four centuries later, fell in twice and had to be restructured, perhaps because it was too shallow.) The octagonal void Filippo was now called upon to cover was about 142 feet across, its rim 220 feet above the floor, and there was no known method of achieving so vast and so complex an enterprise. To raise a scaffold from the ground on which to rest shaped woodwork forms for "centering"—supporting the arches while they were abuilding, i.e. before they could stand up by themselves—would have been time-consuming and extremely costly; timber was scarce, nor was technology advanced enough to guarantee success. According to tradition, a proposal was put forward to pile up earth inside the structure all the way to the top and salt it with gold florins so that people would be eager to remove it later. Filippo finally decided to build the cupola without ground support, using, perhaps, a minimum of centering in its uppermost regions, where the sharp curvature made it desirable, and where he could put the wooden forms on masonry rings already in place. For the rest, movable platforms for his workmen and materials would be used. Exactly how he did it remains a mystery, as there are no surviving records of his day-to-day procedure. He may indeed have wanted to keep some secrets to himself. We know that he constructed, on the ground, a giant hoist of his invention, whose precision mechanism, powered by oxen, was capable of lifting the huge blocks needed on top. During the fourteen years of work-in-progress, the machine is thought to have averaged fifty hauls a day. Florentines liked to hitch rides into space on it until the practice was forbidden. Filippo had installed a kitchen and canteen on the octagon rim so workmen would not have to use the lift to have a hot lunch. Construction started, with a rimside toast, on 7 August 1420. Laying down ring upon ring, he deviated from his plan as he saw fit, proceeding, on the whole, empirically—while Florence held its breath. The major problem was the tendency of domes to burst, and it had been decided to contain this outward thrust within its structure, without resorting to unsightly tie-rods crossing the interior space, or outside buttresses to counteract the pressure. The principal insurance against spread was the steep profile of the dome. Filippo reared eight sandstone ribs—marble-faced on the outside—rising almost vertically from the octagon's eight corners and curving gradually inward toward the top. Two more, invisible and thinner, upright ribs divided the triangles between them, so that there were, in all, twenty-four ribs. He closed the open spaces between them with a double skin of specially baked flat bricks laid, at strategic points, in herringbone patterns for increased cohesion. Working from the rim upward, he thus built two separate shells, one contained within the other, four feet apart at the bottom, and nearly five feet apart toward the top. The upright ribs are deep enough to bridge the distance between the shells, serving as stays for both; apertures in the ribs accommodate the walkways needed for inspection and re-pairs and the narrow stairway winding to the summit. Filippo's heavy-duty inner shell is seven feet thick at the base and tapers to a five-foot thickness at the top. The outer shell—"magnificent and billowing" in the words of his prospectus—tapers from two-and-a-half to one-and-a-quarter feet and gives the cupola its splendid skyline. As a final precaution against bursting, Filippo ringed the shells with loops of iron-cramped stone blocks, built into the masonry at various heights, and with one wooden "chain" in the lower section, made of twenty-four huge chestnut logs passing through the ribs and visible in the interstices be-tween them. He thus obtained a stiff, tough, roughly beehive-shaped, 125-foot-high fabric. The double-shell idea was an old one, probably dating back to the fourth century. The Pantheon has a single cupola, while the Florence baptistery—fifth to twelfth centuries—facing the cathedral has a double one. The inner shell, often decorated on its underside, is thus protected from the weather by a light-weight umbrella, and the straight upward view from the ground into the void above is made less dizzying. (Recent studies have called attention to the rather striking similarity between Filippo's structure and the early-fourteenth-century octagonal, roughly 165-foot-high, mausoleum of the Mongol emperor Oljeitu at Sultaniya in Azerbaijan, Persia. Sultaniya, at the time, lay in an Italian-administered diocese. But though communications between Italy and Persia were open, it is doubtful whether Brunelleschi had heard of the imperial tomb, or seen a drawing of it. And, as its cupola is onion-shaped, its influence, if any, could not have been important.) One of the wonders of the Western world, Brunelleschi's cupola is neither Romanesque nor Gothic. It is new. And while some of the techniques employed, as well as the steepness of its pitch, echo the Gothic, in keeping with the body of the church itself, the marble lantern topping it, completed after the master's death from his design, proclaims the Renaissance. "Who would be so dull or jealous," writes Alberti (almost thirty years his junior), "as not to praise Pippo, the architect, when he beholds this grandiose structure soaring heavenward, big enough to cover with its shadow all the people of Tuscany, made without the aid of centering—a work, if I judge rightly, that was unimaginable in our time, and unknown even in antiquity." And R. J. Mainstone, in his *Developments in Structural Form,* calls Master Pippo's accomplishment one "which was, and still must be, counted as one of the greatest in all structural history." Towering to a height of 351 feet (including the metal ball and cross), visible from afar, Filippo's brick-red, white-veined dome remains the pride of Florence and the major landmark of the lovely countryside around it. He had stood the egg on its end. He died laden with honors, and a tomb was voted him in the cathedral he had finished. Long lost, it was rediscovered in 1972.

C A E S A R ' S   D E A T H . Gaius Julius Ceasar (B.C. 100–44), statesman and general, was born on the twelfth of July—the month named in his honor. The descendant of a prominent family, he started his political career as a populist and rose to high offices in the Republic only to become its gravedigger. Tall, narrow-faced, possessed of great intelligence and energy, he was of delicate health, suffered from epileptic fits, but steeled himself to endure hardships. He was a fine horseman, a strong swimmer, an untiring walker, and a busy lover. Known as a dandy, he took some trouble in his later years to cover his baldness with his few remaining hairs. Having advanced by shrewd maneuvering, bribery, useful alliances, and opportune marriages; having conquered Gaul (France) and twice landed in England during a nine-year campaign described in terse Latin in his *Commentarii;* having won a civil war against Pompey; having amassed a major fortune; having loved Cleopatra, queen of Egypt, who gave him a son; he climaxed his career by accumulating all important government positions, reducing the Senate to impotence, and making himself dictator for life. Statues of him were raised in public places. His head appeared on coins. Although he used his power beneficially, his undisguised monarchic tendencies alienated many, especially the nobility, which in the past had exercised considerable leverage through its hold on the Senate. Various groups of malcontents plotted his downfall. On 15 February 44 B.C., on the Feast of the Lupercalia, an old fertility rite when Rome went wild, Caesar was addressing a crowd from the speaker's platform, the *rostra,* in the Forum. Suddenly, Mark Antony, his protégé and his fellow consul for that year, appeared before him in the costume of a Lupercalia priest, nude except for a strip of animal skins, and tried to crown him with a royal diadem. Although Caesar rejected it, his enemies prepared for action. More than sixty patricians, led by Marcus Junius Brutus and Gaius Cassius, banded together to assassinate him. They were a mixed company of men, some of whom, like Publius Servilius Casca, hated him, while others, like Brutus, who had fought on the losing side of the civil war and owed their lives to his generous pardon, joined the conspiracy in order to save the Republic. Their first plan was to hurl him from a bridge. But when a Senate meeting was scheduled for 15 March, the Ides (from an Etruscan word meaning "divide") of March, it was decided to kill him in the meeting hall of Pompey's theater, where the Senate was to sit that day. Caesar was warned by the soothsayer Spurinna, an Etruscan, to beware of misfortune that would strike no later than the Ides. The night of the fourteenth, strange birds were seen settling in the Forum. A violent storm blew open doors and windows in Caesar's house, and his wife, Calpurnia, sleeping by his side, dreamt that he was being murdered in her arms. With an agitation out of keeping with her usual calm, she implored him not to go. Caesar seriously thought of canceling the meeting. He left the house, full of misgivings, when one of the conspirators dropped in and asked him not to keep the Senators waiting all day. On the way, someone handed him a small scroll revealing the conspiracy; he gave it to an aide, unread, as was his habit. Passing the stand of the soothsayer Spurinna, he joked, "You see, the Ides have come!" "Not over yet," said the Etruscan. The Senate rose as Caesar entered and took his seat. One of the conspirators, Tillius Cimber, who had been one of his supporters, approached him to beg a favor. When Caesar motioned him away, he grabbed his toga as if trying to pull it off his shoulders. Casca now stabbed him with his dagger in the neck, but managed no more than a glancing blow. Caesar caught his arm, crying, "Cursed Casca, what are you doing?" Leaping to his feet and seeing himself beset by men with unsheathed daggers, he tried to dodge their weapons, shouting. The Senate did not stir. In the confusion, some of the murderers stabbed one another. When Brutus, whom Caesar had always treated with paternal love, added his blow, Caesar is said to have murmured in Greek, *Kai su, teknon* ("You too, son?"), and drawing his toga over his head, he sank down in silence. He fell against the statue of Pompey—his erstwhile friend, later his enemy, murdered four years before in Egypt—splattering the pedestal with blood. A doctor viewing his body concluded that, of twenty-three dagger wounds he had received, only one was fatal. Three slaves placed his body on a litter, with one arm hanging down, and carried it to his house. Of the two principal histories of Caesar's life and death, written by Suetonius (c. A.D. 70–c. 140) and Plutarch (c. A.D. 46–c. 120), the latter was the source of Shakespeare's *Julius Caesar* (c. 1599). We are in the crowded Forum, where Caesar's body is laid out for burning on a pyre and where Mark Antony delivers his immortal funeral oration:

> Friends, Romans, countrymen, lend me your ears;
> I come to bury Caesar, not to praise him. . . .
> He was my friend, faithful and just to me:
> But Brutus says he was ambitious;
> And Brutus is an honorable man. . . .
>
> . . . .
> If you have tears, prepare to shed them now.
> You all do know this mantle: I remember
> The first time ever Caesar put it on;

'Twas on a summer's evening, in his tent,
That day he overcame the Nervii.
Look! in this place ran Cassius' dagger through:
See what a rent the envious Casca made:
Through this the well-beloved Brutus stabbed;
And as he plucked his cursed steel away,
Mark how the blood of Caesar follow'd it, . . .
For Brutus, as you know, was Caesar's angel:
Judge, O you gods! how dearly Caesar lov'd him.
This was the most unkindest cut of all;
For when the noble Caesar saw him stab,
Ingratitude, more strong than traitors' arms,
Quite vanquish'd him: then burst his mighty heart; . . .
O! now you weep, and I perceive you feel
The dint of pity, these are gracious drops. . . .

. . . .

Here was a Caesar! when comes such another?

Whether or not Mark Antony's shrewd eloquence was needed
to turn the populace against the killers, there is no doubt that
people felt bereaved and dazed by Caesar's disappearance. The
conspirators, aware that they lacked popular support, left town.
There followed a long, bloody struggle. Brutus and Cassius
raised an army in Greece and, at Philippi (42 B.C.), fought
a pursuing force led by Mark Antony and young Octavian,
Caesar's grandnephew and adopted son. Defeated, they committed suicide. Octavian and Antony, rivals for Caesar's mantle,
then fell out, and Antony, after an extravagant love affair with
the irresistible Cleopatra (who bore him twins), was decisively
defeated by Octavian at Actium, Greece, in 31 B.C. He too committed suicide. Shortly afterwards, Cleopatra, according to tradition, killed herself by holding her nude arm out to an asp,
brought to her in a basket of figs (she is said to have first tried
the snake on her slave girls), when hearing that Octavian
wished to exhibit her at his triumph in Rome. Octavian was
now the sole master of the Roman realm. In 27 B.C., under the
name of Gaius Julius Caesar Octavianus, to which an adulating
Senate added the honorific *Augustus* ("the Exalted One"), he
became Rome's first emperor. The nearly five-hundred-year-old
Republic was dead, replaced by an empire that, in the West, was

to last until A.D. 476. "Caesar," the dead dictator's family name, henceforth became a title; it survives in the Russian, *Czar*, and the German, *Kaiser*. It was in Octavian's reign that a star shone in the Eastern sky: "And it came to pass in those days, that there went out a decree from Caesar Augustus, that all the world should be taxed," we read in Luke 2 : 1.

CAPELLO (or Cappello), Bianca (1548–87). Grand duchess of Tuscany, a skeleton in the Medici closet. Beautiful, strong-willed, cunning, skilled at repartee, and utterly unscrupulous, she was born in Venice of a patrician family that had given the republic outstanding statesmen, admirals, ambassadors, and men of letters. Her uncle, Cardinal Grimaldi, was patriarch of Aquileia. Aged fifteen, she eloped from the family palace to Florence with a Florentine clerk, Pietro Buonaventuri, by whom she was with child. When a shocked Venice demanded her extradition, Florence refused. The two were married and a son was born. In Florence, Bianca caught the eye of Francesco de' Medici, the eldest son of Cosimo I, who was married to the humorless, sickly Joanna of Austria. Bianca became his mistress and moved into a noble mansion, which Francesco had remodeled for her, on Florence's Via Maggio. The crest of the Capello family, showing a hat (*cappello*), still adorns its façade. In 1572, after her husband, who had been bought off with money and honors, was found murdered, she and Francesco made their liaison public. He was much in love with her, and his poems to "Madonna Bianca" have been preserved. He also evinced an almost Leonardesque interest in the sciences, particularly chemistry, and ballistics. Grand duke upon his father's death in 1574, he proved an able ruler. As he had no male heir, Bianca, in order to secure her position, feigned pregnancy and, after nine months, presented him with the newborn son of an unknown working-class mother, who was baptized Antonio. Though she had taken care to murder every one of her accomplices, her fraud was discovered. Francesco seems to have taken it good-humoredly, contenting himself with excluding little Antonio from the line of succession. In 1578, Joanna died, and Bianca and Francesco were married, to the joy of the Capellos, and to the indignation of the Medici—who, were, however, in no condition to moralize. Two years before, Francesco's brother, Pietro, had killed his wife, Eleanor of Toledo, and his sister, Isabella, was strangled by her husband, Duke Paolo Orsini. Installed as Tuscany's grand duchess, Bianca behaved with decorum. The Republic of Venice recognized her, and all was forgiven. She and Francesco might have ended their days blissfully had it not been for the smoldering hatred of Francesco's ambitious younger brother, Cardinal Ferdinando. In October 1587—a delectable time of year in Tuscany and good for hunting—husband and wife were stopping at the Medici villa at Poggio a Caiano, an ancient fortress rebuilt for Lorenzo the Magnificent, who enjoyed falconing there. With its huge, frescoed hall, its splendid garden, and its sweeping view, it is one of the most alluring of the great houses around Florence. There, suddenly, and without visible cause, Francesco died after a hunting banquet. Bianca died the next day, just as unaccountably. There was talk of poison, and suspicion fell on Cardinal Ferdinando—who, to no one's surprise, stepped in as the new grand duke. He soon renounced his clerical status and married Christine of Lorraine as part of a political pact with France which greatly benefited Tuscany. They were to have nine children. Ferdinando patronized the arts, drained the unhealthy marshes, developed the port of Leghorn (Livorno), and, with the help of France and Austria, made Tuscany a power to be reckoned with. Grand duke Francesco was fittingly laid to rest in the family vault at S. Lorenzo, while Bianca is said to have been buried, wrapped only in a sheet, in the mass grave for the poor in the main part of the church.

CARAVAGGIO, Michelangelo Merisi da (1573–1610). One of Italy's most original painters, whose violent temper made him his own worst enemy. Born in Caravaggio, near

Milan, he was apprenticed to a minor Lombard painter in his youth. Aged about twenty, he appeared in Rome, where he lived among the city's poor, pocketing handouts and occasionally working for various painters. His talent aroused the interest of Cardinal del Monte, an influential art collector, who took him into his palace and commissioned several paintings. "A most eccentric brain!" he marveled. Though a child of the High Renaissance, Caravaggio rejected its "grand manner"—the classical, heroic style popularized by Leonardo and Raphael. His characters were culled from among the unwashed, sunburned street peddlers and workmen he knew so well. But who had ever painted biblical figures with sweat-soaked clothes and dirty feet? His Paul, in the *Conversion of St. Paul* in Rome's S. Maria del Popolo, is a rough common soldier, and the horse from which he has been thrown by the "great light" from heaven is a raw work horse off the nearest farm. For his *Death of the Virgin* (Paris, Louvre), Caravaggio is said to have used the bloated body of a girl fished out of the Tiber as a model for the Mother of Christ. Potential clients, scandalized by such liberties, often rejected his works as indecorous. But his magisterial compositions and the freshness of his style gradually silenced his detractors. At the age of twenty-four, he was referred to as "most famous." It was his own unruly spirit that was to trip him up. The story of the last ten years of his brief life is written in police records. He inflicts a sword wound on a captain of the papal guards, is under house arrest for circulating scurrilous verse, attacks a waiter in a tavern, is jailed for throwing stones at the police, insults an officer who wants to see his license to carry arms, is jailed for bothering two women, wounds a notary in a fight over a prostitute of Piazza Navona. One Sunday night in 1606, Caravaggio fatally stabbed a companion in a brawl after a ball game. He fled and, two years later, surfaced in Malta, the island fortress then belonging to the Knights of St. John. The knights, delighted with the paintings he produced for them (among them the superb *Beheading of St. John the Baptist*, still in the Cathedral of Valletta, the island's capital), received him into the order and presented him with a golden chain and two slaves. But, within weeks, Caravaggio landed in the dungeon for insulting an official, was removed from the order "like a fetid limb," and, after a spectacular escape, turned up in Sicily. On his way back to Rome where a papal pardon awaited him, he was set upon by thugs in a Naples tavern, disfigured, and reported dead. Landing at Port'Ercole, a Spanish enclave one hundred miles northwest of Rome, he was arrested by mistake and, on his release, was told that the felucca that had brought him there had sailed away with his belongings—which were, in fact, safe at the customs house. He died a few days later of a fever—caused, legend has it, by a fit of exasperation. (All of this final act is poorly documented.) His ruthless realism and his striking light effects were to influence the art of painting for years to come in Italy, Spain, France, and Holland. "Darkness gave him light," the painter Henry Fuseli (1741–1825) said of Caravaggio.

CARRIERA, Rosalba (1675–1757). Venetian painter, the daughter of a ship's captain and a lacemaker, famous for her pastel portraits. She began as a miniaturist, painting snuffboxes; a charming miniature on ivory, called *Innocence,* showing a wide-eyed little girl fondling a dove, is at the Accademia di San Luca in Rome. She soon was in demand as a portraitist by the Venetian aristocracy. The British consul and collector, Joseph Smith, whose Venice house was a way station on the Grand Tour, became her patron and agent. Foreign visitors, to whom he showed her pictures, often went home with several of them. Pastel, which until then had not served as a vehicle for serious art, was the ideal medium for her tender touch which, with its subtle shadings, succeeded in evoking the feel of well-groomed flesh. Her males, such as the *Cardinal de Polignac* (Venice, Accademia) with his penetrating eyes and noble features, look virile and intelligent. Her bejeweled females, with their generous décolletages, painted eyebrows, lace dresses, fur collars, and flower-garnished hair (of which a stray curl may fall, by accident, on a nude shoulder), look at the beholder proudly or coquettishly. Besides portraits done from life, Rosalba excelled at allegorical figures, such as the elements (air, fire, water, earth) and the four seasons (Dresden, Gemäldegalerie). A lovely little *Virgin Mary* is in the Cà Rezzonico, Venice. As Carriera's fame spread, she became the darling of Europe's ruling houses and, with her crayons and her fingertips, immortalized the gay artificiality of a powdered, perfumed, pleasure-seeking leisure class. Maximilian II, elector of Bavaria, who visited Venice in 1704, sat for a portrait and ordered pictures of "all of the most beautiful women in Venice." King Frederick IV of Denmark followed his example a few years later and commissioned a dozen portraits of Venetian beauties. Augustus III, elector of Saxony and king of Poland, amassed the largest collection of her works, many of which are still in Dresden. The art-collecting banker, Pierre Crozat, one of the richest men in France, repeatedly invited her to Paris. Having accepted at last, she traveled there in 1720, accompanied by her mother, two sisters, and her brother-in-law, the painter Gian Antonio Pellegrini (1675–1741). Paris gave her a whirl. The cultured and vivacious lacemaker's daughter, who carried with her all the lure of Venice, was presented at court, taken to the theater and balls. She met and painted the elite (portraits including a posy, or a hand or two, cost more than a mere head), and was elected to the French Academy of Painting, a signal honor for a woman and a foreigner. Her social presence was enhanced by her talent as a harpist. As to her looks, there is some confusion. A youthful self-portrait (stolen from the Cà Rezzonico in 1972) shows a pleasing, finely-chiseled face with large, luminous eyes; a portrait of her, painted in 1705 by Sebastiano Bombelli (1635–1719), presents a pretty and engaging countenance. Yet, she was said to be ugly, and a contemporary caricature as well as a later self-portrait (Venice, Accademia) confirm this; whether the two self-portraits, both laurel-crowned, are really portraits of herself, however, is debated. In Vienna, which she visited in 1730, she portrayed the Holy Roman emperor, Charles VI, and gave painting lessons to the empress, Elizabeth Christine. Her Venice palazzo remained her headquarters, where visitors from many lands stopped their gondolas to view her latest pictures. As other painters had done before her, she ran a workshop with several assistants. She never married. "To find a husband worthy of Rosalba," a friend remarked, "you'd have to bring back Guido Reni!"—the much-admired Bolognese painter (1575–1642). And though Rosalba was, perhaps, not one of the great figures of Venice's resplendent eighteenth century—Oxford scholar Francis Haskell (*Patrons and Painters*) calls her work "delicate and flimsy"—her handsome paintings constitute a precious album in which the Venice of Goldoni mixes with the France of Louis XIV. Her blossom-strewn life ended with a blast of winter. She lost her eyesight, briefly regained it after an operation, lost it again, and died deranged, aged over eighty.

CASANOVA, Giacomo (1725–98). Prototype of the Latin lover, exemplar of all the charm and the permissiveness of eighteenth-century Venice, author of twelve volumes of candid memoirs, and one of the grand adventurers of all ages, Casanova began his career as a candidate for the priesthood and finished as an obscure librarian. He worked, occasionally, as a fiddler, silk merchant, lottery agent, and magician. He also was a writer—his works include a partial translation of the *Iliad,* a description of a voyage to the center of the earth, and numerous librettos. Five-foot-nine-inches tall, he had intense dark eyes, a large, curved nose, and full lips. His swarthy face and a few pockmarks gave him a rather fierce appearance. He liked good food and wines and gambled avidly. His actor parents, always on the road, left him in the care of his maternal grandmother, who sent him to school in Padua, lodging him in a vermin-ridden boarding house. A kindly priest took the glum boy in and Giacomo began to flourish. He received his doctorate in civil and ecclesiastical law when he was barely seventeen, took minor orders, and dressed in a cassock. Ambitious, he already saw himself a cardinal. But, being offered a job as assistant to a bishop, he took one look at the dismal southern Italian town where he was expected to live and left. There now emerges the characteristic Casanova pattern. Employed as secretary by the influential cardinal Aquaviva in Rome, he worked for a few months, became involved in a scandal—presumably a love affair with the mistress of a nephew of the pope—and went to seek his fortune in far-off Constantinople, wearing a blue-and-silver uniform of his own invention. When a rich Turk offered him a career in business and his daughter as a wife if Casanova would become a Moslem, he fled. Down and out in Venice, where he played the violin at weddings, he saw a red-robed senator step into a gondola and drop a letter in the process. He picked it up, and the pleased dignitary asked him aboard. No sooner were they off than the old man suffered a stroke. Casanova jumped ashore, found a doctor, and accompanied doctor and patient to the latter's palazzo. Recovering, the senator invited him to live with him. Giacomo spent most of the next three years brawling and gambling. Having pinked a man with his sword, he left the city in a hurry. Ever since he had first tasted love, at the age of sixteen, he had drifted from one amorous adventure to the next, discovering that his virility made him uncommonly attractive to the fair sex. There were blondes and brunettes, rich ones and poor ones—several hundred, by his own estimate—but there was none like Henriette. He met her at an inn. She was French, and beautiful. She was dressed as a man, had no luggage, and was vague as to her plans. Perhaps she was a noblewoman who had left her husband. "I have a very comfortable carriage," said Casanova, and went out and bought one, secondhand. They spent three blissful months together, most of it in hiding from some unknown danger. He hired seamstresses and had her fitted out with a new wardrobe. But what she dreaded most did happen. She was recognized and had to take the long road home. At a Geneva inn, they parted. Alone, Casanova stepped up to the window of their room. Scratched with a diamond into the glass were the words, "Henriette too you will forget." Four years and many kisses later, Giacomo, back in Venice, was ready for a new attachment. Catherine—discreetly called "C.C." in his *Memoirs*—was a teen-age fledgling who enchanted him with her "innocent vivacity." He took her to the opera. "I feel as safe with you," said the girl, "as with my brother!" Having just won a hundred gold pieces at gambling, he bought her a dozen pairs of silk stockings and as many white gloves. They raced each other in a park, laughed, ate an omelette, and rushed into each other's arms. But when the lover asked her respectable parents for her hand, they put her in a convent. Once Casanova had a solid job, she would be his. "I was devastated," Casanova writes. Police reports of the time depict him as an all-round rake. After reciting an "impious poem in a wineshop," he was arrested and taken to the *Piombi* (the "Leads"), the stiflingly hot prison cells separated only by a low attic from the lead-decked roof of the doge's palace, from which no one had ever escaped. Casanova had been sentenced by a secret tribunal to a five-year term for practicing black magic, but no one had informed him. He decided to make a break for freedom. After working for three months sharpening an iron rod he had picked up during an exercise walk in the corridor, he cut a hole through the floor under his cot. When the hole was discovered, he was moved to another cell, but had the time to smuggle the instrument to a prisoner next door, a monk named Balbi. Balbi cut through the thin ceiling of his own cell, climbed into the attic, and broke through to Casanova's cell. Having pried loose one of the lead plates of the roof, they found themselves under the starry sky, hugging the steeply slanting shoulder of the roof. How to get down? By a fantastic stroke of luck, they came upon a ladder left there by repairmen, but Casanova lost his grip and slid down the leaden incline until he dangled from the gutter, ninety feet up in space. With his last ounce of strength, he pulled himself back up. Armed with the ladder, they crawled through a dormer window into a dark room, where Casanova collapsed with exhaustion. Dawn was about to break when he awoke. Traversing offices and archives, forcing locks, they reached the ground floor. Giacomo slipped into the clothes which he had worn at his arrest fifteen months before and which he carried in a bundle. Wearing a plumed hat, flanked by the trembling monk, he swept past an astonished doorman, hailed a gondola, and was soon gliding through the sparkling waters— thanking the Lord and weeping like a child. Critics long doubted the veracity of his account, published during his lifetime, but the repair bills for the doors and windows damaged by his escape have since come to light. Places visited by Casanova during the next eighteen years include Paris, Amsterdam, Genoa, Rome, Munich, Florence, London, Berlin, St. Petersburg, Vienna, Madrid—Casanova slept here. There was little method to these ramblings. It was a feast-or-famine life. When there was money jingling in his pocket he lived like a prince. In Paris, he rented a palatial mansion, kept two carriages, gave exquisite dinners, and was invited by the cream of French society—until he went bankrupt and vanished, a jump ahead of the police. In Spain, he was about to be put in charge of a project for colonizing a deserted mountain region, but fell out with his sponsors. In Warsaw, he fought a duel with a Polish count over a pretty ballerina. The only world in which he felt at home was the floating world of dancers, singers, actors, impresarios, harlequins, and mountebanks, to which he, the son of actors, had ready access. In any town that had a theater or concert hall, he found good friends—Italians—who gave him a feeling of belonging. To please them, he occasionally wrote a play and acted on the stage. He was, by now, a living legend. His reputation as a jailbreaker, combined with his grand style and learning, gave him a halo of distinction. In St. Petersburg, he discussed the merits of the Russian calendar with Catherine the Great. Benjamin Franklin, representing the United States in Paris, asked him to a session of the French Academy. Frederick the Great of Prussia offered him a job instructing his cadets, which Giacomo turned down. Voltaire listened attentively to his opinions. Pope Clement XIII laughed at his jokes. At the same time, the cheat was never quite asleep in Giacomo. His prize dupe was a rich Frenchwoman, the Marquise d'Urfé, whom Casanova promised to turn into a baby boy who would grow up to command occult powers. During the seven years of preparations for the miracle, he bilked her of a fortune. Still, they parted on the best of terms. His amorous encounters followed one another in quick succession. A tender and devoted lover, he made each woman feel that he was there for her alone. "You're not my first, but you'll surely be my last," he told them all, and meant it. When he was rich, his lady friends found themselves overwhelmed with presents—lace dresses, furs, rare china, diamonds. He gave a studious girl a hundred precious books. Poor girls received a dowry and, sometimes, a husband picked by Casanova. Though he proposed several times and was accepted, something always came up to save him. "Marriage," he once said, "is the tomb of love." In London, where he went in 1763 in the vain hope of launching a state lottery, he fell deeply in love with Pauline, a Portuguese lady of noble blood. It was his last completely happy romance. Approaching fifty, and homesick, Casanova now obtained a pardon from the Venetian government. He spent eight quiet years in Venice, living with a poor seamstress, managing a troupe of actors, and working for the government censorship office—which had given him some trouble in the past. Then, spurred on by his evil demon, he published an attack against the ruling families of the republic and was exiled for life. We find him installed as librarian in the remote Bohemian country seat of Dux—now Duchcov in Czechoslovakia. There, the ageing gallant recorded the story of his life. Written in French (available since 1962 in an unexpurgated English edition), these famous memoirs show Casanova as a consummate storyteller and observer. As to his loves, three stand out from the rest—"C.C.," Pauline, and, above all, Henriette. "No," he writes, "I have not forgotten her." Batches of love letters addressed to him, found among his shabby belongings, bore witness to the feelings the great lover had inspired.

CASTIGLIONE, Baldassare (1478–1529). Author and diplomat. The cult of the gentleman (and of the lady), rooted in Italian court life, was first codified by him in *Il cortegiano (The Courtier)*, one of the most renowned books of the sixteenth century. Born of an aristocratic family in Casatico near Mantua, Castiglione received a classical education and was trained in the fine points of chivalry, including horsemanship, fencing, and wrestling. After a few years' service at the Gonzaga court in Mantua, he joined the group of humanists and artists gathered around the duke of Urbino, Guidobaldo da Montefeltro, and, after the latter's death in 1508, remained there under his successor, Francesco Maria della Rovere, nephew of the warrior pope, Julius II. He was an aide to Duke Francesco Maria when the latter led a papal army against Venice, and he was at the side of Julius himself during the siege of fortified Mirandola—a service for which he was made a count. Later, he went as Urbino's ambassador to the court of Pope Leo X in Rome; in 1525, he was sent to Spain by Pope Clement VII as papal nuncio to the emperor Charles V. He liked the courtly life, fine horses and expensive clothes, had many friends, including Pietro Bembo, was happily married, and, between jobs, lived quietly on his estates near Mantua. His portrait by Raphael, painted in the Venetian manner and in a pose resembling that of Leonardo's *Mona Lisa,* shows the prepossessing face of a man of high intelligence (Paris, Louvre). Castiglione wrote most of the *Courtier* between 1513 and 1518. The book takes the form of a series of conversations. Its characters are visiting papal attendants as well as gentlemen and ladies of the local court— among them Giuliano de' Medici, the brother of Leo X and duke of Nemours; Frisio, a German diplomat who thinks the role of women is to cook and spin; Elisabetta Gonzaga, the childless, much-liked wife of Guidobaldo; her witty companion, Emilia Pia, who was to die discussing the *Courtier;* and Pietro Bembo, who plays the trump card with his discourse on Platonic love. The imaginary conversations are held during four evenings in the Renaissance palace of the duke of Urbino and turn on the ideal of the courtier, who should be brave and good-looking, well-read and well-spoken—with no small taste for art and music—and discreet. In sports and in the arts, he should not seem professional, but retain his status as an amateur. He must be smooth in dealing with his lord, never bear bad news, cultivate his reputation, avoid mixing too much with the common people, and change his manner to suit his interlocutors. Above all—and this is one of the book's subtler points—he must appear aloof, never betraying his emotions, such as anger and frustration. If we detect in this composite portrait a shade of snobbery, even hypocrisy, such flaws are more than balanced by the courtier's virtues, which comprise a capacity for friendship and loyalty to his employer. As for milady, she ought to be, "in fashions, manners, words, and gestures, much unlike the man. For while it is well for him to show a full and steady manliness, so it is well for her to have a tenderness, soft and mild, and show her womanly sweetness in every gesture . . . always behaving in such a way as to commit no faults and not be blemished with suspicion." Published in 1528 by Aldo Manuzio's firm in Venice, less than a year before the author's death in faraway Toledo,

Spain, the *Courtier* quickly went through numerous Italian editions. But it was outside Italy that the book celebrated its main triumphs. In 1561, it was translated into English by Sir Thomas Hoby—a long-time resident of Italy, and English ambassador to France—and became, overnight, a manual of manners for the upper classes, then looking eagerly to Italy for cultural and intellectual guidance. (Castiglione himself had visited England in 1506 to receive, as Guidobaldo's proxy, the Order of the Garter.) The English gentleman is shaped, largely, by Castiglione. Polonius's famous admonitions to his son Laertes, in the first act of Shakespeare's *Hamlet* (1600–1601)—"Give thy thoughts no tongue. . . . Be thou familiar, but by no means vulgar. . . . Take each man's censure, but reserve thy judgment"—reflect Castiglione's prescripts. Indeed, Hamlet, the "sweet prince," himself is thought by many scholars to be modeled after Castiglione's hero, while the sharp-tongued Emilia Pia lives on as Beatrice in *Much Ado About Nothing.* Was Baldassare himself the courtier? The emperor Charles V, on hearing of his death at the age of fifty-one, exclaimed, "I tell you, one of the world's great *caballeros* is dead!"

C E L E S T I N E V (Pietro Angeleri da Morrone, born c. 1215). The reluctant pope. The conclave held after the death of Nicholas IV was hopelessly split between the powerful Colonna and Orsini clans, both represented by cardinals. In July of 1294, after two years of futile haggling, an outsider was picked. The choice of Pietro, an aged hermit haunting the wilderness of the Abruzzi and known for his supernatural powers—he was said to have once hung his monk's robe on a sunbeam—responded to the popular desire to see a messianic pope, *papa angelicus,* restore the church to apostolic poverty. This hope was fostered by the "spiritual" branch of the Franciscans, and the ascetic branch of the Benedictines, which Pietro himself had founded. When the bishops carrying the summons to the papal throne found the emaciated figure with a matted beard in the remote mountain hut where he was doing penance, they fell to the ground—and so did he. On seeing that the message was authentic, he tried to scamper away, then, on the plea of fellow monks, reluctantly accepted. A crowd of some two hundred thousand, among them cardinals and princes, flocked to the Abruzzi to see the poor old man invested with the glittering insignia of papal power. Charles II ("the Lame"), the Angevin king of Naples, led the ass that carried the unfortunate hermit to nearby Aquila where he was crowned. In need of papal backing for his intended conquest of Sicily, Charles forthwith secured the new pope's person, prevented him from reaching Rome, and kept him in a cell in his own Naples palace. The absurdity of the conclave's choice now became manifest. Celestine, uneducated and unworldly, was utterly unequal to the functions of a pontiff. Surrounded by a camarilla of schemers, he obediently signed every document put before him. Legend claims that Cardinal Benedetto Gaetani (or Caetani), close friend of Charles, who wanted to be pope himself, spoke to him through a tube at night, urging him to lay down the tiara. True or not, Celestine did resign. On 13 December 1294, dressed once again in his monk's habit, he publicly announced his resignation, over the protest of an irate crowd that viewed him as a savior. (The unnamed shade in Dante's *Inferno* [III: 60] guilty of "the great refusal made out of cowardice" is sometimes thought to be Celestine.) The tragedy was far from over. Elected pope and taking the name Boniface VIII, Gaetani felt threatened by the hermit's popularity and sent him as a prisoner to Rome. But Celestine, falling back on the instincts of a creature of the wilds, escaped into the woods and, after weeks of wandering, reached the Adriatic coast where he boarded a boat bound for the freedom of mountainous Dalmatia. Alas, an adverse wind threw the vessel back on shore. He was arrested and incarcerated in the papal fortress of Fumone, where he died less than two years later. Sainted in 1313, he is an object of much veneration in his beloved Abruzzi. Many pray at his Renaissance marble tomb in S. Maria di Collemaggio, Aquila.

CELLINI, Benvenuto (1500–71). Florentine goldsmith and sculptor, famed for his bronze statue of the hero Perseus (in Florence's Loggia dei Lanzi), a wondrously wrought gold saltcellar (Vienna, Kunsthistorisches Museum), and a breezy, readable autobiography. Impetuous, vain, facetious, he was involved in brawls and murders, hasty love affairs, arrests, hairbreadth escapes. Florence, Rome, Fontainebleau were his main scenes of action; Duke Cosimo I of Tuscany, Pope Clement VII, King Francis I of France, his patrons. Many of his creations, among them coins and medals, are lost. But what remains makes him one of the finest sculptors of his generation. Michelangelo often visited his studio and, writes Cellini, "praised my work." Among his picaresque adventures (for which he is our only source) is his role during the Sack of Rome, when he killed, with one lucky harquebus shot from the ramparts, Charles de Bourbon, commander of the attacking rabble. Then, having squeezed into Castel Sant'Angelo (the redoubt of the papal court) just before the portcullis came rattling down, he manned a big gun, killing many of the enemy who were already in the city and saving the fortress from capture. Years later, imprisoned in the same stout stronghold by Pope Paul III, whose tiara he was (falsely) accused of having stripped of jewels, he escaped in daredevil fashion, breaking his leg in the process. Perhaps the most exciting episode of his career, however, is the casting of his masterpiece, the *Perseus,* for Duke Cosimo I in Florence. The clay model, showing the hero raising high the severed head of the Gorgon Medusa, was so complicated that it was doubtful whether it could be cast in one piece. Cosimo said the Medusa head would not come out. Cellini wondered whether Perseus' right foot would be all there. Having built a special furnace in his workshed, heaped the cauldron with lumps of copper and tin which would fuse into bronze, and positioned the mold so it would receive the flow of liquid metal, he lined up ten assistants, lit the fire—and collapsed. Shouting to his men to proceed, he took to his bed, where he writhed with a devastating fever, gasping that he was about to die. After a while, he saw one of his helpers shuffle in with a long face—the bronze had caked and wasn't flowing; all was lost! Benvenuto, raging, hitting and kicking everyone in sight, rushed to the furnace, sent for some oak logs, and started a fierce fire—so fierce that it not only liquefied the metal, but blew off the furnace lid into the bargain, and set the roof on fire. In an instant, he realized that the intense heat had burned the tin out of the bronze, leaving behind almost pure copper, less fusible, less handsome, and too soft for sculpture. Detailing men to take care of the blazing roof, he ordered others to fetch all his pewter pots, pans, tankards, bowls and dishes—nearly 200 pieces. These he dropped, one by one, into the seething stew, which their high tin content restored to bronze. The mold filled nicely as the hissing alloy flowed through opened vents. Benvenuto, miraculously cured, sank into a happy sleep. The statue came out nearly perfect, the only missing part being the toes of Perseus' right foot, which the master had to put on afterward. He died seventeen years later in Florence and was buried with high honors. A vagabond at heart, he never married. He supported six nieces. His only child, an illegitimate son, was inadvertently smothered by his nurse at the age of two.

THE CENCI MURDER CASE. The events leading up to the public execution of Beatrice Cenci in 1599 have stirred the imagination of dramatists and poets through the centuries, not merely because of the girl's youth and reputed beauty—"a most gentle and amiable being, a creature formed to adorn and be admired" (Shelley)—but also because the story raises the fundamental question of what it takes to justify a murder, and parricide at that. Her father, Francesco (1549–98), an influential Roman nobleman and landowner, had been in and out of court for criminal offenses ever since he was eleven years old.

In 1593, his mistress, "la bella Spoletina" ("the beauty from Spoleto"), brought suit against him for extreme cruelty. The same year, his valet accused him of heavy beatings and of having locked him up, naked, for two days. The next year, he nearly killed a man, who suffered serious injuries. Also in 1594, Francesco was tried by a papal court for sodomy and cruelty and, when his accusers persisted in their charges under torture, found guilty, but allowed (as he had been allowed in other run-ins with the law) to buy impunity for a large sum of money paid into the papal treasury. In 1563, he had married a rich lady, Ersilia Santa Croce, whom he treated abominably and who, nevertheless, bore him twelve children, seven of whom survived early childhood. His son Cristoforo was murdered over a love affair; another, Rocco, exiled for various crimes, secretly returned to rob his father's house, and was eventually killed in a duel. One of his two daughters married into the Savelli family, a noble Roman clan. After his first wife's death, Francesco married Lucrezia Petroni, a widow with three daughters, to each of whom he gave a generous dowry. In the vast, spooky Cenci palace on the edge of Rome's ghetto, domestic life was made unbearable by Francesco's violent nature. In 1595, he took his wife, Lucrezia, and Beatrice, his eighteen-year-old daughter, to the lonely castle of La Petrella, a Colonna stronghold southeast of Rome of which he had the use, and locked them up in its upper rooms, where he brutalized and threatened them. Although there is no evidence of incest with his daughter, his passion for her is generally accepted as a fact. Beatrice is said to have found temporary solace in an affair with Olimpio Calvetti, warden of the castle. Finally, driven to extremes, she conspired with Olimpio and two of her brothers, Giacomo and Bernardo —who had quarrels of their own with their father—to murder him. The deed was done, on 9 September 1598, by Olimpio and a hired assassin, Marzio Catalano, who hammered a nail into the sleeping Francesco's head, then threw his body from a balcony into a tree and fled. The family went into mourning. Olimpio was captured and killed. Catalano was taken alive and confessed, whereupon Lucrezia, Beatrice, Giacomo, and Bernardo were arrested. Beatrice, tortured, at first clung to her denial of all guilt, but confessed her part in the conspiracy under a more severe degree of torture. Though her defense insisted that she was driven to her crime by her father's behavior, she was condemned to death. A groundswell of popular sympathy backed pleas for a papal pardon. But Pope Clement VIII (the same who, shortly afterwards, had the freethinking philosopher, Giordano Bruno, burned as a heretic in Rome's Campo dei Fiori, where he now has a monument) turned a deaf ear to all petitions. Only the boy Bernardo was sentenced to life imprisonment and released after a year. On 11 September 1599, Beatrice, aged twenty-one, and her stepmother, Lucrezia, were beheaded on the square facing Castel Sant'Angelo across the Tiber. Giacomo was torn with red-hot tongs, killed with a mace, and drawn and quartered. Beatrice was buried in a nameless tomb in S. Pietro in Montorio. She had left money for masses to be said for her soul. The murdered Francesco's extensive holdings were confiscated by the pope; this, Romans said, was the real motive behind the executions. The best-known literary efforts dealing with the events are Shelley's lyric tragedy, *The Cenci*, and Stendhal's romanticized account in *Chroniques Italiennes*. More recently, the Italian writer Alberto Moravia and the French playwright Antonin Artaud have written plays about the Cenci case.

C H I G I , Agostino, "The Magnificent" (c. 1465–1520). Plutocrat. Member of an old Sienese (originally French) family, he came to Rome in 1485 to join the Sienese banking house of Spannocchi, which soon became his own. His immortality is vouchsafed by two landmarks of Renaissance Rome—his villa by the Tiber and his funerary chapel in S. Maria del Popolo. The former, now known as "La Farnesina" for its later owners, the Farnese family, was designed on a palatial scale by Baldassare Peruzzi (1481–1536) and decorated with resplendent frescoes by a group of artists that included Il Sodoma (1477–1549)—whose *Marriage of Alexander the Great* in one of the villa's bedrooms is his masterpiece—and Raphael, who painted

Galatea gliding over the waves in a paddle-wheel chariot drawn by dolphins. Here, Chigi entertained popes, artists, cardinals, and princes in a riverbank portico. Choice food was served on silver dishes (some say gold), which were then tossed into the Tiber— to be recovered, when the guests were gone, by way of a large net spread previously for the occasion. As treasurer to Pope Julius II, Agostino handled the finances of the church and officiated as *éminence grise* of the papal court. He operated his own fleet of seagoing merchant vessels and maintained branches of his bank in several Italian cities and warehouses in London and Constantinople. Julius, in a rare gesture of familiarity, permitted him to join his own name, della Rovere, to his and to quarter the Chigi family arms—six hills topped by a star—with the Rovere oak. Leo X further enriched him by granting him the concession to exploit the papal alum mines at Tolfa, northwest of Rome, whose product, needed in the manufacture of fast dyes for the Mediterranean wool trade, yielded large revenues. Chigi collected art on a grand scale and sponsored archaeological digs. He introduced young Pietro Aretino to society and was rewarded by that charming rascal's lifelong adulation. The Chigi Chapel, designed for Agostino by Raphael, is graced by an admirable altar painting by Sebastiano del Piombo, another of his protégés. There, Agostino and his brother Sigismondo are buried under pyramids of magenta-colored marble. Agostino's fortune was soon dissipated. Sigismondo's progeny, however, achieved worldly prominence as princes of the Holy Roman Empire. One of his descendants, Fabio Chigi, became Pope Alexander VII in 1655. He was an enthusiastic patron of Bernini, who built on his behalf the portico around Piazza S. Pietro.

CHRISTINA, Queen of Sweden (1626–89). Lutheran convert to Catholicism, long-time resident of Rome, a greedy art collector, and a "case." Unpredictable, self-willed, often called "mad," she left her imprint on the age of the Baroque.

Daughter of the great warrior-king Gustavus Adolphus ("Lion of the North"), who died in battle without leaving a male heir, she was raised as a boy. Even late in life she was admired for her sure hand with a hunting gun and for her lightning takeoff on a horse. Physically unattractive, indifferent to dress, she was an insatiable reader, spoke several languages, and excelled by her quick wit, her erudition, and her passion for the arts. These gifts enabled her to gather learned men around her, including the philosopher René Descartes, who died of pneumonia after giving her lessons in the freezing royal palace at five in the morning. Crowned in 1644, she made herself a virtually absolute ruler, but shocked her counselors by declaring that she would not marry and produce children to perpetuate the Vasa dynasty. A male cousin was proclaimed heir to the throne. Christina's penchant for Catholicism, a faith the royal family was legally forbidden to embrace, made her seek the advice of the Jesuits, who sent two priests, in disguise, to Stockholm to instruct her. In 1654, she abdicated, rode out of Stockholm dressed as a man, and became a Catholic in Brussels. The papacy looked on her conversion as a major triumph, and her entry into Rome, in 1655, was one of the most ostentatious events of the period. Bernini had decorated the Porta del Popolo for the occasion (the inscription, *Felici Faustoque Ingressui* ["to a happy and well-boding entry"] is still there), and Pope Alexander VII (Chigi) himself escorted her to the high altar of St. Peter's. But she soon raised Roman eyebrows by her lack of manners, her often vulgar speech, her disdain for formal piety, and her financial zigzags which forced her, at one point, to pawn her dresses. Restless, ambitious, scheming, she meddled in affairs of state. Eager to play queen again, she went to France where she was promised the crown of Naples if the French succeeded in taking that city from the Spaniards. Christina had retained juridical authority over her court, and when her equerry and favorite, Marquis Giovanni Monaldeschi, betrayed the plot to the Neapolitans, she condemned him to death and had his throat cut— an "execution" that lost her most of the sympathy of Catholic Europe. "I have no cause for regret," she wrote. Back in Rome, her rented palace remained the meeting place of a select group of churchmen, artists, writers, and musicians. Her concerts, given by her own orchestra, were the joy of connoisseurs, especially when she appointed Alessandro Scarlatti her music master. Operas were dedicated to her. She founded an academy of erudite men. Bernini came to see her frequently, created several sculptures for her, and advised her on her art collection. Cardinal Decio Azzolino, papal secretary of state, became her financial manager and, many said, her lover. Among her interests were alchemy, astrology, and archaeology; she organized digs and actually found a statue of Venus. Her collection had its origins in Stockholm, where she had been presented with several bargeloads of works of art looted by Swedish armies from the Hapsburgs during the Thirty Years' War. At the end of her life, she owned one of the richest private collections ever put together. Her statuary, consisting of more than two hundred pieces, included the famous marble group of the Muses found in Hadrian's Villa near Rome. Among her 300-odd paintings were two great Titians, a Madonna by Raphael (her favorite painter), Correggio's celebrated *Danaë,* and a portrait of Sir Thomas More by Hans Holbein the Younger. There were important drawings by Raphael and Michelangelo, two-thousand-odd precious manuscripts, and an assortment of rare coins and medals. These treasures were dispersed, soon after her death, and are now to be seen in the world's principal museums and libraries. The queen is buried in St. Peter's—remembered, in her own assessment, as "one of the monuments of Rome."

C I C E R O , Marcus Tullius (106–43 B.C.). Statesman, orator, one of the greatest trial lawyers of all times. Well documented by his works and his correspondence, he has left behind a clear image of himself. A provincial without family connections, he captivated Rome with his political orations in the Forum and soon was asked to represent people in court. His election to the post of *quaestor* (treasury official) made him, automatically, a life member of Rome's most powerful body, the Senate. After studying under famous orators, he opened a law practice. He rose to fame through his proceedings against Verres, governor of Sicily, who was defended by Rome's leading lawyer. The case was heard before a special claims court, the jury being formed by senators. Cicero's clients were the Sicilian people whom Verres had exploited and oppressed, and he came to the trial with a stack of evidence gathered by interviewing hundreds of witnesses and examining local records. It was summer; Rome was filled with out-of-towners, many of whom crowded the court in hopes of seeing a smart young lawyer get the better of a high-and-mighty viceroy. Verres, Cicero charged, had stolen temple statues for his art collection, had taxed the farmers out of house and home, had cruelly put to death innocent people. Demolished by Cicero's sharp sallies, Verres decamped before the trial ended and sailed for France. Cicero emerged as a national figure, meeting with cheers wherever he set foot. Fifty-eight of his grand orations have survived. Their lucid style, their sarcasm, their irresistible appeal to the emotions, make them forensic works of art. Out of sixty-nine criminal cases in which he appeared, usually for the defendant, he lost ten, and he was equally successful in civil law suits. He never shouted—"Why take a horse when you can walk?"—and suffered from stage fright. Tipped off that Catiline, a rabble-rouser with a large following, was plotting to burn Rome and massacre its leading citizens (including himself), Cicero delivered his famous orations against the bold adventurer in the Senate, where Catiline himself was sitting. Beginning, "How long will you abuse our patience, Catiline?" they were so loaded with invective that Catiline fled Rome before he could be arrested. Later, dismayed by the civil war between the two colossi, Pompey and Caesar, Cicero spent most of his time writing at one of his country places. Many of his works were Latin adaptations of Greek classics (he once translated one of Aristotle's books entirely from memory during a journey), making him the chief transmitter of Greek thought to his—and our own—civilization. Latin was still a simple language of the soil, and Cicero created, in large part, the abstract vocabulary needed to convey ideas. He left a heritage of some eight hundred personal letters, written with uncommon freshness and revealing him as a compassionate human being who could weep bitterly at the death of a slave. Toward the end of his life, he divorced his wife, Terentia, to marry another. His son and daughter knew him as a loving father. Placing liberty above life, he rejoiced at the murder of Julius Caesar in the Senate. "Our liberators," he wrote, "will be forever famous." (It is said that Brutus raised his bloody dagger in a salute, calling out, "Cicero!") But when the dead man's heir, Mark Antony, continued Caesar's autocratic rule, Cicero—to the surprise of all concerned—stepped from retirement into the Senate and, by his harangues against Mark Antony, became the voice of liberty. "I would gladly offer my own body if with my death I could redeem the freedom of our country." He had signed his death warrant. For centuries to come, Rome would be ruled by despots. Proscribed as a public enemy, Cicero left Rome. Soldiers caught up with him in a pine-woods near the sea. He told his bearers to set his litter down, and silently stretched forth his neck. A centurion struck off his head. Thus died a Roman. "I may be wrong," he had written in his booklet *On Old Age,* "in my belief that the soul is immortal. If so, I'd rather err than part with this belief, which gives me so much happiness."

COATS OF ARMS. Wherever he goes in Italy, the traveler is faced by a profusion of armorial bearings, painted in bright colors, or sculpted on large, weighty stone shields, looking down on him from palaces and churches, fortresses and public buildings. Emblems of noble families or of towns and guilds, these coats of arms are a characteristic Old World institution, going back to feudal times, and reaching its richest flowering in form-and-color-happy Italy. They may have been invented to distinguish friend from foe and were useful in identifying visored knights to spectators at tournaments, like jockeys' colors in a modern horse race. Many of them originated during the Crusades (1096–1270) when they appeared on flags and banners. In Italy, the conqueror of a town would lose no time in placing his escutcheon on the town hall. The Medici arms—six balls, usually arranged to form an upright oval, which, as the family ran a bank, may be the origin of our pawnshop shingle—are to be found all over Tuscany, their hard-won duchy. (According to others, they are pills—a pun on the family name, which means "physicians.") Combinations of two or more bearings on a single shield usually point to a marital union between families, or acquisition of more territories. Puns are popular. The lords of Anguillara, near Rome, used an eel (*anguilla*) in their ensign; when the Orsini family took over Anguillara, the eel slid into their own, much subdivided crest, which is upheld by two bears (*orsi*). Popes and cardinals ("Princes of the Church") choose coats of arms, unless their family already has one, upon their installation; two escutcheons placed at equal height on the façade of a church in Rome identify the building as a cardinal's "titular" church (the church assigned to him) and show his bearings and those of the reigning pope. Memorable papal emblems are the two blue waves of the Gaetani (Boniface VIII); the column of the Colonnas (Martin V); the Borgia bull (Calixtus III and Alexander VI); the Piccolomini's five crescents (Pius II and Pius III); the Rovere oak (Sixtus IV, Julius II); the fleur-de-lis, or lily, of the Farnese (Paul III); and the Boncompagni dragon (Gregory XIII). Pope Pius XII (1939–58), whose family name was Pacelli, chose a dove holding an olive branch—*paco* ("Peace")—a motif already used, though in a different design, by Innocent X (Pamphili, 1644–55). Roses and comets form the crest of the Torlonia, a rich, once-powerful Rome family. Famous Venetian crests are the three dolphins, for Dolfin, and the twin roses of the Mocenigo, both ducal families. In Florence, three crescents stand for Strozzi, three hunting horns for Guicciardini, two dolphins and five crosses for Pazzi, a moor's head means Pucci. Among city crests, the best known is the winged lion of Venice, attribute of its patron saint, Mark. The vertically divided bearings of Milan show, in the right half, a city gate and, on the left, a serpent devouring a child—the ancient coat of arms of the Visconti, who lorded it over Milan from c. 1200 to 1447. Rome proudly displays the classic S.P.Q.R., the abbreviation used in antiquity in promulgating official decrees and commonly assumed to stand for *SENATUS POPULUSQUE ROMANUS*, though the "Q" may stand for *Quirites* ("Roman citizens in their civil capacity").

———————•◆•———————

COLONNA FAMILY. The Italian Constitution of 1948 abolishes all noble titles, but does not interdict their use— and few Italian aristocrats will go through life simply as *signor* or *signora.* Titles are used on visiting cards and formal invitations, as well as in the telephone directory. They are, in ascending order, *barone* ("baron"), *conte* ("count" or "earl"), *marchese* ("marquis"), *duca* ("duke"), and *principe* ("prince"). All of them are hereditary. Values attached to them, however, are relative; a baron with a thousand-year-old title might consider himself of bluer blood than a third-generation prince. (Pius XII [1938–58] was the last pope to grant papal titles.) Heavily intermarried, welded together by bonds of business and friendship, Italy's aristocracy still operates as an exclusive club. Among the most illustrious princely houses are the Colonnas (an old baronial clan with roots in the countryside near Rome), sometimes called, "Italy's first family." Mentioned by Dante and Petrarch, long dreaded for their armed exploits, they were so deeply and so bloodily involved in Rome's vicissitudes during the Middle Ages that it is often said that the Colonna story is the story of medieval Rome. For the last nine centuries, the family has nurtured an astounding number of prominent and able individuals, among them some thirty cardinals, one pope, outstanding condottieri, statesmen, and at least one famous lady, Vittoria Colonna. Their drama, continued through the Renaissance and into modern times, has a Shakespearean ring, and many of their men have borne Shakespearean-sounding names: Aspreno, Fabrizio, Prospero, Ascanio, Pompeo, Marcantonio. Marriages with other potent dynasties—the Montefeltro, Aragon, Gonzaga, Doria, Barberini, della Rovere, and even their archenemies, Orsini—reinforced the native power chromosome. Colonnas were endowed with a remarkable capacity for bouncing back after a fall. Though they were Ghibellines (imperialists)—their princely title, added to their baronies and dukedoms in the six-

teenth century, makes them princes of the Holy Roman Empire
—they frequently aligned themselves with the papacy, switched
back and forth, and, on occasion, fought in two opposing
armies. Their claim of direct descent from the *gens Iulia*—
the family that fathered Julius Caesar (and that, in turn,
claimed descent from the goddess Venus)—is no longer seriously maintained. Colonnas are first heard of in the eleventh
century, when one Piero de Columna ("column")—it is not
known which came first, the name or the family crest—was lord
of several strongpoints in the Roman countryside, among them
Palestrina. Numerous and resourceful, they built up their feudal
sway, more land giving them more peasant-soldiers and more
wealth. By 1212, they had their first cardinal, Giovanni, who, a
Ghibelline at heart, threw in his lot with the Holy Roman
emperor, Frederick II, in that ruler's struggles with the papacy.
It was at this point that the Colonnas first clashed with the
Orsinis, rival nobles in the Roman region and inveterate Guelfs
(pro-papal)—who were to have three popes. They took Giovanni
prisoner and ravaged the Colonna villages. For centuries, the
bitter feud was to continue under the slogan "Colonna for the
people—Orsini for the Church." By the middle of the thirteenth
century, however, the Colonnas were Rome's paramount clan,
commanding a ring of fortified estates that cut across major
highways, giving them a stranglehold on the city. In Rome itself, they held a large chunk of what is now the downtown area,
which they had turned into a formidable fortress, bristling with
towers and surrounded by a wall. One member of the Rome
branch, also called Giovanni, serving as senator (at the time,
chief magistrate) of Rome under Pope Nicholas IV (1288–92),
enjoyed such popularity that he was taken to the Capitol in triumph and hailed as "Caesar" by a populace ever in search of
civil leadership. When, after the abdication of Celestine V in
1294, Benedetto Gaetani ascended the papal throne as Boniface
VIII, he at once bestowed positions and estates on his own
family. Finding themselves pushed into the background, the
Colonnas, captained by their two cardinals, Jacopo and Pietro,
rose in rebellion against Boniface, branding him a usurper, since
Celestine's abdication was, in the view of many, an illegal act.
The pope, seeing a chance to crush the clan forever, struck back,
proclaiming a "crusade" against it. Proud Palestrina was de-

molished and, in 1298, the humbled cardinals, in sackcloth and with ropes around their necks, knelt before Boniface—who pardoned them, but did not reinstate them. Landless, but far from finished, the Colonnas found new friends abroad. In September 1303, a small French force, led by Sciarra Colonna and Guillaume de Nogaret, chief minister of the French king, who resented Boniface's meddling in French affairs, descended like a lightning bolt on Anagni, near Rome, the pope's birthplace, where he was residing. The papal garrison was massacred or fled, and the two chiefs, swords drawn, rushed over corpses into the burning and deserted palace, where they found the octogenarian pontiff enthroned in his robes of state. Sciarra pulled him off the throne, and had to be restrained from killing him. (The oft-repeated story of Nogaret's slapping the pope is probably a myth.) Incarcerated, Boniface was rescued by the people of Anagni and escorted to Rome where—haunted, perhaps, by the ghost of Celestine—he is said to have gone mad. He died within a month. Before the year was over, the Colonnas were restored to their former status—and free to engage in years of warfare with the Gaetanis and Orsinis. It is against this somber background of anarchy and chaos, with Rome and the Campagna devastated by the feuding clans, that we must view the rise of Cola di Rienzo, dictator of Rome, who, in the battle by the gate of S. Lorenzo (1347), utterly vanquished a baronial force consisting of Colonnas, Gaetanis, and Orsinis. Eighty slain nobles, among them three Colonnas, were left lying naked in their blood. Surely, the end! Yet, we soon see the family resume its former role—and, at long last, in the person of Oddone Colonna (Pope Martin V, 1417–31), clutch the ultimate prize. Martin, a peaceable and cultured man, started restoring Rome, reduced organized crime, and called great artists to his court. At the same time, he established new Colonna footholds in central Italy and caused his neighbor to the south, Queen Joan II of Naples, who needed his support, to grant him titles and estates within her kingdom as insurance against the jealousy of future popes. Close relatives of Martin emerged as counts of Celano, dukes of Amalfi, princes of Salerno. When Naples, soon afterwards, came under Spanish domination, we find Colonnas as grand constables (commanders-in-chief) of Naples, leading Spanish armies against the French in northern Italy, or strutting about in gorgeous

Spanish dress on their estates south of the border. It was, presumably, their southern connection that prompted them to stage the typically Neapolitan feast of the Cockaigne—named for a never-never land of idleness and plenty—in the Church of the Holy Apostles adjoining their Rome palace. There, every first of May, fat fowl were released, and a roast pig was suspended from the ceiling for the crowd to jump for and be doused by bucketsful of water from above. In 1526, with tension growing between the Holy Roman emperor and king of Spain, Charles V, and Pope Clement VII, an Imperial force of three thousand infantry, eight hundred horses, and a battery of buffalo-drawn cannon, led by Pompeo Colonna, broke into Rome. It plundered St. Peter's and the Vatican and withdrew across the Neapolitan border, having given the pope a foretaste of the "Sack of Rome" of the following year. The apex of Colonna glory came with the naval battle of Lepanto (1571), in which armed Christendom decisively defeated the advancing Turk, with Marcantonio Colonna commanding the papal galleys holding the center of the Christian line. He got a hero's welcome and was granted a triumph in Rome. The Colonna story, henceforth, continues in a more settled mood. In 1870, a young cavalry officer, Fabrizio Colonna, rode with the liberators into Rome through the breach at Porta Pia in the assault that was to topple the popes' secular power over Rome and pave the way for Italy's unification. (Fabrizio's son, Ascanio, as Mussolini's ambassador to Washington, had the sorry duty of declaring war on the United States in 1941.) Today, the Colonnas, while still holding large estates near their ancestral seat of Paliano, east of Rome, are found in managerial jobs, in banking, business, and professional life. Their sprawling palace, in the capital itself, was remodeled in the late seventeenth century. It boasts a 250-foot-long, 40-foot-wide hall with frescoed ceilings, columns of rare yellow marble, sculptured baroque furniture, statues, crystal chandeliers, mirrors, paintings, and gilt stucco work.

CONDOTTIERE, pl. condottieri. A captain-adventurer, hired for pay, leading a mercenary army—usually several thousand strong, most of them heavy cavalry—in the perennial wars among Italian states. Condottieri flourished, approximately, between 1250 and 1450. As city dwellers became too soft, or too busy, to take up arms, these tough professionals, whose forces contained many stragglers from foreign armies, were much in demand. Condottieri were liberally paid. Battles were fought with relatively little bloodshed, as soldiers were too precious to be sacrificed, but the countryside suffered heavy damage as village after village was given over to plunder. Condottieri frequently switched sides, transferring their loyalty to the higher bidder, and often fought against a prince or republic that had been their employer in the recent past. One of the greatest condottieri was an Englishman, Sir John Hawkwood (c. 1320–94), known as Giovanni Acuto ("Sharp"), the son of an Essex tanner. After fighting with the English forces in France, he strayed across the Alps and became captain of a roving band of Englishmen, Frenchmen, and Germans—the dreaded "White Company," originally formed by a German, Albert Sterz. As captain general of Pisa, he applied the lessons he had learned in the French wars—his troops were highly disciplined, excelled at rapid movements, and saw to their equipment—and soon was Italy's most respected military leader. After successful campaigns for the Visconti of Milan, he spent several years commanding the armies of the Florentine republic. He died a citizen of Florence, where his equestrian portrait, painted by Paolo Uccello, is in the cathedral. The ruggedness of famous condottieri brought out the best in some Italian artists. The bronze equestrian monument of Erasmo da Narni (c. 1370–1443), *Gattamelata*, by Donatello stands in front of the Church of S. Antonio in Padua; Bartolommeo Colleoni (1400–75), commander of the Venetian armies and greatest tactician of his time, lives on in Verrocchio's celebrated monument in Venice. He lies buried in a sumptuous Renaissance tomb in Bergamo, near Milan. Another prominent condottiere serving Venice, Francesco Carmagnola, was recalled from the battlefield, tortured and tried for conspiring with the republic's enemy, the duke of Milan, his erstwhile employer, and beheaded as a traitor in 1432 between the two columns of the Piazzetta, in front of the doge's palace.

A number of condottieri carved out their own principalities or dukedoms and founded dynasties—such as the Montefeltro of Urbino and the Malatesta of Rimini—renowned for the humanistic culture and the artistic life of their courts. The founder of the Sforza line which ruled Milan from 1450 to 1535, sponsoring Leonardo da Vinci and Bramante, was Muzio (1396–1424), a peasant from Romagna called "Sforza," from sforzare ("to force"). He fought as condottiere for Queen Joan II of Naples and for Pope Martin V and drowned in his last campaign. A curious case is that of the condottiere in priestly garb, Giovanni Vitelleschi (d. 1440), who started as a scribe, became a priest, then chose the career of a condottiere, in which he displayed considerable talent and a cruelty unusual even in his age. Pope Eugene IV (1431–47), a weak man in need of a strong arm, took a liking to him. After consecrating him a bishop, he appointed him military governor of Rome, in which capacity Vitelleschi took on the troublesome baronial clans of the Campagna, as Cola di Rienzo had done a century earlier. In waging this war, which he obviously relished, he destroyed some thirty towns—including Palestrina (stronghold of the Colonnas), destroyed before by Pope Boniface VIII (1294–1303) and since rebuilt—leaving them smoking piles of rubble. He turned the Campagna into a desert, promising his soldiers a hundred years' remission of punishment for sins for every olive tree cut down. Survivors were sold into slavery. Others were killed or thrown into dungeons where they perished. Coming upon a minor condottiere, Antonio da Pontedera, whose hungry soldiers were plundering what was left to plunder, he hanged him from the nearest tree. As a reward for his victory, Eugene made this monster—as humanist Lorenzo Valla called him—archbishop of Florence and titular patriarch of Alexandria. Vitelleschi returned to Rome in triumph, riding under a golden baldachin carried by leading citizens and escorted by a procession of torchbearers, clergy, musicians, and people waving olive branches. They had reason for gratitude, for the barons would no longer harass them and the bread price had come down. "Long live the patriarch!" Vitelleschi was presented with a goblet filled with gold. One Poncelletto Venerami, who had led a conspiracy against Eugene—the Pope (at this time presiding over the Council of Ferrara and Florence) had escaped in disguise, in a rowboat, down the Tiber—was dragged through the streets, pinched with red-hot tongs, and drawn and quartered. For his services, Eugene rewarded Vitelleschi with a cardinal's red hat. Soon afterwards, the pope received word that his trusted paladin was plotting to betray him and grab the papacy for himself. Caught in an ambush when he was separated from his men, the condottiere-cardinal was wounded and pulled off his horse. He died—presumably of poison—in Castel S. Angelo, the papal fortress, three weeks later. The last great Renaissance condottiere, Jacopo Piccinino, called *Cavallo* ("Horse"), son of the equally famous Niccolò, is remembered for a remarkably frank exposition of the condottiere's calling recorded by Pope Pius II (1458–64) in *Memoirs of a Renaissance Pope,* translated by Florence A. Gragg, edited by Leona C. Gabel. (Published here with the permission of G. P. Putnam's Sons.) During a lull in the warfare between Ferdinand, the Spanish king of Naples, and John of Anjou, the French claimant to the same throne, Piccinino, fighting for the French, found himself confronted by superior forces commanded by the condottiere Alessandro Sforza, son of Muzio and brother of Duke Francesco of Milan. Invited into Sforza's camp under safe-conduct, Piccinino, determined to avoid battle, addressed the assembled officers roughly like this: "I ask you, Comrades, whom will you defeat if you beat Piccinino? Is it not I who support you? While I am a captain and disturbing the peace, you are called out to war when otherwise you would be idle. Is it not I who got you the gold with which you glitter, your arms, horses, dress? Do you then persecute me—me, the source of your well-being? Suppose I am taken prisoner or killed in battle. What good would it do you? Who finds peace advantageous except merchants and priests? You will fatten the priests if they are not already fat enough. You will enrich the merchants. Unless Italy is ablaze with war, we can scratch no profit out of her. In peace, we are looked down upon and forced to the plow. In war, we are famous. Our business is to bear arms. Do not let them rust! Take my word for it, we can easily siphon off the wealth of pope and cardinals and merchants. How? Just don't try to win. Let us prolong the war, for when it ends, a soldier's income ends." His words, we read, were greeted with approval by his opponents. Sforza, turning to his staff, said, "Have no fear. Italy will never be without war until it is governed by one lord. When this war is over, we shall be called to bigger ones!" Piccinino, closeted with Sforza, was persuaded to come over to the side of Naples, and the French lost the war. In 1465, less than two years after this conference, he walked into a trap and was murdered in a Naples dungeon—at the behest, it was said, of Duke Francesco Sforza, who nursed a grudge against him.

COSMATI. Cosmatesque work, enlivening medieval churches in and near Rome, is frequently attributed to a family of stone and marble workers, the "Cosmati," active between 1100 and 1300. The generic term is a modern invention, based on the fact that several of the craftsmen whose signatures have been preserved (and about whom we know little else) bore the Christian name Cosma. In fact, several Roman families, among them the Oderisi and Vassaletti, specialized in colorful mosaic work—work that evokes memories of childhood games as the beholder's eye follows the complicated geometric patterns and color combinations. Looking for precedents, we find them in ancient Rome's taste for polychrome marble inlays, exemplified by remnants in the Roman Forum and, more magnificently, in the Imperial living quarters of Tiberius's (A.D. 14–37) cliff-top "Villa Jovis" on Capri (one of whose finest portions has been transferred to Capri's Church of S. Stefano). Byzantine and Moslem decorations, in Sicily and elsewhere, may also have served as an inspiration. Still, the Cosmati created something wholly of their own, a rejoicing in color that breathed a playful spirit into somber Romanesque church architecture. Their work-shops, turning out meticulously fashioned squares, oblongs, lozenges, and roundels of rare stones, were at their most productive at a time when successive popes were sponsoring a renewal of Rome's churches. Drabness gave way to light and color. Cosmatesque church floors, reminiscent of Oriental carpets, are inlaid with slabs of many shapes and sizes, from small white marble wedges to large purple disks of precious porphyry. Bright yellow and deep green are among the favorites. There was little in a medieval church these fantasists did not enrich with ribbons of kaleidoscopic splendor. Altars and altar screens, paschal candlesticks, architraves, tombs, pulpits, bishop's chairs, and corkscrew columns fringing cloisters were decked with glittering stone and glass-paste mosaics of blue, red, yellow, gold, and silver. In Rome, Cosmatesque work may be seen in S. Clemente, S. Maria in Cosmedin, S. Maria in Trastevere, S. Maria d'Aracoeli, and in other medieval churches. Occasionally, the Cosmati tried their hand, successfully, at architecture and sculpture in combination with their decorative work. The beautiful cloisters of St. John Lateran and St. Paul's-Outside-the-Walls are, wholly or in part, the creations of two Vassalettos, father and son. How far these Roman craftsmen were prepared to travel is demonstrated by the Cosmatesque decorations of the shrine of Edward the Confessor and the tomb of Henry III in Westminster Abbey, London. But the Cosmati's most original work is the Ionic portico of the cathedral of Civita Castellana, a small town thirty-five miles north of Rome. The portico itself, with its high central arch and its spare, vigorous mosaic bands, is the work of three generations of artisans, as vouchsafed by the signatures, dated 1210, of Jacopo, *civis romanus* ("Roman citizen"), son of Lorenzo, and *his* son, Cosma.

COUNTER REFORMATION. In 1517, when Martin Luther, Augustinian friar and theology professor, nailed his Ninety-five Theses to the door of the palace church in

Wittenberg—modern scholars doubt that he did so, believing
that he circulated them—the Roman Church was faced with a
revolt that was to carry off whole nations. It was also faced with
itself. Prelates acknowledged that the papacy was scandal-ridden
and corrupt, that Christians went to church only on major feast
days, and that the selling of "indulgences," promising the remission of purgatorial punishment for sins, was an ungodly business. These massive sales were Luther's prime target. A Dominican, John Tetzel, had outraged the Germans by selling thousands
of indulgences off a cart with a money slot:

Sobald das Geld im Kasten klingt,
Die Seele aus dem Fegefeuer in den Himmel springt.
(As soon as the money clinks in the chest,
The soul jumps from purgatory into heaven.)

Such huge amounts of money were involved in this strange
trade—which partly financed the rebuilding of St. Peter's—that
the Augsburg banking house of Fugger was charged with handling them. Voices in Rome argued for reforms before it was
too late, and ranking Catholics saw in the 1527 Sack of Rome
the Lord's just visitation. "We are not citizens of holy Rome but
of unholy Babylon. Let us reform!" a bishop told the Sacred
Rota, tribunal of the Holy See, in 1528. Reform, taking the
wind out of the spreading Reformation, appealed to the papacy.
The last great Renaissance pope, Paul III (Farnese), after
fathering four children, "got religion" and ordered priests to
behave decorously, wear their habits, and say mass every Sunday.
He instituted year-round preaching (rather than merely during
Lent), promoted regular church attendance and confession, confirmed, in 1540, the Jesuit order as the Church militia, and forbade prostitutes to solicit in church. With more profound reforms
in mind, he convoked the Council of Trent, in the Italian Alps,
which sat, with major interruptions, from 1545 to 1563, turning itself into the workshop of the Counter Reformation. Its decrees dealt with the veneration of saints, the sacrament of matri-
mony, the appointment of bishops, the concept of purgatory, and
the reform of religious orders. The first seminaries for priests
were set up. Trent did not say much about art. While
endorsing the presence of holy images in churches as an aid
to piety, it insisted on their "accuracy" and modesty and en-

joined the clergy to keep a watchful eye on art and artists. The figure that emerged as standard-bearer of the Counter Reformation was Cardinal (Saint) Charles Borromeo (1538–84), nephew of Pope Pius IV, and archbishop of Milan. A man with an ascetic face and a remarkably long nose, strong-willed and intelligent, an art collector and a scholar, he put into practice Trent's decrees by visiting the one thousand parishes of his strategic diocese and setting up conferences of churchmen and artists at which the latter were told what rules to follow, under threat of punishment. For all his strictness, St. Charles was respected and beloved, especially for his courageous care of the sick during the Milan plague of 1576. As leader of the radical reform group, he obtained the papacy for Pius V (Ghislieri, 1566–72), the Grand Inquisitor, who wore a hair shirt under his Dominican habit, killed a number of heretics, excommunicated Queen Elizabeth I of England, and, it was said, wanted to turn all Rome into a monastery. A book on church construction and furnishings published by Borromeo in 1577 defined the Counter Reformation style already pioneered by Palladio's chaste Venetian churches. Borromeo insisted that churches be big enough to hold large congregations (the Franciscans and Dominicans, 350 years before, had followed the same principle), and contain nothing "profane" or "obscene" or "impudent" or otherwise disruptive to pious concentration. Churches should stand at least three steps above the ground and not be hemmed in by taverns, smelly shops, or noisy fair grounds. The watchword was Austerity. Inspired partly by St. Charles, the Jesuits became the great church builders of the day. Of some twenty-five churches that went up in Rome in the half-century after the "Sack," one of the most impressive is Vignola's Church of Il Gesù ("Jesus"), the order's Mother Church and prototype of Jesuit churches throughout Europe, a single-aisled, wide-open structure accommodating some two thousand worshipers. Still, the drab Counter Reformation style, so un-Italian in its joylessness, could not endure. From about 1620 onward, a jubilant Baroque flooded the naked churches, and art, instead of following St. Charles's sober guidelines, became a propaganda weapon, making the humble citizen —kneeling amidst statues, pictures, gold, jasper, agate, and rare marbles—think himself in heaven. The Gesù itself—where Bernini was a regular worshiper—soon decked itself with such baroque scenography as Il Baciccia's illusionistic ceiling fresco and Jesuit Andrea Pozzo's silver, gilt, and lapis lazuli tomb of the order's founder, St. Ignatius of Loyola. While the Counter Reformation did not advance the visual arts—which was hardly its purpose—it achieved many of its aims. The clergy came out of it more disciplined and less corrupt. The office of "pardoner," handling the sale of indulgences, was abolished. And Italy, thanks to the lynx-eyed Inquisition, yet with a minimum of bloodshed, was kept Catholic.

DANTE (Durante Alighieri, 1265–1321). Italy's greatest poet. His 14,233-line *Divine Comedy* (*La divina commedia*)—*divina* added by a publisher in 1555—is both a compendium of medieval theology and an allegory describing the journey of the human soul through sin and doubt toward salvation. It is composed in *terza rima* ("triple rhyme"), a chain of interlacing rhymes, each rhyme occurring thrice in every five lines, making for a cascading rhythm. Divided into three books—*Inferno, Purgatorio, Paradiso* (hell, purgatory, paradise)—and subdivided into one hundred cantos, the work describes the poet's imaginary voyage, lasting one week, through the great beyond. Lost in a dark wood—life's wild confusion—Dante encounters a friendly specter who offers himself as guide. He is the Roman poet Virgil (70–19 B.C.), Dante's spiritual master, whose own *Aeneid* contains a journey to the underworld. Together, they enter the *Inferno,* whose gate bears the inscription *Lasciate Ogni Speranza, Voi Ch'Entrate* ("Abandon All Hope, You Who Enter"). Hell is an immense, funnel-shaped pit, whose nine circular tiers fall off to the center of the earth. Vast enough to contain rivers, deserts, and a whole flaming city, it is a terrifying place filled with "sighs, lamentations, and loud wailings." Souls undergo worse punishment on each lower tier, according to their sins. As Dante and Virgil descend, the poet interviews the sinners, many of whom reveal themselves as well-known personages, placed there by the

omniscient author with poetic license. Several of them ask for
news—"Is there peace or war?"—and send messages to friends
and relatives in Florence, Dante's birthplace. He shows no re-
straint in depicting the elaborate torments—some shades are immersed in boiling pitch, some are split down the middle, others
are trees that bleed and moan when Dante breaks a twig. Corrupt popes and priests are wedged into hot holes, head downward.
One of the most moving episodes of the descent is the encounter with two lovers, Paolo and Francesca, who even in hell
cling close together, whirled about by a brutal wind. The beautiful Francesca, who had been married for political reasons to
Giovanni Malatesta, the repulsive son of the lord of Rimini, tells
Dante how she and her husband's handsome brother, Paolo,
were reading the romantic love story of Lancelot and Guinevere
together, when their eyes met. "That day we read no further."
Her husband, surprising them, put both of them to death. Francesca's simple tale of their surviving love, in which the word
amor (pron. *amòr*) recurs like a heartbeat, is language turned
to music—a music no translation can render:

> Amor, ch'al cor gentil ratto s'apprende,
> Prese costui della bella persona
> Che mi fu tolta; e'l modo ancor m'offende.
> Amor, ch'a nullo amato amar perdona,
> Mi prese del costui piacer si forte,
> Che, come vedi, ancor non m'abbandona.
> Amor condusse noi ad una morte.

> (Love, which quickly finds its way into the gentle heart,
> caused him to be enamored of the fair body
> of which I was deprived; and I am still afflicted.
> Love, which allows no loved one not to return it,
> attracted me so strongly to his beauty that,
> as you see, it does not leave me even now.
> Love led us to one death.)

Penetrating deeper into the pit—at one time, the two visitors
ride on the back of a flying monster from one tier to the next—
they reach, at last, its bottom. There, Satan sits, a three-faced

hideous colossus with six flapping bat wings, surrounded by eternal ice. They have to get past him to reach hell's back door, and start clambering down his shaggy body, holding on to his matted fur. Arriving at the waist, they carefully reverse themselves, for they have passed the center of the earth, and now their heads are where their feet had been. Through a shaft, they emerge on the other side of the earth, where they behold, rising from an ocean, the mount of purgatory. Dante's portrait in the Bargello, Florence (probably from a drawing by his contemporary, Giotto, much restored), shows a tall figure with a gaunt face, a bony nose, a disdainful mouth, and a firm chin, wearing a scholar's stocking cap. At the age of nine, he fell in love with a shy girl, Beatrice Portinari, whom he worshiped at a distance. Although she married a banker and died young—while he married a gentlewoman by whom he had several children—Beatrice remained the "glorious lady of his mind." His father was an impoverished aristocrat. He lost his mother at an early age. Dante studied Latin, grammar, rhetoric, and, later, philosophy, in religious schools. He read so much that he saw the stars "blurred by a white mist." He moved among the city's noble youths and, with them, took up the art of poetry, which had been largely in the hands of France's troubadours. Before he was thirty, he published *La vita nuova* (*The New Life*), a collection of love poems and prose pieces, composed, for the most part, in the *dolce stil nuovo* (the "sweet new style") of free-flowing vernacular. Creating his own language out of bits of local dialects, with the main stress on the virile Tuscan idiom, he became, in fact, the father of modern Italian. One of his poems, *Donne ch'avete intelletto d'amore* ("Ladies, you who know much about love"), was soon on everybody's lips and made him famous. Meanwhile, he did his military duty as a cavalryman and saw action in at least one battle. Dante's aggressive temperament and public spirit propelled him into local politics. He joined one of the guilds (that of the pharmacists and physicians, considered closest to his calling of philosopher) in order to be eligible for a communal office. He was elected to several policy-making committees and held important posts. Florence was basically Guelph (pro-papal), but the Guelph party had split into two factions, the anti-papal

"Whites" and the pro-papal "Blacks." Dante, a dedicated "White," admired for his eloquence and distinguished presence, was sent on a series of embassies. On his way home from a mission to Pope Boniface VIII, who had territorial designs on Tuscany, he learned that the "Blacks" had taken power in Florence, plundered his house, and sentenced him on trumped-up charges to banishment and a heavy fine. When he did not return, as he could have done, to plead his case, he was condemned to be "burned to death" should he ever set foot in Florence. Thus began Dante's bitter exile which was to last the rest of his life. He loved his native city, and, throughout his wanderings, he dreamt and wrote of Florence—now with nostalgia, now with spite. He was "a ship without rudder, carried hither and yon by the dry wind of poverty." He tells of climbing stairs in strangers' houses and smelling food prepared for others. Still, even as a wanderer, he worked, expressing his opinions in a series of polemical pamphlets. He came out vigorously for a true Italian language—his own!—that would supplant Latin as a medium of Italian letters, which had "turned literature into a harlot" by addressing itself only to the elite; as for himself, he wanted to communicate with "uninstructed men and women." As his reputation grew, he was given asylum by some of Italy's most powerful rulers, among them the cultured Can Grande della Scala, lord of Verona. He was no longer a Florentine politician but a celebrity whose fame had spread across the Alps. In his Latin pamphlet, *De monarchia* (*About Monarchy*), written from a true European point of view, he exalted the Imperial dignity and condemned the perennial conflict between pope and emperor, which was splitting the Western world asunder. Why should the two not live in peace together, the one providing for mankind's bliss on earth, the other for its bliss in heaven? When Henry VII, count of Luxemburg (c. 1275–1313), became the German king in 1308 and marched into Italy to be crowned Holy Roman emperor, Dante pinned all his hopes for lasting peace on this new savior from the North—hopes that were shattered when Henry died in Italy after his coronation. (Learning that Florence had held out against the German monarch, Dante called his home city a "viper." Later, Florence offered him a conditional pardon, which he indignantly rejected.) Having at last settled in Ravenna, where he lived in peace and comfort, surrounded by his family, Dante devoted the rest of his life to finishing the *Divine Comedy*. As he ascends the mount of purgatory, where lesser sinners do temporary penance prior to entering paradise, he is suddenly deserted by Virgil, his trusty guide—who, as a pagan, has no access to the top. About to panic, the poet hears his name called by a woman's voice, and there is Beatrice, his childhood love, come to take charge of him. With her, he soars through space and, to the strains of celestial music, to God's heaven. What troubles him is his own weightlessness, and Beatrice smilingly explains, "You are not on earth! Lightning never moved so fast as you are moving now." They briefly stop on the moon—the "eternal pearl"—and, looking down on earth, the poet is amused by its "miserable appearance." In the tenth, highest heaven, Beatrice leaves him. With a blinding vision of divinity itself, "the Supreme Light," in unity and trinity—a vision he feels incapable of describing—the poet stops, "like the good tailor who cuts the coat according to the length of cloth he has." His last line tells us that it is *l'amor che move il sole e l'altre stelle* ("Love that moves the sun and the other stars"). Dante died shortly after finishing the work, aged fifty-six, of malaria. According to tradition, the last three cantos of *Paradise* could not be found until the poet told his son Jacob in a dream where he had put them, whereupon Jacob found the missing batch in a hole in the wall. More than five hundred surviving copies of Dante's work, all dating from the years shortly after his death, bear witness to its instant popularity. Many took the account of the poet's seven-day trip through underworld and heaven for a factual report and, when they met the author in his later days, when he had grown a beard, concluded, from its slightly singed and sooty look, that he had really been to hell and back. The *Comedy* was soon expounded in universities and churches as the most important moral and religious textbook of its time. Today, thousands of Italians know lengthy passages by heart. And although Dante lived and labored in a medieval world, there is, in his great poem, a first glimpse of the bright new age—of humanism, of the Renaissance—that was to dawn three generations later. It is the noble individual—even in hell—that triumphs in the *Divine Comedy*. Dante is buried in Ravenna, and the elaborate tomb his conscience-stricken native city built for him in S. Croce remains empty.

DA PONTE, Lorenzo (1749–1838). Venetian adventurer, poet, and, in later life, resident of the United States; author of three librettos for Mozart operas. He was born on the Venetian mainland. When his widowed father, a Jewish leather merchant, and his three young sons were baptized into the Catholic Church, the family changed its name from Conegliano to that of the local bishop, Da Ponte, and Emanuele became Lorenzo. A promising boy, he studied for the priesthood and, aged twenty-four, celebrated his first mass. But his loves and imbroglios did not go with the cassock. He was expelled from the seminary of Treviso, where he taught, ostensibly for liberal ideas. Having found an upper-class protector in Venice, he plunged into that city's labyrinth of pleasures, where he encountered, and made friends with, Casanova. His debonair ways, and a flair for improvising verse, gave him entree into society; but, after involvement in some dark affairs, he left to try his luck elsewhere. From Dresden, where he served as poet to the Italian opera, he gravitated to Imperial Vienna, a beehive of theatrical and musical activity. The lingua franca of the world of entertainment was Italian. Lorenzo, armed with no more than brashness, a quick wit, and a gift for using anybody who might help him—including courtesans whom he charmed off their feet—climbed to the prized position of poet of the Imperial theaters. Envied, the center of intrigues and feuds, he rushed through stormy love affairs and shady machinations. But he kept the job, which yielded a high salary plus royalties, for nearly ten years, during which he wrote some twenty librettos, nearly all of them mediocre. The three shining exceptions were *Le nozze di Figaro, Don Giovanni,* and *Così fan tutte,* written for Wolfgang Amadeus Mozart (1756–91), whose name he insisted on spelling "Mozzart." Their collaboration, perhaps the most felicitous partnership between composer and librettist in the history of opera, covered four Vienna years, 1785–89. Of the three joint masterpieces, *Don Giovanni* is the most renowned, and many critics consider it the greatest opera ever written. Like *Figaro,* which was an adaptation of Beaumarchais's revolutionary play, *The Marriage of Figaro* (1784), it was based on a pre-existing plot. The story of the libertine who meets his punishment goes back to an old Spanish legend, first dramatized in a play attributed to Tirso de Molina (c. 1571–1648). Because of its universal appeal, it became the theme of countless plays—among them one by Molière (1665)—and even puppet shows. Da Ponte, fired by the spark of Mozart's genius, came up with a spine-chilling drama whose hero, Don Giovanni, sets himself above all moral laws, seduces 2,065 women in five countries, hankers for more, kills a father who tries to protect his daughter, and is consigned to flaming hell (on stage) by the walking statue of the murdered man. The opera, with its dazzling arias and glacial terror, was created for Prague, the Austrian empire's second city. Mozart took the unfinished score with him and dashed off the overture during the night before the gala opening (29 October 1787), while his wife, Constance, kept him going with punch. The orchestra played the overture at sight. Mozart conducted. The evening was a resounding triumph. Among the spectators was the ageing Casanova, whom Da Ponte is said to have consulted on details of the plot, and among whose effects were found, after his death, scraps of a libretto he himself had essayed for the opera. But opera-goers are fickle, and both composer and librettist were soon to fall from public favor. In 1791, the year of Mozart's miserable death, Da Ponte left Vienna. In Trieste, he fell in love with the presumably half-English Nancy Grahl, his future wife. With her he was about to go to Paris to seek the patronage of Marie Antoinette when the hapless queen, soon to die on the guillotine, was arrested. The trip was canceled. There followed eleven obscure years in London, where Da Ponte, in and out of debtor's prison, was victimized by usurers and prima donnas, and by his taste for speculative ventures, while he and Nancy were raising their four children. An invitation from Nancy's mother, living in America, saved them from utter ruin. Lorenzo's journey—Nancy had preceded him—took fifty-seven days; he traveled with a box of violin strings, all he had to his name. In New York, then a city of one hundred thousand, he ran a spice-and-soap store, which he sold because of sickness. The

Hebrew scholar, Clement Moore—author of *'Twas the Night Before Christmas*—whose father was president of Columbia College (now University), took a liking to the indestructible immigrant and persuaded him to give Italian lessons. Soon, Lorenzo dealt in Italian books and directed theatrical performances, but after a disastrous involvement with a distiller, fell again on evil days. He briefly tried to gain a foothold in Philadelphia, but at the age of seventy, returned to New York where he ran a bookstore and taught at Columbia. After presenting some Italian operas, including *Don Giovanni,* he opened, with much fanfare, an Italian opera house—which closed after twenty-eight performances. His last years were tragic. "The author of 36 dramas," he wrote to a friend, "the poet of Mozart, who gave America the Italian language, Italian literature and music, lies abandoned and forgotten, like a fugitive convict." His wife and his favorite son had died, he lived on handouts, and, after vain attempts to return to Italy, died, nearly ninety years of age, in his house on Spring Street. But the world suddenly remembered his romantic past, and his funeral was attended by a crowd of admirers. Like Mozart's tomb in Vienna, his resting place is lost. His bittersweet *Memoirs* convey, along with insights into young America, a picture of eighteenth-century Europe in its decadence and splendor, and offer glimpses of its madcap, Italian-dominated theater community.

DELLA ROBBIA. A Florentine family of sculptors, active for three generations, renowned for its large output of glazed and painted terracotta sculpture, most of it in the form of relief roundels and lunettes. Hundreds of Della Robbia madonnas—graceful and serene white figures on a sky-blue ground—are in the town and village churches for which they were originally made. Other works are scattered through the world's museums. Leon Battista Alberti, in his dedication of *Della pittura* (1436), gives Luca della Robbia (c. 1400–82), founder of the workshop, equal honors with Brunelleschi, Ghiberti, Donatello, and Masaccio—perhaps an exaggerated compliment. Trained as a sculptor in marble, Luca tended toward classical forms. We do not know his master—possibly Ghiberti—but we do know that he worked hard at drawing when a youth, and that, sitting up late at night in his cold room, he often put his feet in a basket of wood shavings for warmth. His best-known work is the marble choir gallery sculptured from 1431 to 1438 for Florence cathedral. It shows children and adolescents singing, dancing, and making music, in illustration of Psalm 150: "Praise him with the sound of the trumpet: praise him with the psaltery and harp." Now in the Museo dell' Opera del Duomo, it faces its slightly younger companion piece by Donatello. Both works, until 1688, confronted each other under the dome of the cathedral. From roughly the 1440s on, however, Luca's production was predominantly in terracotta ("baked earth" or fire-hardened clay), a medium used by sculptors for millennia before him. Vasari states that Luca had studied accounting and, after laboring at works in marble as well as on the bronze doors for the "New Sacristy" of the cathedral, sat down to figure out their cost to him on a time-is-money basis, concluding that he could not afford them. More probably, he and his clients were much taken with the possibility, inherent in glazed terracotta, of wedding firm, smooth shapes to brilliant colors. In its moist state, clay yields to the touch of a finger. The finished work is baked at a high temperature, usually in a specially built kiln, then coated with a liquid glaze made of the same ingredients as glass and mixed with various metallic oxides; the pigment is applied to the dried glaze, with which it will unite in a second firing. Glazed terracotta is extremely durable. Two of Florence's loveliest Renaissance interiors, Brunelleschi's Pazzi Chapel on the grounds of S. Croce and the Chapel of the Cardinal of Portugal in the Church of S. Miniato al Monte, contain Luca's reliefs—Apostles in the former, the Virtues and the Holy Spirit in the latter. Luca was succeeded by his almost equally gifted nephew, Andrea (1435–1525), to whom we owe the row of white-and-blue medallions with babes in swaddling clothes on the façade of Brunelleschi's Ospedale degli Innocenti (the foundlings' home) in Florence. Three of his finest works, among them a large *Annunciation* in white and blue, are at the Franciscan forest sanctuary of La

Verna. Of Andrea's seven sons, five continued the production of glazed terracotta sculpture, the most talented being Giovanni (1469–1529), who, with two pupils, fashioned the multicolored frieze of the various works of mercy on the Ospedale del Ceppo, a charitable institution in Pistoia. A younger brother, Girolamo, spent nearly forty years as a sculptor and decorator in the service of the kings of France. But the Italian demand for Della Robbia work had become so vast that the family workshop turned itself into a veritable factory, whose product, growing cruder and more garish, came close to folk art. Even so, Italy would be the poorer for the absence of the dash of color injected by the Della Robbias into Renaissance sculpture. One facet of their appeal is their affinity to nature. Luca had started the trend with a set of colored tiles framing his marble tomb of Bishop Federighi, now at S. Trinita in Florence, painted with roses and lilies, foliage and pine branches, and every kind of fruit. Soon, the festoons grew three-dimensional and, forming decorative garlands or frames for circular reliefs, became a Della Robbia trademark. As the viewer picks out the fir cones, apples, pomegranates, lemons, oranges, quinces, grapes, and pears, painted with nature's own greens, browns, and yellows, he almost smells the earth of Tuscany. (A close relation of glazed terracotta sculpture is the Renaissance ceramic ware used for table services and vases. Called *majolica* for the island of Majorca, in whose ships glazed Spanish pottery arrived in Italy during the fourteenth century, Italian majolica was produced in, among other centers, Gubbio, Urbino, Deruta, and Faenza—whence the French term, *faïence*. Specimens aglow with a metallic, iridescent lustre and often decorated with coats-of-arms or mythological scenes, some of them based on paintings by great masters, went to a princely clientele which used them largely for wedding gifts, and probably never ate off them. Italian wares were Europe's finest for about a century, after which Northern Europe took the lead.)

DORIA, Andrea (1466–1560). Genoese admiral, statesman, soldier of fortune. Born on the Riviera, seventy miles west
of Genoa, he was the offspring of one of the maritime republic's
oldest and most powerful Ghibelline (imperialist) families, first
recorded about 1100, which had given Genoa a series of outstanding sea captains and civic leaders. A Doria, in the twelfth
century, commanded a fleet fighting the Moors of Spain. A Doria
fought under King Richard the Lion-Hearted at Acre in the
Holy Land. Oberto Doria, captain of the people, won the naval
battle of Meloria, in 1284, in which the Genoese crushed forever
the rival Pisans; no fewer than two hundred and fifty of his kin
are said to have fought under him. Branca Doria, who murdered
his father-in-law at a banquet, was placed by Dante into his
Inferno. Pagano Doria, in 1352, defeated a joint force of Venetians, Catalans, and Byzantines, before Constantinople, and
shortly afterwards captured the whole Venetian fleet. Andrea,
born into this dynasty, brine in his veins, had a tradition to
uphold. Situated at the head of the Tyrrhenian Sea; protected by
the Apennines; in easy reach, by way of Alpine passes, of all
Europe; blessed with a natural harbor through which the fertile
Po plain could ship its produce, "Proud Genoa" was made for
trade. "A Genoese, therefore a trader," was the saying. As
bales and crates and barrels piled up along its docks, money
flowed into the coffers of the local merchant clans, whence
it trickled down to the industrious, freedom-loving people.
The city's population, by 1300, was one hundred thousand.
Economically dominated by the Bank of St. George, one of
the continent's most affluent, Genoa evolved such durable
institutions as the joint stock company and maritime insurance.
Part of Sardinia and Corsica were hers, as well as a long stretch
of the Ligurian coast extending to the east and west of her stout
walls. A far-flung sea-borne empire was Genoese-ruled. So were
Pera, a thriving suburb of Constantinople, and Caffa, in the

Crimea, whence, in 1347, three Genoese galleys unwittingly exported the black death. Genoa, was, in sum, the counterpart of Venice, which occupied a similar position at the head of the Adriatic, enjoyed the same freedom under an oligarchic constitution, carried on the same maritime trade, and built a similar empire. The bloody rivalry between these twins long darkened their relations. Andrea lost his parents when still a child. His early years are the erratic ventures of a condottiere. He proved his mettle, on land and sea, in the service of various Italian princes, including the della Rovere, lords of Urbino. In 1513, he became admiral of the Genoese fleet and showed himself a leader worthy of his forebears in chasing Turks across the deep. In the struggle for control of Europe between King Francis I of France and Charles V, the Holy Roman emperor and king of Spain, Genoa was under French influence. When Charles took the city, Andrea joined the French, who eagerly appointed the already famous sailor admiral of their Mediterranean fleet. But, finding that King Francis did not show him the respect, or pay him the large wage to which he felt entitled, he suddenly deserted him and, in 1528, went over to the side of Charles, whom he picked, rightly, for a winner. Aware that he had just secured, by a dramatic about-face, the ablest fighting captain in the Mediterranean, Charles paid Andrea what he asked and, in 1532, salved his ego by making him prince of Melfi, a wealthy bishopric in southern Italy. In switching to Charles's side, Andrea drove a bargain that proved him both a patriot and an accomplished statesman. Genoa was to enjoy complete autonomy under an invisible Spanish umbrella. Her fleet was to be a chosen instrument of Spain's expanding trade, allowing Genoa to play a major role in exploiting the new worlds across the ocean; and Spanish gold, from the unfathomed treasures of the colonies, was to be her reward. Grateful Genoa named him "Liberator of the Fatherland" and presented him with two fine palaces. He now proceeded to work out a new constitution, under which the republic would be administered by a "Consul" elected for a two-year term, balanced by a senate made up of members of the leading families, with himself as the ultimate arbiter. He turned down the title, "doge," but accepted that of *sindacatore* (roughly, "inspector"). At large, he was engaged in almost constant warfare with the advancing Turks and their friends, the Barbary pirates, ever preying on Mediterranean shipping from their bases in North Africa. When Charles, at last, in 1535, struck out in person for Tunisia, Doria commanded the Imperial navy, and the capture of Tunis was largely due to his superior strategy. But when, in 1538, the emperor made common cause with Venice and Pope Paul III in order to deliver the death blow to the master pirate Khair ed-Din, known as the "Sword of Allah," Doria was late for the rendezvous off the small Greek port of Preveza, deliberately dragged his feet, and caused the allies to retreat in disarray—just to spite the Venetians whom he disliked more than the Turks. Meanwhile, decisively assisted by Andrea, whose naval tactics proved unbeatable, Charles made himself lord of all Italy and of much of the western Mediterranean. A magnificent portrait of Andrea by Sebastiano del Piombo (Rome, Doria) shows a face illuminated by a wakeful intellect, with a pair of sea-wise eyes and a silky short white beard. He was rounding eighty and at the summit of his fame, when a conspiracy against him and his rule was mounted by Gian Luigi Fieschi (known as "Fiesco"), the young, ambitious scion of an old Guelph (pro papal) family that had given the Church two popes and Genoa many high office-holders. Encouraged by Pope Paul III and King Francis I, aided by kinsmen and the still important pro-French party, Fiesco brought armed men in from his lands. In the dead of a dark January night in 1547, he occupied the city gates and shipyards and was about to seize the admiral's galley, when, crossing a gangplank to a ship, he fell off and drowned. That was the end of the rebellion. Andrea, whom the rebels had meant to kill, had managed to get out of town, but his favorite nephew and chief lieutenant, Giannettino, was felled as he came running to the scene. Doria was icily vindictive. Among the ringleaders tortured and put to death was one of Fiesco's brothers. Another brother was captured and executed eight years later. More jealous than ever of his city's freedom, the aged Doria effectively vetoed an imperial project to place a Spanish garrison in Genoa as a protection against the French. The Genoese could take care of themselves! When the French did occupy Genoese Corsica as a base for an attack, the old salt launched a naval expedition financed and captained by himself and spent two years in inconclusive fighting on the island. His last military action consisted in outfitting yet another expedition against the Turks, in 1560, which he did not accompany. He died that year, aged ninety-four, and was buried in the crypt of the Doria family church of S. Matteo, where his sword was hung over the altar. Having married late in life (a widowed noblewoman, Peretta Usodimare Cybo), Andrea left no progeny, and his line became extinct. Another branch of the family continued to prosper and, intermarried with the Pamphili, made famous by Pope Innocent X (1644–55), styled itself, upon that family's extinction, Doria Pamphili. Settled in Rome, the family acquired one of the city's largest and most sumptuous palazzi (where it still lives, and which now houses its excellent art collection). The world moved on. Eleven years after Andrea's death—and thirteen after that of Charles V—the Turks were finally defeated by an allied fleet at Lepanto. But Genoa's sea-borne empire was crumbling. Today, the city, still Italy's leading port, looks on the princely mariner as one of its two greatest citizens, the other being Christopher Columbus, born—presumably in or near Genoa—some fifteen years before Andrea Doria.

ESTE. A north-Italian dynasty descending from a line of Lombard nobles already powerful in the tenth century. Without them, luminous Ferrara, which they ruled from the thirteenth to the sixteenth centuries, might have been little more than a fat market town. Along with several accomplished rulers, they presented Italy with the leading lady of the Renaissance, Isabella d'Este, marchioness of Mantua. The first marquis of Ferrara to bear the papal title "duke" and reign over a territory greatly enlarged by an Imperial grant was Borso (1413–71), a dedicated falconer and owner of the finest pack of hounds in Italy. His two enduring contributions to Italian culture are the frescoes he commissioned for the upper story of Ferrara's Palazzo Schifanoia and the two-volume, wondrously illuminated Bible that is known by his name. He was succeeded by his half brother, Ercole I (1431–1505), a generous patron of the arts. With the

latter's children—Beatrice, Isabella, Ippolito I (archbishop of
Milan), and Alfonso I (Ercole's successor)—the height of Este
grandeur was attained. Ferrara, prosperous and, on the whole,
benignly governed, traversed by wide, straight streets, lined with
palaces and gardens—provided even with a public park—became
the continent's first modern city. A gathering of humanists and
artists made it a fulcrum of the Renaissance. Alfonso I (1486–
1534)—the husband of Lucrezia Borgia—was known both as
an artillery expert and a patron of Titian, from whom he ordered
three of that artist's greatest pictures: the *Worship of Venus* and
the *Andrians* (both in Madrid, Prado), and *Bacchus and
Ariadne* (London, National Gallery). It was Alfonso's and
Lucrezia's son, the worldly cardinal Ippolito II, who built
Villa d'Este, with its terraces and fountains, at Tivoli near Rome.
But it was Isabella (1474–1539), wife of Francesco Gonzaga,
marquis of Mantua, who was the dynasty's outstanding personality. Intelligent, a lover of antiquity, poetry, and music, she
was surrounded by some of the high-minded spirits of the century. Bembo, Castiglione, and Ariosto were her friends. (Ariosto's poem, *Orlando Furioso*, published in 1532, is an exaltation
of the House of Este.) Though she has often been called "beautiful," contemporary portraits show crude features and a willful
expression. Vibrant with energy, she virtually ran her husband's
marquisate and, when Francesco was held prisoner in hostile
Venice, obtained his release with the help of Pope Julius II.
Widowed, she was her reigning son's chief counselor and pro-
cured a cardinal's hat for his brother. Her favorite pastime was
the decoration of her *studiolo* ("private study") in the palace.
Wishing to be "well served," she dealt with leading artists as if
they were dressmakers, instructing them in detail on how to com-
pose the mythological allegories she desired. Giovanni Bellini
let her know that "artists resent such strict directives, preferring
to let their imagination roam." Nevertheless, she did persuade a
number of great painters—Correggio, Perugino, and her court
painter, Mantegna, among others—to work to her specifications.
The seven major paintings that embellished her apartment are
now in the Louvre. She begged Leonardo for just "a little picture" of the Madonna—and later for a painting of a young
Christ, done "with the sweetness that distinguishes your excellent work"—but received no reply. On Giorgione's death, she

asked her agents to buy one of his paintings, but there were none for sale. She sent as far as Asia Minor for ancient statues. When Cesare Borgia sacked the palace of Urbino, she at once tried to obtain—in vain—two looted statuettes she had always coveted. (When Cesare put to death his top lieutenants, she sent him her congratulations, with a present of one hundred masks for the approaching carnival.) For years, she pestered Mantegna for a Roman statue he possessed—and received it, late in his life, when he badly needed money. Still, for all her rapaciousness, she showed discerning taste, and her collection of paintings, sculptures, manuscripts, and musical instruments was among the best in Italy. Her pretty sister, Beatrice (1475–97)—who married Ludovico Sforza, duke of Milan ("the Moor"), and died in childbirth—was the softer, and more amiable, of the two. She also had her entourage of artists and musicians. But she delighted most in riding to hounds, and in gay festivities, in jewels, and in dresses—of which she owned several hundred, keeping eighty-four in her hunting lodge for a quick change. Although her marriage was arranged, in line with the dynastic custom of the age, she made her husband fall in love with her and get rid of his mistress. The Este dynasty became extinct in the male line in 1597, and Ferrara was swallowed by the papacy, which had long had its eye on it. One branch clung to the affiliated duchies of Modena (where the rich Este art collection and library, including Borso's Bible, are now public property) and Reggio until 1803, while another branch, Austria-Este, ruled Modena, with great brutality, from 1814 to 1859. Mantua and its palace were sacked by Imperial troops in 1630, and a large part of Isabella's treasures was eventually acquired by Cardinal Richelieu, "Red Eminence" of King Louis XIII of France.

ETRUSCANS. Italy's unsolved mystery. A people flourishing in Central Italy between 800 and 300 B.C., they have puzzled generations of scholars. Their territory, Etruria, was little more than a loose confederation of cities, of which impressive remnants—portions of temples, stone walls, houses—have been unearthed. The greater part has disappeared, or is still waiting for the archaeologist's spade. We know that some of the chief towns were of substantial size. Veii, near Rome, was enclosed by a four-and-a-half-mile-long wall. Many Etruscan sites are tucked away in rough, formerly bandit-ridden country, riven by somber chasms. Others lie in smiling pasture land—with grazing sheep, occasional clumps of oak, and masses of wild flowers. Who were the Etruscans? Most Etruscologists have given up guessing. Some hold that they reached Italy from Asia Minor. Others consider them native Italians. Their language, preserved in brief inscriptions, is incomprehensible. Though we can read the characters—archaic Greek imported from the Aegean island of Euboea—the meanings of most words, as well as grammar and pronunciation, are unknown, as is the language group (non-Indo-European) to which Etruscan belongs. Whoever they were, the Etruscans were rich, enterprising, and imaginative. Their natural wealth included copper and iron deposits. Their ships carried on trade with many countries, particularly Greece, with which Etruria maintained close cultural and commercial ties. Imported artifacts, among them some of the most beautiful Greek painted vases in existence, have been found in Etruscan tombs. These tombs—new ones are being uncovered every year—are of particular interest. Among Etruscan cities of the dead, some of them consisting of elaborate rock-hewn chamber tombs arranged like dwellings of the living, are Tarquinia, Veii, Cerveteri, Vulci. They point to a profound belief in an afterlife, borne out by swords, adornments, furnishings, toys, and household articles deposited in them. A chariot, its four iron wheels and part of the wooden body still intact, was found in a tomb near Rome in 1980. (Tombs have for centuries been robbed by *tombaroli* ["grave robbers"].) The Etruscans excelled at painting, sculpture, and goldsmithing. Frescoes of dancers, wrestlers, horsemen, and musicians embellish many tombs. Gold jewelry is delicate and charming, sometimes decorated with tiny animals or incredibly fine granules. Sculpture was executed in bronze, stone, and terracotta. Outstanding terracotta works are a group of winged horses (Tarquinia, Museo Nazionale); and a lifesize Apollo statue (Rome, Villa Giulia). One of the most remarkable bronzes is the she-wolf (symbol of Rome) at Rome's Capitoline Museum, attributed to a late-sixth-century B.C. Veii sculptor called Vulca. (The baby twins, representing Romulus and Remus, were probably made by the Florentine, Antonio Pollaiuolo [1431–98].) In Rome, Etruscans were known as flutists, soothsayers, and surgeons. Possessors of a well-developed urban culture when Rome was still a cluster of muddy villages, the Etruscans passed on to their gradually evolving Roman neighbors important elements of their civilization: among them were land reclamation; the keystone arch; the layout of the Roman house, with its characteristic atrium, as we still see it in Pompeii; and the structure of the Roman temple, sitting on a high podium and meant to be viewed frontally, dominating the space before it. Of Rome's legendary seven kings, two may have been Etruscans: Tarquinius Priscus and Tarquinius Superbus (seventh to sixth centuries B.C.). The former, presumably the son of a Greek immigrant, is said to have been the guardian of the sons of Rome's King Ancus Marcius, and to have usurped the throne on the latter's death—eventually to be murdered by his wards. He drained the swampy Forum, may have laid out the Circus Maximus, and perhaps began construction of a city wall and the Jupiter temple on the Capitol, Rome's supreme sanctuary. Tarquinius Superbus ("the Proud") is thought to have killed his predecessor, King Servius Tullius, and to have set up a cruel tyranny. The rape of Lucretia, a virtuous married woman, by his son, Sextus, led to his expulsion from the city and the establishment of the Republic. When an Etruscan army attempted a reconquest, a valiant Roman, Horatius Cocles, according to legend, held off the enemy single-handedly by defending a bridge which his fellow citizens were demolishing behind him, saving himself at the last moment by plunging into the Tiber and, in full armor, swimming to safety. Lucretia, who stabbed herself after the deed, has been the subject of innumerable paintings, and of a long poem, *The Rape of Lucrece,* by Shakespeare, while the story of Horatius at the bridge is told by Thomas B. Macaulay in his *Lays of Ancient Rome.* Lacking political organization, the Etruscans were eventually brought under Roman rule and absorbed into the Italian population. For all their fascination, there is something slightly off-putting about them. "All of Etruria is a tomb," the Romans say.

———————·———<<◆>>———·———————

FLORENTINE PAINTING. At the threshold
of the Florentine Renaissance stands Giotto di Bondone (c.
1267–1337), the "founder" of Italian painting. Born in the
pastoral Mugello Valley, north of Florence, he is believed to
have been the pupil of Cimabue (c. 1240–1302), about whose
life and work little is known. But Giotto soon found his own
style. His compact figures are more alive than their medieval
predecessors; their gestures convincingly convey emotions, and
the space surrounding them has a new depth. His frescoes at
Padua (Scrovegni Chapel), Assisi (S. Francesco), and Florence
(S. Croce) are milestones in the history of European painting.
Famous in his lifetime— his contemporary, Dante, mentions him
as being "all the rage"—he was named architect to the city of
Florence, though he had no training in that field, and began
building, but did not complete, the campanile of the cathedral,
still known as Giotto's tower. Like other great precursors, he
remained a voice crying in the wilderness. Though we find
traces of his style in the works of some of his successors, fourteenth-century Florence was still largely dominated by "International Gothic," whose chief exponent, the roving painter Gentile
da Fabriano (c. 1370–1427), specialized in fashionably dressed,
frail-looking personages inspired by French court art. It remained for Masaccio—Tommaso di Mone (1401–28)—born
in the Arno valley above Florence, to take up where Giotto
had left off three-quarters of a century before. His art, breathing
the humanism of the Early Renaissance, was equaled only by
the sculpture of Donatello, fifteen years his senior. Masaccio's
frescoes in the Brancacci Chapel of S. Maria del Carmine in
Florence—begun by the more traditional Masolino da Panicale
(c. 1383–c. 1440)—revolutionized Italian art. Commissioned
by the merchant Felice Brancacci, whom Florence had sent to
the sultan of Egypt in order to open up trade with the Orient,
they depict, along with other biblical scenes, the life of St. Peter.

The figures, defined by volume rather than by contour, are molded by gradations of light and shade, and move in such a way as to let us perceive the living body inside their heavily draped clothes. Gestures, calm and subdued, are natural, never contrived. Perspective is applied, for the first time in fresco painting, so scientifically that the viewer, standing in the center of the chapel, has the illusion of looking into the depth of every picture. Among the best are the *Paying of the Tribute Money, Peter Healing the Sick with his Shadow,* and, above all, the *Expulsion from Paradise,* a shattering representation of human grief. Masaccio's work was recognized immediately as a unique achievement, and the Brancacci Chapel assumed the function of an academy of painting, where Fra Angelico, Botticelli, Raphael, Michelangelo, and many others spent days on end scanning and sketching. Florence's quattrocento (lit. "four hundred")—short for the 1400s, or the fifteenth century—was launched. In cluttered studios young acolytes were studying under great masters. Painters and sculptors, philosophers and literati, were cross-fertilizing one another's minds in the warm Medici sun. The churches, many of them new, were crammed with scaffolds from which painters were decorating the blank walls. Like Giotto, Masaccio was too much of a phenomenon to be accepted at once. The linear Gothic style fought back against the new plasticity, and individual artists struggled free, progressed, relapsed. Two less-known Florentine painters belong to the vanguard: Paolo Uccello (1397–1475) and Andrea del Castagno (c. 1421–57). The former, son of a barber, was raised on International Gothic in Ghiberti's studio. But he soon let himself be shaped by the vital force of Donatello, whom he followed to Padua. To him we owe such original conceptions as the (much-damaged) *Deluge* frescoes in the "Green Cloister" of S. Maria Novella in Forence; the equestrian portrait of the condottiere, *Sir John Hawkwood,* in Florence cathedral; and three panels (Florence, Uffizi; London, National Gallery; Paris, Louvre), once in the bedroom of Lorenzo the Magnificent, of the *Battle of S. Romano* (1432), in which the Florentines routed the Sienese: armored knights, mounted on heavy-duty chargers, clash among orange trees. Uccello's peer, Andrea del Castagno, the virile heir of Donatello and Masaccio, is celebrated for his frescoes of *Famous Men and Women,* and of the *Last Supper*

(Florence, ex-convent of S. Apollonia). His equestrian portrait of Niccolò da Tolentino (who captained the Florentines at S. Romano), next to Uccello's earlier *Hawkwood* in the cathedral, echoes Donatello's *Gattamelata* statue, three years its senior. Castagno was known for his violent temper, and the grim-faced severity of many of his figures may reflect his character. Having painted the executed members of a Florentine conspiracy on the façade of the Bargello—some of them hanging by their heels— he was called "Andrea of the Hanged." Vasari presents him as a ruffian of great physical strength—a former cowherd, liberal with his fists—and accuses him of having murdered the painter Domenico Veneziano, who died four years after him. Two books affected the Early Renaissance painter's status and his work. One, circulating around 1400, though published later, was Giovanni Villani's chronicle of Florence, completed by his nephew, Filippo (1345–1405), which advocated the artist's liberation from the medieval bonds of anonymity. His separation from the mass of artisans, begun with Giotto, now became a general process. The other book was Leon Battista Alberti's *On Painting* (1436), which, besides its famous exposition of Brunelleschi's laws of perspective, gave painters a few useful tips, pointing out, for example, that a dead body must appear "dead to the fingernails," while "every tiny particle" of a living person must be vibrant with life; that white and black should be mixed with other colors to obtain light and shadow; and that dogs must never be as big as horses.

———————<❖>———————

ST. FRANCIS OF ASSISI (c. 1181–1226). Founder of the Franciscan order, patron saint (with St. Catherine of Siena) of Italy, one of the most loved and venerated of saints. After a stormy adolescence, he emerged from a spiritual crisis disdaining worldly goods, rejecting an orderly career, and wishing to lead the life of an ascetic. Aged twenty-four, he was sued by his father, Piero Bernardone, a well-off cloth merchant, for restitution of missing money. Francis—a slight, unprepossessing fellow—admitted that he had sold some of his father's merchandise, along with the horse he had ridden, so that he might use the cash for the repair of a small church. Its priest had not accepted it, and here it was! With that, to the astonishment of the public and the bishop sitting as judge, the young man stripped to the skin, returning to his irate father the clothes he was wearing, along with the money. Plaintiff had won the case and lost a son. "From now on," Francis is reported to have said, "I shall serve one father only—God." A shabby workman's cloak was given him. He marked it with a cross and went his way, singing God's praises. In a woods some two miles from Assisi, he came to a neglected chapel dedicated to St. Mary of the Angels. The site on which it stood, called *Porziuncula* ("parcel of land"), appealed to him, and he remained there. At a service, he heard a priest read Jesus' admonition to the Disciples (Matt. 10: 9–10): "Provide neither gold, nor silver, nor brass in your purses; . . . neither two coats, neither shoes, nor yet staves." At this, Francis cast off the last of his possessions, even his staff and leather belt. Henceforth, he wore a tunic of undyed wool, the kind worn by the poorest laborers and peasants, patched with coarse rags, and held together by a simple cord around the waist. Barefoot, he set out to preach the Word, greeting passing strangers with "God give you peace." Soon, the first companions joined him, attracted by his way of life. Among them were a merchant, a priest, a peasant, and a troubadour. "Minstrels of the Lord," carrying no possessions, they roamed the country, drinking from springs, begging when they were hungry, sleeping under hedgerows or in abandoned barns. They preached, cared for the sick, and cleansed the lepers. Francis had no intention of forming a religious order; monastic life behind thick convent walls did not appeal to him. Contact with people was his element. Yet, though he was a foe of convention, he wished to function inside, rather than outside, the Church. In 1209, when his little band had grown to twelve, he went to Rome in order to obtain credentials for his brotherhood. His ragged appearance, his contempt for protocol—he is said to have walked straight into the pope's study—met with displeasure at the papal court. But Innocent III, after much hesitation, approved the rule, or constitution, Francis had brought along. The brethren were to be friars, free to move—not monks tied to a monastery. (Seven years later, the Dominican order, based on a similar rule, was founded.) It was a farsighted decision. The clergy, content with reeling off the Latin liturgy which few Italians understood, had become alienated from the ignorant and poor. And here were ordinary men (Francis was not a priest and looked on too much erudition as excess baggage) who, emulating Christ and his Disciples, were walking the paths of the country, addressing villagers and townsmen in the vernacular, and thus making religion, once again, a popular concern. Francis's twelve, in a few years, were several hundred, and the *Poverello* ("the Little Poor One"), as he was affectionately called, was a well-known figure. Church bells were rung at his approach. His voice, we read in contemporary reports, was vibrant, sweet, and clear. Joy shone in his long, pale face. Sometimes, on the spur of the moment, he would grab a stick while preaching, hold it like a fiddle, and with another stick scrape away. When a cardinal invited him to preach before the pope, Francis so utterly forgot himself that his feet started dancing while he spoke. One of his favorite themes was the humanity of Christ—a humanity that had long been obscured by the prevailing fashion that visualized Him as a crowned and sceptered monarch, rather than as the intimate of publicans and fishermen. Francis spoke of a Christ born in a stable, poor, suffering, naked on the Cross. This human image of the Lord was Francis's gift to Christendom. It transformed religious art and Christian hymnody. Spending a winter with some brethren at the hermitage of Greccio, high in the wooded Apennines, he set up what may have been the first crib, with manger and live ox and ass, and preached a Christmas sermon about Bethlehem. The *Poverello* lived up to his name. He called nothing his own except one threadbare tunic, his drawers, and his cord. When someone forced a cloak on him, he gave it to the first beggar who came his way. A painting in the Basilica of St. Francis at Assisi, by an unknown master, shows Francis's marriage to a haggard woman, Lady Poverty; a thornbush growing at her feet turns into roses. He and his companions worked with their hands, often continuing their former trades, or helping farmers with the harvest. Francis himself was good at making earthen vessels and is said to have labored as a goatherd on occasion. When work was lacking, they would beg food, sharing what scraps they could collect. Told that a well-meaning visitor had left behind some cash for them, Francis ordered it thrown on the dung heap. Having installed themselves in a derelict farm shed by a pleasant stream outside Assisi, the brethren left without a murmur when a rustic pushed his donkey through the door, claiming the building as a stable. Shortly afterwards, the Benedictine monks owning the Porziuncula offered the site to Francis as a gift. He accepted, but only as a tenant, and paid a bucket of fresh fish as annual rent. The little community made its headquarters there, living in wattle huts, or cells, in the surrounding forest clearing. Francis left a strip of fallow ground around the kitchen garden, so that, in season, wild flowers would come up "to praise the beauty of the Father of all things." But when some brethren, taking advantage of one of his absences, put up a stone house as a shelter from the elements, Francis, returning, climbed onto the roof and started throwing down the tiles. The brethren, much ashamed, helped him pull down the structure. Francis had many arguments with Brother Jackass, as he called his body. His self-willed chastity was often hard to bear. Nor was his suffering purely physical. One moonlit winter night, he made himself a family of seven snowmen—a wife, two sons, two daughters, and two servants for good measure. "They're dying of cold," he murmured. "Hurry up, clothe them!" Francis was no fanatic. He allowed those who could not tolerate wool next to their skin to wear a shirt. And tender-footed brothers might use sandals. Umbria, the region between Rome and Florence where Francis was born, is marked by darkly wooded mountains, rocky outcroppings, and crystal brooks. Francis often prayed and meditated amidst its oaks and boulders, or retired to its caves. His way with birds and beasts has given rise to some engaging stories. He is said to have tamed a fierce wolf by speaking sternly to him, and to have addressed a sermon to a gathering of doves and jackdaws. At the Porziuncula, a cricket whose song he enjoyed became so friendly that it sang for him all week and hopped onto his hand when called. Assisi's citizens, who had once laughed at him, flocked to hear him when he was invited by the bishop to preach there. Among those who came under his spell was Clare, the beautiful, high-spirited daughter of a nobleman. Determined to join the order's saintly life, she slipped out of the back door of her family palace one night and ran to the Porziuncula, where Francis—who, so far, had made no provision for nuns—cut off her hair and gave her a rough habit. He placed her temporarily in the care of Benedictine nuns in a nearby convent. When two sisters, her widowed mother, and several other women followed her, he housed the little tribe in a convent of their own, where they lived by the Franciscan rule, observing rigid poverty. Such was the birth of the Order of Poor Clares. Francis saw as much of Abbess Clare as the rules permitted, and her affection and wise counsel comforted him to the end of his days. In 1219, Francis, accompanied by a few brethren, took ship for Egypt where the Crusaders were besieging Moslem-held Damietta. He was warmly welcomed in the Christian camp. During a lull, he walked toward the Moslem lines, aware that the sultan had put a price on any Christian's head. Seized by guards, beaten and fettered, he cried, "Sultan! Sultan!" and soon stood face to face with Melek-el-Kamel, who received him with Oriental courtesy. During a stay of several days, Francis was asked to preach before the ruler, but failed to convert him. Still, Melek begged him to stay with him forever and, when Francis left, asked him to pray for him, "so that God may reveal which of our two religions is the better." On his return to Italy, Francis found that Lady Poverty was being snubbed by the order's rank and file. Franciscans were handling money, wearing sandals, donning soft garments, settling in houses, building up libraries! More than a principle was involved. Could an organization several thousand strong really manage without houses, especially in colder climes? And what was to be done with fortunes, in cash and land, that pious persons left the order in their wills? Finally, was it fair to society to let this quickly multiplying horde of beggars prey on it? Francis did not feel equal to solving these weighty problems. He resigned as minister general. "Lord, I give you back this family which you entrusted to me." In the fragrant Tuscan forest of La Verna, he built himself a hut. One dawn, as he rose from his prayers, he was aware of a perturbing physical sensation—his body bore the stigmata, the wounds of Christ. Though Francis always hid these wounds, which he considered tokens of divine grace, by pulling down his sleeves and wearing socks, more than fifty witnesses touched them upon his death. His health was now deteriorating fast. Barely past forty, he was an ageing man. Poor food, exposure to the elements, and worry over the future of the order had worn him down. Emaciated, prevented by the stigmata from walking, he continued preaching, riding a donkey from place to place. He happened to be near Clare's convent of San Damiano at Assisi when he could ride no further. The nuns prepared a hut of rushes in the adjacent vineyard for him. His shelter was soon swarming with mice, running over him as he lay down. After a sleepless night of prayer, he composed the *Canticle of the Creatures,* expressing his all-embracing faith in simple language:

> Praise be to you, my Lord, and all your creatures,
> Particularly Brother Sun
> Who rules the Day and gives us light from you,
> And is beautiful and radiant in his splendor.
> From you, Most High, he takes his power.
> Be praised, my Lord, by Sister Moon and the Stars
> You made in Heaven, luminous and precious.
> Be praised, my Lord, by Brother Wind, and by the Air,
> And every kind of Weather, clouded or fine,
> By which you give sustenance to your creatures.
> Be praised, my Lord, by Sister Water,
> Which is very useful and humble and precious and chaste.
> Be praised, my Lord, by Brother Fire,
> through whom you brighten the night,
> And he is beautiful and cheerful and strong.
> Be praised, my Lord, by our mother, Sister Earth,
> who feeds and governs us,
> and brings forth many kinds of fruit, and flowers of many
>   colors, and herbs.
> Praise ye and bless the Lord, give thanks,
> And serve him with humility.

He sang it to a tune of his own making. Sister Death was approaching. Francis asked to be carried to his beloved Porziuncula, the heart of the Franciscan movement, which held so many memories of his own life. Soldiers escorted the slow litter-bearers. In one of the familiar huts, he lay down on the floor. He hemorrhaged. On 3 October 1226, having whispered the words from

Psalm 141, "Lord, I cry unto thee: make haste unto me," he died. A flock of skylarks rose in jubilation from the roof, as if escorting Brother Francis to heaven.

FREDERICK II (1194–1250). King of Germany, Sicily, and Jerusalem; crowned Holy Roman emperor in 1220. One of the most imposing and perplexing medieval rulers—soldier, administrator, poet, patron of the arts—whose byname, *Stupor Mundi* ("Amazement of the World"), was meant to be a compliment. A member of the Hohenstaufen family, which ruled Germany from 1138 to 1254, he was the grandson of Emperor Frederick I, Barbarossa ("Redbeard"), a promoter of knightly ideals, who had descended into Italy six times, and drowned while leading a Crusade in Asia Minor. Frederick's father, Henry VI, had acquired a claim to the crown of Sicily and southern Italy by marrying Constance, daughter of the Norman king, Roger II. Born near Ancona, Italy, Frederick spent his childhood in Palermo, Sicily. His dream was to unite Italy and Germany. Like his predecessors, he frequently collided with the reigning popes, who cherished territorial ambitions. He was excommunicated thrice. Of his three wives, the third was Isabel, a daughter of King John and sister of Henry III, of England. Heading the Fifth Crusade, he rode into Jerusalem, where he crowned himself king, and, by a friendly treaty with the Sultan, obtained Jerusalem, Bethlehem, and Nazareth for the Christians. Deterred by political unrest in Germany, he concentrated on ruling Italy, which he brought almost totally under his scepter. In Sicily, he set up a model administration, resting on a civil service— a revolutionary notion. Installed in one or the other of his southern Italian castles, shielded by 10,000 Saracens, Frederick presided over a court filled with artisans and scholars. He spoke several languages, including Arabic, and had a number of Greek texts translated into Arabic. He kept a zoo and sometimes traveled with a procession of exotic animals from one of his castles to another. His book on falconry reflects his pleasure in the hunt and his knowledge of the habits of birds. The poems attributed to him, composed in the Sicilian vernacular, are among the earliest specimens of a truly Italian poetry. His law code, the "Melfi Constitutions," broke the feudal tradition by substituting written law for "custom." Henceforth, his subjects were no longer to be judged by feudal overlords but by qualified judges. He was versed in geometry and medicine, and one of his contributions to Western culture was the founding of Naples University. His hunting lodge, Castel del Monte, sitting, like an imperial crown, on a lone hilltop amidst the almond groves of Apulia, southern Italy, is one of the most handsome secular structures of the Middle Ages: an octagon, with an octagonal inner court, eight octagonal corner towers, and eight rooms on each of its two floors—geometry, or perhaps magic, in stone. Yet, this *Stupor Mundi* was a savage persecutor of suspected heretics. A year before his death, he suddenly imprisoned his closest collaborator, Piero della Vigna—poet, jurist, diplomat, and outstanding Latinist—on a (probably baseless) suspicion of treachery; horribly tortured, he dashed his brains out in his prison cell. (Dante consigns Frederick to his *Inferno,* while defending della Vigna.) No more than a few clumps of masonry remain of Castel Fiorentino, where he died—dressed, it is said, in the rough habit of a Cistercian friar. He is buried, next to his forebears, in a porphyry sarcophagus in the Cathedral of Palermo. The Hohenstaufen dynasty collapsed soon after his death. His grandson, Conradin, last of the line, was decapitated in 1268 at Naples on order of the usurper, Charles of Anjou. Frederick's natural son, Enzio, spent the last twenty-two years of his life in a Bologna prison, eating his heart out with nostalgia for the South.

GALILEI, Galileo (1564–1642). Astronomer, physicist. Born in Pisa, the son of an impoverished Florentine nobleman, he was educated in a monastery, learned to play the organ, and

briefly studied medicine. According to tradition, he was drawn
to mathematics while watching a lamp swinging overhead during
a service in the cathedral of Pisa; timing its movements, he found
that every swing, regardless of its length, employed the same
amount of time—the isochronal principle of the pendulum, later
applied to clocks. Another basic law he discovered—some say by
dropping objects from the Leaning Tower of Pisa—is that bodies
of different weight fall with the same velocity. He understood the
gravitational pull exerted by a larger body upon a smaller one,
demonstrated that the path of a projectile is a parabola, and
first explained the laws of dynamics—concerning the motion of
bodies and the forces that impel them—fully developed by Isaac
Newton (born the year of Galilei's death). As a mathematics
professor at the University of Padua from 1592 to 1610, he had
to lecture out of doors because no classroom was large enough
to hold his students. Having heard of the Dutch invention of an
optical instrument that, with the help of lenses, made far objects
appear nearer, he built the world's first powerful telescope, with
a magnifying power of thirty-two, and used it to look at the sky
—man's first step into space. Among his discoveries were sun-
spots, mountains on the moon, four of Jupiter's satellites—the
first celestial bodies spotted with a telescope—and the true nature
of the Milky Way. Here began his troubles. Arguing that the sun
is the center of our planetary system; that the sun rotates; that
the earth, revolving daily on its axis, moves around the sun, Galilei contradicted the teachings of the Church which held, with
the second-century A.D. Greek scholar, Ptolemy, that the earth
was the fixed center of the universe. Galilei, by contrast, accepted
the theories of the Prussian, or Polish, astronomer, Nicolaus Copernicus (1473–1543), anathema to Church authorities, which
his own observations proved correct. His *Letters on the Solar
Spots* brought him a summons to Rome, where, in 1616, he was
forced to promise never again to propagate the doctrines of
Copernicus. Having given up his university career to become
"First Philosopher and Mathematician" to the grand duke of
Tuscany, Cosimo II, Galilei now went to live quietly in Florence.
Unfortunately, the published result of his continued research,
Dialogue on the Two Principal Systems of the World, clearly
spelled "Copernicus." A runaway success, it infuriated the
papal Curia. Called to Rome, once again, Galilei—in spite

of his poor health, his age (he was seventy), and his great fame—was made to face the Inquisition on the suspicion of heresy. Threatened with torture (the instruments, it is said, were shown to him), he recanted and, on his knees, "abjured, cursed, and detested" his "erroneous" beliefs. "And yet it (the earth) moves!" he murmured after the humiliating act— his best-known, if undocumented, statement. His prison sentence was commuted to house arrest by Pope Urban VIII, but he was condemned to silence and his works were placed on the Index —the Church's list of forbidden books—where they remained until 1835. Spending the last eight years of his life on his small property near Florence, Galilei continued to write, smuggling his manuscripts out of the country to have them printed abroad. An accomplished stylist, he set forth his ideas with exceptional clarity, and his vitality shines through his every line. The overriding principle of his teachings is the physical unity of the universe: the same laws rule all motion, here below and in the skies. Far from being an atheist, he recognizes, in this unity, the ultimate affinity of the divine and human minds. His suppression involved more than the silencing of an independent thinker whose writings "contradicted Scripture." As churchmen saw it, Galilei's bold assertion that "the book of Nature is written in mathematical characters"; his absolute reliance on observations and experiments; his insistence on the freedom of pure science, were likely to bring the whole edifice of ecclesiastical teaching tumbling down. One Galilei, they argued, "can do more harm than Luther and Calvin put together." What was at issue was nothing more or less than Pilate's question, "What is truth?"

GARIBALDI, Giuseppe (1807–82). Adventurer, guerrilla leader, liberator, the most dashing among the founding fathers of the Italian nation, and one of the romantic figures of modern European history. Born on the fourth of July, 1807, in Nice (then under French occupation), the second son of the skipper of a coastal vessel, he was destined for the priesthood; but the strong-willed, blond youngster went to sea instead, working on ships plying the Mediterranean and the Black Sea. He was hardy, fearless, a fine swimmer. He also was a patriot. True, the Italians had never formed a nation, not even in Roman times. But they were thinking of themselves as but a single people, and now their land was parceled out, like Africa, among great foreign powers. The one exception—allowing for the special status of the Papal States and the twenty-four-square-mile Republic of San Marino—was the Kingdom of Piedmont-Sardinia, ruled by the Alpine dynasty of Savoy, with its capital at Turin. Garibaldi, during his years as a merchant sailor, had become a passionate republican. In 1833, he joined the subversive society *Giovine Italia* ("Young Italy"). Its leader, Giuseppe Mazzini (1805–72), who had already served a prison term as a member of the Carbonari (lit: "charcoal burners"), a secret liberation and unification movement, entrusted him with a perilous mission. Garibaldi was to sign on as a sailor on a Piedmont warship, subvert the crew, and bring it in on the side of a Mazzini-led coup against the Piedmont monarchy. The coup failed. Hundreds were arrested. Garibaldi jumped out of a window during his interrogation, got away, and reading in a newspaper that he had been sentenced to death—"The first time I saw my name in print" —escaped to South America. There followed twelve years of adventure, during which he formed a legion of marauders, whose cheap, durable uniform was the red shirt worn by slaughterhouse men. Most of these soldiers of fortune were, like himself, Italian exiles. As their leader, Garibaldi first fought for the Republic of Rio Grande do Sul, which had seceded from Brazil, and, after its collapse, for Uruguay, then trying to hold its own against its giant neighbor, Argentina. Once, captaining a Rio Grande boat, he was attacked by two Brazilian river barges and was hit by a bullet that went clear through his neck. On land, he evolved tactics used by guerrillas to this day, avoiding head-on clashes with superior forces, moving at night, pouncing at the opponent's weak points, and making the best of a terrain unfavorable to large, slow-moving units. On one occasion, he was caught and tortured; later, when the official who had supervised the torture was brought before him as a prisoner, he ordered his men not to harm him. His most spectacular success was the victory of San Antonio del Salto, Uruguay, in 1846, where he routed an enemy force of 1,500 with a bayonet charge of 250 Redshirts. The Uruguayan government, which he had saved, bestowed on him and all his men the title "Meritorious" and offered him the rank of general, which he declined. He had other things on his mind. In 1839, cruising in Brazilian waters on a captured schooner, he spotted, in a little house on shore—or thus he later told the story—a beautiful girl. He disembarked, walked up to her, and said, "Angelo, tu sarai mia"—("Angel, you'll be mine"). The lovely Anita (Anna Maria Ribeiro da Silva), who was already married or engaged, came with him. During the next ten years, she shared the hardships of his campaigns, fired a rifle like a man, and, in the course of their long, happy union, finally sanctioned by marriage, gave him four children, three of whom survived. Their sons, Menotti and Ricciotti, became famous soldier-adventurers. Garibaldi now yearned for his homeland, where liberal and patriotic forces were on the move, and where he could fight for a cause that was his own. The ship on which he sailed was called *Speranza* ("Hope"). His fame had traveled before him. During the brief Roman spring of 1849, when Pope Pius IX had fled the seething city and a republic had been set up, he watched the ramparts. The French, to whom the pope had urgently appealed for help, were on the march with 40,000 well-armed men. Garibaldi, entrusted with the republic's defense, concentrated his 7,000 volunteers, among them many Italian exiles returned from South America, in the exposed northwestern perimeter hinged on the Janiculum. There was no lack of bravura. One of his officers captured single-handedly 500 Frenchmen by grabbing their commander by the hair. As battles swirled around each isolated villa outside the walls, with Garibaldi in the thick of it, he lost some of his closest friends. His faithful Negro adjutant, Anghiar, fell by his side. Once, when he was dining with his staff at headquarters, a grazing cannon ball swept food and silver off the table. With French artillery bombarding Rome, Garibaldi kept on fighting with his saber, while many of his men were down to daggers. At last, he rode up to the Capitol and strode into the republican assembly of which he was a member to say that Rome had to accept defeat. With that, the two-month-old republic gave up the ghost. (Today, Garibaldi's equestrian statue looks down on

Rome from the top of the Janiculum.) During his retreat northward across enemy lines with a tattered remnant of his legion,
Anita, who had joined him during the last days and who was
with child, died in a farmhouse—to remain an unforgotten
heroine. Piedmont regulars took Garibaldi forcibly to Turin,
where he received an official scolding for having fought for the
republic without royal authority. Dejected and perplexed, the
sailor went to sea again, dropping anchor at Hong Kong, Liver-
pool, Lima, and New York. For a while he worked on Staten
Island as a salami- and candlemaker. When he returned to Italy,
Turin watched him closely (aware that he would not sit still),
ready to prevent him from making contact with revolutionary
groups. The rift in the Italian liberation movement could no
longer be patched up. While Garibaldi championed an Italian
republic, Piedmont's "gentleman king," Victor Emmanuel II,
wanted an Italian monarchy ruled by himself and his descendants. In 1852, Camillo Benso, Count Cavour (1810-61), became prime minister. A shrewd and cultured nobleman, a
military engineer, expert in agriculture and finance, he was, like
Garibaldi, a patriot. He, too, was for *Italia Una* ("One Italy").
It was he who had popularized the term *Risorgimento* ("Resur-
gence"), which was the title of a newspaper he published and
soon became the label for the entire struggle for unity and freedom from foreign rule. But he was a born statesman, and what
he had in mind was a nation that would take its place among the
world's great powers. Free Italy, in order to endure, must be admitted to the European drawing room. The price he paid for such
respectability was the dispatch of an Italian expeditionary force
of 15,000 men to the Crimea, where they fought with France and
England against Russia. As a result, Cavour was invited to the
Paris peace conference closing the Crimean War, which thereby
acknowledged Piedmont as representing all of Italy. Henceforth,
by an alliance here, a conference there, he steadily promoted his
grand design. In January 1859, the king made his historic speech
about the "cry of pain rising from all the peoples of Italy" to
which he could not close his ears. It was, perhaps, no mere coincidence that, a few weeks before, Garibaldi had been summoned
to an audience with Cavour. The two were destined to be enemies
for life. Yet, they knew that they needed each other and that
Italy needed them. Garibaldi, the best fighting officer in Italy,

reluctantly accepted an appointment as major general in the Piedmont army. Forming a corps of irregulars from all over Italy, the Alpine Hunters, he conducted a fast, victorious guerrilla war against the Austrians in the mountains, while the king's regulars fought the big battles. Milan was taken. But an untimely armistice, signed by Cavour for reasons of state, stopped Garibaldi from rushing on to Venice. His next venture—well described in Alfredo Venturi's *Garibaldi* (De Agostini, Novara, 1977; in Italian)—was the Expedition of the Thousand, aimed at the liberation of the South from the Spanish Bourbons, who had long ruled it by the *forca* (the "gallows"). His slogan was "For Italy and King"; he was willing, as he privately put it, to "make Italy with the Devil himself." Leaving the small port of Quarto (near Genoa) at dawn on 6 May 1860, with two steamships, he asked, "How many are we?" "More than a thousand, with the sailors," was the answer. "So many!" he exclaimed. With their three field pieces, the Redshirts disembarked at Marsala, some seventy miles southwest of the island's capital, Palermo. At Calatafimi, on their march inland, they routed a Bourbon force of 5,000. The capital itself was heavily garrisoned. Using a strategy he had developed in South America, Garibaldi drew the defenders from Palermo by moving small detachments of his Redshirts into the mountains, where they were eagerly pursued by the duped enemy, while he himself, marching with the main body at night, suddenly appeared before the depleted capital. He took it—with the enthusiastic help of its inhabitants—while the British and American fleets stood by, observing, and sending marveling dispatches to their governments. As the Redshirts advanced further, losses on both sides were heavy. When all of Sicily was theirs, the Thousand had dwindled to four hundred. But reinforcements had arrived, both volunteers and regulars, and Garibaldi, defying orders from the king, who was worried about his clamorous success, took some 4,000 men across the straits to the Italian mainland. To Rome! On landing, they captured thirty cannons. Next, 9,000 Bourbon soldiers surrendered. Several other units panicked; hundreds deserted; King Francis II of Sicily and southern Italy (the "Two Sicilies") left Naples, his capital; the Neapolitan fleet passed to Piedmont's side; and, just three weeks after his invasion of the mainland, Garibaldi rode into Naples. After a last, dramatic victory at the Volturno River, the road to Rome was open. At this point, Turin exploded. Whose war was this, the Redshirts' or the king's? Piedmontese troops were sent south in large numbers, and Garibaldi had to swallow hard when the king published a manifesto ("I hereby close the revolutionary era") and high-handedly annexed the liberated lands to Piedmont. Near the small town of Teano (north of Naples), Victor Emmanuel and Garibaldi, both on horseback—one in a braided and bemedaled uniform, the other in red shirt and poncho—held a chilly roadside meeting. There was to be no march on Rome. Behind Victor Emmanuel's caution loomed the ambivalent figure of his imperial sponsor, Napoleon III, nephew of the first Napoleon, who did not want to lose Catholic support by backing an attack against the pope. Stopped in his tracks by politics he could not understand, Garibaldi—Italy's most admired citizen, the symbol of Italian freedom — retired to the island of Caprera, off the Sardinian coast, where he had bought a farm, and where he raised his children. (After a one-day marriage to the daughter of a marquis, who turned out to be pregnant by another man, he lived with Francesca Armosino, by whom he had three sons, and whom he married at the age of seventy-three.) The Risorgimento now rolled on without him. In 1861, Victor Emmanuel was proclaimed "King of Italy," a title that was premature. Venice was still Austrian (it would be peacefully united with Italy, through Napoleon III's mediation, in 1866); and the pope had no intention of donating his dominions to the nascent nation. As Garibaldi brooded over his country's fate, the idea of liberating Rome became an obsession, drawing him back into action. And there ensued the tragicomedy of Garibaldi charging off, time and again, to conquer the Eternal City, and the king putting him back in his box before he could attain his goal. In 1862, having raised another volunteer corps, he was again marching on Rome from Sicily. "O Roma o Morte!" ("Rome or Death!") In the Aspromonte Mountains, near the toe of the Italian boot, Piedmont regulars barred his way. He held his fire, but his men were fired on, and he himself was wounded. "The fatal day of Aspromonte," reflects Joseph Conrad's Signor Viola in *Nostromo,* "when the treachery of kings, emperors, and ministers had been revealed to the world." Clearly, Garibaldi was becoming an embarrassment to the Italian kingdom, which could not tolerate freelance adventures that ran counter to its foreign policy. After being imprisoned in a fortress for a month, to the astonishment of the Western world, the enfant terrible was bundled off to his island. But who could keep him down? Soon, Garibaldi was at large again and, having fought the Austrians in Italy's third war of independence, veered toward Rome. Promptly shipped back to Caprera, he was told to stay there. A naval squadron watched the island day and night. So, one October evening, the old man got into a rowboat, his oars muffled by rags. Leaving behind a friend dressed to resemble him, he glided through the naval cordon and rejoined his men on the mainland, ready to invade the papal states. The action was an utter failure. The French defenders, armed with new rapid-firing rifles, proved invincible. After a bloody battle, the Redshirts were disarmed by regulars. Garibaldi was carried bodily into a railroad carriage and, in exchange for a promise not to make further trouble, escorted, for the last time, to Caprera. When the Italians three years later (20 September 1870) rode through the breach near Porta Pia into Rome, *Italia Una* had become reality. But Garibaldi wasn't present, and Cavour was dead. What kind of man was Garibaldi? Of slightly more than medium height, sturdily built, with a massive forehead and a square, reddish beard, he had about him the aura of a natural-born leader. Wearing his red shirt and poncho, and usually smoking a cigar, he was an object of love and devotion, inspiring his often ill-fed, poorly armed men to deeds of gallantry. *"Avanti* ["forward"], boys!" "At them, you whoresons!" The chance of quick promotion and the atmosphere of camaraderie caused many regulars to join his ranks—to be shot as deserters if caught by the king's men. His bayonet charges, which he often led in person, were so dreaded by the foe that fear became his strongest ally. Wherever there was a collision, it was gory. Once, in Sicily, he suddenly perceived a mounted enemy officer race toward him, brandishing his saber; drawing his own, Garibaldi cut off his head with a single stroke. He was well-read, liked to recite the Italian classics, was a discursive letter writer, and wrote poor, always touching, poetry. During an official visit to London, in 1864, he sent the public into waves of enthusiasm. In politics, he was a liberal. He belonged to a society for the abolition of capital punishment, was violently anticlerical, and wished to do away with noble titles. But politics was not his element. In the Italian parliament, of which he was a member to his death, he delivered childish harangues and declared that he "could not breathe" in that stuffy environment. He was, at heart, a condottiere. With Napoleon III taken prisoner by the Prussians at Sedan in the Franco-Prussian war of 1870–71, and with a French republic in the offing, he joined the hard-pressed French as leader of an international force of 20,000 volunteers. Against tremendous odds, he won the three-day battle of Dijon, captured the only regimental flag the Prussians lost in the entire war, and was acclaimed as the only general on the French side who wasn't beaten. Prussia's top military experts highly praised his tactics. After the French defeat, he was elected to the constitutional assembly in Bordeaux; but when he wanted to speak in favor of a democratic state, he was shouted down by the monarchical majority, and left for home—once more embittered and resentful. The Garibaldi drama, which sometimes sounds like a Sicilian puppet show, ends on his farm, where he lives, with his large family, on a generous government pension. Plagued by rheumatic pains and by his wounds, he spends most of his days in a wheelchair. At his island home, the "White House," visitors from all over the world are treated to fresh shrimps and memories of the eighty-odd battles he has fought on two continents. The ships of the Italian navy, once standing off Caprera to keep watch on him, fire a last salute as he is buried. He had made Italy "with the Devil," and the Devil had his way. His country was a kingdom, ruled by the Savoy dynasty until the abdication, in 1946, of King Victor Emmanuel III, and the termination, by a referendum (12,717,923 votes to 10,719,284) of his son Humbert's— Umberto II—one-month reign. *Italia Una* was, at long last, a republic.

GOLDONI, Carlo (1707–93). Venetian playwright, founder of modern Italian comedy. The sparkle of eighteenth-century Venice illuminates the work of this nimble dramatist who revamped the Italian stage. The son of a doctor, he ran away from school and, aged fourteen, joined a company of strolling players. He later resumed his studies, acquired a law degree, and practiced law in Venice and Pisa. But the play was the thing. His is the merit of having toppled Italy's conventional commedia dell'arte (the prototype of England's Punch and Judy show), whose actors represented such stock characters as Arlecchino ("Harlequin") and Pulcinella, wore masks, and depended largely on witty improvisations and slapstick hilarity. Inspired by the human comedies of Molière, Goldoni felt that the theater should reflect the realities of life as it is lived on every social level, presenting flesh-and-blood characters and their every-day problems, in an entertaining vein. He wrote with incredible speed, tossing off sixteen plays in a single winter season. Many of his 150-odd comedies and librettos are written in Venetian dialect. He is at his best when depicting the world of the poor. The tribulations of courtship are often at the bottom of his plots, and he is a master at blending the lighthearted with the sad. Having written successfully for theatrical companies in Venice, he was harassed by jealous rivals and in 1762 accepted an invitation to direct a theater in Paris. He caught on rapidly, was engaged to teach the royal princesses Italian, and wrote a play in French for Louis XVI's wedding, *Le Bourru Bienfaisant* ("the Rough Diamond"). He fell from grace as quickly as he had risen. The Revolution had no use for him. He lost his pension and died in poverty in Paris. He remains one of Italy's most popular playwrights. His statue graces many piazzas, he is read in high school, and his plays—such as *La Locandiera* ("the Lady Innkeeper")— are frequently performed. His memoirs, penned at Versailles, are a bemused, amusing record of his times.

GRAND TOUR. A loose term, first heard in English toward the end of the seventeenth century, designating a gentleman's leisurely circuit of the European continent. Institutionalized by the British upper class in the seventeen hundreds, its beginnings reach further back. We hear of a Prince of Jülich and Cleves, in the northern Rhineland, who went to look at Italy in 1575 with an escort of sixty horse and died in Rome. But Europe did not really open up to peaceful travel until 1648, when the end of the Thirty Years' War made the main highways relatively safe, and the movement of sightseers, thereafter, fluctuated with the continent's political vicissitudes. A blend of motives lay behind the Tour. It was, for one thing, a status symbol—back home again, you would be able to talk about narrow escapes from robbers, a duel or two, your impressions of the Laocoön statue at the Vatican. It also meant keeping up with the Lord Joneses, who were doing the same thing. But the Grand Tour was, primarily, a way for the young Englishman of "good birth" and ample means to round out his education, polish his social manners, improve his dress, and absorb "culture." He'd spend a year or more visiting the major centers of civilization and enjoyment, lingering at Paris, perhaps at Vienna, seeing the mighty Rhine, crossing the frozen Alps, and making sunny Italy the main dish of his varied menu. Germans, too, hit the southward trail, impelled by a romantic longing to "know the land where the lemon trees bloom; where gold oranges glow among dark foliage," as Goethe wrote. (The German poet went to Italy in 1786–88 in order to escape from his administrative chores at the provincial court of Weimar and in vain hopes of finding the *Urpflanze,* ancestor of all vegetation.) But the Americans were latecomers, arriving—not counting a few early scouts—in the mid-nineteenth century, when the tour was no longer "grand." The typical English Grand Tourist was eager to see, with his own eyes, the ancient monuments he had read so much about. He had studied the Latin classics, at Oxford or Cambridge, and would recite them at the drop of a hat. James Boswell (1740–95)—best known for his *Life of Samuel Johnson*—who made the Grand Tour in his mid-twenties, could rattle off forty of Horace's 102 *Odes.* Edward Gibbon (1737–94) visited "each memorable spot where (he fancied) Romulus stood, or Tully (Marcus Tullius Cicero) spoke." He conceived the idea for his monumental *Decline and Fall of the Roman Empire* while brooding among the ruins of the Capitol in Rome. But although the "milords," as the Italians called all

Englishmen, dutifully toured art galleries and churches (where Catholic pomp troubled their Protestant consciences), few of them knew what to make of Italian art, especially that of the Middle Ages and of the Baroque. They did enjoy the social life, however, so much less hidebound than at home. Many of them were armed with introductions to noble families and were readily welcomed at their palaces and villas. If they were traveling with a tutor, they did their best to get away from him, timing their itinerary so as to abandon themselves, in early spring, to the "frantic, bacchanalian," and delightfully un-English, carnival. Sex was predominantly on their minds. Italian women, known for their dark-eyed beauty, were reputed to be easy game, and Boswell claims that, whenever he admired a lady, married or not, he was told, "Sir, you can have her. It would not be difficult." Nevertheless, as he wrote to Jean-Jacques Rousseau (1712–78), he had "no success at all with the ladies of Piedmont," perhaps because his approach was too direct. But he did indulge his passion in Naples, where "the ladies resembled country chamber maids," and carried on a serious love affair with the wife of the *capitano del popolo* (roughly, "mayor") of Siena, Girolama ("Moma") Piccolomini, a woman considerably older than himself. He lingered in her arms until his pa, Lord Auchinleck, ordered him back to Scotland. Freedom from puritan morality seems to have been one of the reasons why British fathers sent their sons to Italy, where they would "learn how to live," and where their amorous adventures could safely be left behind. There was an odor of wild oats, and of a corresponding guilt feeling, about the journey south. "Whore-hunting among groves of myrtles," Scotland's national poet, Robert Burns (1759–96), called the Italian leg of the Grand Tour. The more mature milords stopped at cultural way stations they had heard about at their clubs. In Rome, they visited the printshop of Giambattista Piranesi (1720–78) and, later in the century, the sculptor's studio of Antonio Canova (1757–1822); carried on earnest literary and artistic conversations—in poor Italian or fair French—in the salons of countesses and at coffee houses, and, if they were lucky, made the rounds of ancient monuments with the great Winckelmann (1717–68) himself as their cicerone. From Naples, they went on excursions to Pompeii, partly excavated since 1748, and climbed Mt. Vesuvius, whose A.D. 79

eruption had buried it, to enjoy one of Europe's most celebrated views. In Florence, they bought antiques, fake or authentic, and might pick up a Botticelli or a Raphael that is, today, the pride of a museum in England or the United States. In Venice, they forgathered at the house of the British consul, Joseph Smith— "the Merchant of Venice"—to inspect his remarkable collection of rare books and paintings (among the latter, Vermeer's *Lady at the Virginal*), which he later sold to King George III. What one too easily forgets is that these travelers were willing to undergo considerable hardships in order to see Italy. The two-day trip across the Alps, usually by way of Mt. Cenis, was a hair-raising experience. Milord's carriage, unless he wished to take another one on the other side, was dismantled and carried across piecemeal. He himself sat in a rope chair suspended from two parallel poles and was lifted over icy heights by a team of six bearers. Horace Walpole (1717–97), novelist, antiquarian, and collector—who on occasion wore a limewood necktie sculpted by the master wood carver, Grinling Gibbons (1648–1721)—had his lapdog snatched from him by a wolf during the ride. Once in Italy, the tourist found bad roads, dirty inns, and, frequently, poor food. Unless he traveled, like Lord Byron (1788–1824), with a train of five carriages, seven servants, and livestock of his own, could he be really comfortable? Brigands were lurking in romantic ruins. The foreigner was cheated, or thought he was, at every turn. To top it all, a noxious miasma, hanging in the warm night air, brought on malaria, or "Roman fever." (The female anopheline mosquito was not identified as the sole carrier of the disease until 1898—by three Italians: Bignami, Grassi, and Bastianelli.) No wonder, then, that many visitors took an ill-humored view of Italy and its inhabitants. "The people here," wrote Shelley (1792–1822), from Milan (quoted by H. and P. Massingham in *The Englishman Abroad*), "though inoffensive enough, seem both in body and soul a miserable race. The men are hardly men; they look like a tribe of stupid and shriveled slaves, and I do not think that I have seen a gleam of intelligence in the countenance of man since I passed the Alps." And, from Naples: "Young women of rank actually eat—you will never guess what—*garlic!*" Boswell and his traveling companions, arriving at Ferrara, with its resplendent palaces and art treasures, "had a violent dispute as to whether it was necessary to stay to look at the city." This rather jaundiced view was to spill over into nineteenth-century American literature. Henry James (1843–1916), who visited Italy more than once and chooses an Italian setting for a number of his novels, describes Eugenio Giovanelli, devoted escort of his pure, Yankee Daisy (*Daisy Miller*), as a "shiny—but, to do him justice, not greasy—little Roman," and spots in him "the depth of Italian subtlety, so strangely opposed to Anglo-Saxon simplicity." Poor Daisy, after sitting in the Colosseum with Eugenio during a moonlit night, dies, expectably, of malaria. And Nathaniel Hawthorne (1804–64), in *The Marble Faun,* published after a long stay in Italy, writes: "Here was a priesthood pampered, sensual, with red and bloated cheeks, and carnal eyes. . . . And here was an indolent nobility, with no high aims or opportunities, but cultivating a vicious way of life, as if it were an art, and the only one which they cared to learn. Here was a population, high and low, that had no genuine belief in virtue." It remained for Mark Twain (Samuel Langhorne Clemens, 1835–1910) to produce, in *The Innocents Abroad,* the classic spoof of the Grand Tour. Posing as one of the "Innocents" himself, the one-time Mississippi River pilot asks his Italian guide, "Who is this Renaissance? Where did he come from?" In Venice, he tells his gondolier, who sings a serenata, "Another yelp, and overboard you go." In Florence, he observes that the Arno would be "a very plausible river if they would pump some water into it." He wonders why the angels in pictures "wear nothing but wings." Shown a yellow hair said to be from Lucrezia Borgia's head, he confesses to the highest respect for the lady for the "facility with which she would order a sextuple funeral and get the corpses ready for it." Finally, being told, by various cicerones, that Michelangelo designed the Colosseum, the Pantheon, the Tiber, and the Seven Hills of Rome, he enthusiastically cries, "Lump the whole thing! Say that the Creator made Italy from designs by Michelangelo!" Still, the Grand Tour fostered a new appreciation of Italian art, a spate of memoirs of wanderings in Italy, and guidebooks indispensable to twentieth-century Innocents.

GREECE IN ITALY. The traveler in southern Italy is struck by the number of Greek temples, which, for their beauty and their state of preservation, have few peers in Greece itself. The finest specimens, dating from the sixth and fifth centuries B.C., are to be found—set off, in early spring, by wheat fields, flowers and scented herbs—at Agrigento, Segesta, and Selinunte, in Sicily and, on the mainland, at Paestum, some sixty miles southeast of Naples. They tell the story of Greek colonization of parts of Italy that started about 750 B.C. and lasted for three centuries, engendering a brave new world generally referred to as Magna Graecia—Great Greece, or, better, Greater Greece. Here, Greek civilization reached heights of refinement when Rome was barely on the map. Familiar shades frequent these shores—Pythagoras, Aeschylus, Plato, Pindar, Archimedes, visited or lived here. Homeric terrors—among them Polyphemus, the man eating Cyclops; the Sirens, whose sweet voices lure sailors to their death; Scylla and Charybdis, ruination of ships and crews; Circe, the sorceress who changes men into beasts—are at home in Magna Graecia. The process of establishing Greek colonies, both in Asia Minor and Italy, was not based on an imperialist design, but, rather, on the local needs of a cramped, mountainous homeland whose rock-strewn fields yielded but little food. This or that city would send out a shipload of adventurers eager to settle where the grass was greener. They drew other settlers after them, drove the barbaric natives inland, created viable communities which traded the rich crops of their wide-open spaces for manufactured goods, built their own fleets, raised their own armies, struck their own coins—some of them of great elegance—and tirelessly quarreled with one another. Their constitutions ranged from democracies and oligarchies to autocratic regimes lorded over by a *tyrannos*. In Sicily, whose luscious flora amazed the newcomers, one of the earliest landings—about 735 B.C.—was made at Syracuse, on the east coast, a site endowed with two natural harbors, one of them big enough to accommodate a battle fleet. Settled by colonists from mercantile Corinth, it quickly rose to wealth and power. Its prominence was reinforced when Gelon, ruler of Gela, a south-coast colony (where he exercised in an outsized swimming pool along with a squadron of swans), took Syracuse in 485 B.C. and five years later routed the Carthaginians who, from North Africa, kept harassing the young colonies. Governing wisely, he turned Syracuse into a thriving metropolis, whose court attracted artists and philosophers from the Greek mainland. During the reign of his brother and successor, Hiero I, Pindar and Aeschylus visited Sicily. The former sings of "the fruitful land of Sicily and her rich cities" and describes an eruption of Mt. Etna, with "streams of fire and crashing rocks—a wonder to behold and even hear." Aeschylus, whom an oracle had told that he would be killed by a bolt from heaven, died at Gela in 456 B.C., when an eagle, mistaking his bald pate for a stone, dropped a turtle on it to crack its shell. Dionysius I (c. 430–367), a usurper, who assumed the title "Lord of Sicily," had literary ambitions and, having bought the pen and harp of Euripides, contrived some mediocre plays, one of which won him a prize in Athens. Plato (c. 427–348), who visited Syracuse three times, conceived the bizarre notion of transforming it into a laboratory where his theories of the ideal state, as set forth in his *Republic,* would be translated into reality by a philosopher-king, namely, Dionysius' son, Dionysius II. He could hardly have picked a more unlikely candidate. This vain and dissolute young man resented the austerity taught by the master. On his third visit, Plato was imprisoned and released only upon the intervention of influential friends. When Dionysius II later visited Locri, his mother's home town on the Italian mainland, he took over a large hall, had its floor strewn with thyme and roses, and, on this bed, proceeded to make love to local beauties; whereupon the Locrians ravished and killed his wife and daughters. Driven from Syracuse, he ended his days in Egypt as a tambourine-beating priest of the great mother goddess Cybele-Demeter. At the time of the Roman conquest of Sicily in 212 B.C., the most distinguished Syracusan was the mathematician Archimedes, among whose many discoveries was the law of specific gravity. He hit upon it while trying to determine whether a crown, made for the ruler Hiero II, who intended it as a present to the gods, was of pure gold, as specified. Puzzling over this in a public bathhouse, Archimedes observed that the water level in his tub rose in proportion to the volume of the part of his body immersed in it—and had the answer. Not bothering to dress, he ran through the streets, shouting *eureka! eureka!*—"I've found it!" (The specific gravity of silver is lower than that of gold, hence a pound of silver displaces more water than a pound of gold. The crown contained an admixture of silver, and the goldsmith was convicted of fraud.) Archimedes is reported to have delayed the capture of the city for two years by building catapults whose missiles played havoc with the Roman fleet and by using reflecting mirrors to set ships on fire. When the Romans finally took Syracuse, a soldier found him bent over a geometric problem, tracing figures on the ground, and Archimedes is said to have implored the man, as he raised his sword to kill him, not to "disturb those circles." He wanted to have a cylinder enclosing a sphere placed on his tomb, in memory of one of his treatises. When Cicero, nearly 250 years later, served as quaestor in Sicily, he recognized the tomb, forgotten among brambles, by this token. The first Greek colony on the Italian mainland was Cumae (c. 760 B.C.), a steep hill on the Tyrrhenian coast near Naples. (The latter, *Nea Polis*—"New Town"—was founded by Cumaean settlers.) Cumae's most famous, if mythical, inhabitant was the Cumaean Sibyl, one of the prophetesses who, inspired by Apollo, had drifted westward with his cult from Asia Minor. The cave in which she is said to have lived, writing her oracles on leaves, exists in Cumae to this day. According to the legend, she had asked Apollo for the gift of prophecy, and for as many years of life as she could hold grains of sand in her hand, in return for her love, but forgot to mention lasting youth. Unwilling after all to part with her virginity, she could beg no further favors. When she accompanied Aeneas, who had come to Italy from burning Troy—presumably before the year 1000 B.C.—into the Underworld and back again, she had already seen 700 harvests. And Trimalchio, the boastful host of Petronius's *Satyricon*, written in the first century A.D., claims to have seen her shriveled form "hung up in a flask," pestered by urchins who cried in Greek, *Sibylla ti theleis* ("Sibyl, what do you want?"), to which she invariably replied, *apothanein thelo*—"I want to die." (The motto of T. S. Eliot's poem, *The Waste Land.*) This was the Sibyl who offered to Rome's king nine books containing her collected prophecies, at an exorbitant price. At his refusal, she went away and burned three books, then offered the remaining six for the same sum. Refused again, she burned three more, and the king bought the last three books at the original price of nine. They were kept under lock and key in the Jupiter Temple on the Capitol and consulted, on order of the Senate, in major crises. They perished in a fire in 83 B.C., and a new collection of Sibylline oracles was made, which was last consulted in A.D. 363. We probably owe the entrance of Sibyls into Christian lore—and thus into Michelangelo's Sistine Ceiling—to a misreading of Virgil's fourth ("Messianic") Eclogue, published in 37 B.C. In it the Cumaean Sibyl predicts the imminent dawn of a new era, ushered in by the birth of a wonderful boy—a reference to a Roman dignitary whose wife was pregnant, rather than a prediction of the birth of Christ. On Italy's indented southern shore, the sister colonies of Sybaris and Croton, twenty-five miles apart, faced, across the wide, warm bay, the fishermen's republic of Taras (now Taranto). All three were late-eighth-century foundations. Croton's fame rested on brain as well as brawn. Pythagoras, the wizard of the ancient world (one of his major discoveries was the arithmetical ratio of the intervals of the musical scale), having fled his native Samos, settled at Croton about 530 B.C. He rescued it from a depression by establishing a sound currency, based on a new silver coin whose beautiful dies he is reported to have cut himself. Pythagoras also founded a philosophical society, or sect, whose members seem to have believed in the transmigration of souls. Croton produced a line of famous athletes, the most renowned of whom was Milo, a six-time winner of the wrestling crown at the Olympic games, not to mention other all-Greek competitions. He once strode down the length of the Olympic stadium carrying a heifer on his shoulders. His death was equally spectacular. He came upon a tree trunk partially split by woodmen, who had left a wedge in it, and tried to sunder it with his bare hands. The wedge jumped out, and the trunk closed on his hand. Wolves (some say, lions) found him and devoured him. Nearby Sybaris was proverbial in antiquity for the luxury of its upper-class inhabitants. Many of the stories making the rounds, and no doubt containing some exaggerations, were collected by Athenaeus, an Egyptian Greek who lived in Rome (c. A.D. 170–c. 230). The Sybarites, we read, maintained 5,000 cavalry—five times as many as Athens—who paraded in expensive saffron-yellow uniforms and whose horses danced to music. Citizens traveled in carriages, and the roads leading into the country were roofed for shade (probably with canvas). Sybarites gave mixed dinner parties, exceptional in Greek society, and often issued invitations a year ahead, so that the ladies might see to their dresses, and the hosts had time to dispatch ships to the Orient for rare delicacies. Cooks who came up with a new tasty dish were granted exclusive rights to the recipe for one year—the Western world's first patent law. Importers of the purple shell, yielding the precious purple dyestuff, and eel fishers were exempt from taxes, so as to guarantee a steady supply of the two luxuries. The Sybarites invented chamber pots. Noisy trades, such as that of the blacksmiths, were not allowed within the city, nor was it legal to keep a rooster. The Sybarites were good customers of Miletus, in Asia Minor, which turned out the ancient world's most costly woollen fabrics. One Sybarite owned a specially woven himation—a fulllength, ample garment draped about the body—so universally admired that Dionysius I of Syracuse acquired it and later sold it, at a fantastic price, to Carthage. Another citizen went suing for the hand of a Greek lady with a retinue of 1,000 cooks and fowlers. Whence all this wealth? Sybaris dominated a vast, fertile plain, where almost anything would grow. Vineyards, rich forests, and silver mines were situated in its territory, which comprised some twenty-five towns. (Paestum, with its stout walls and splendid Doric temples, was a Sybarite colony, founded about 650 B.C., probably as a trading post with the Etruscans to the north.) Sybaris controlled the overland route, across Calabria, to the Tyrrhenian markets, allowing merchants from the East to avoid the long, perilous sea voyage through the Sicilian straits. Last but not least, Sybaris was generous in granting citizenship to foreigners, many of whom brought in both skills and capital. But the rich colony continuously squabbled with its sibling, Croton. In 510 B.C., when the Sybarites had foolishly put to death all thirty members of a Crotonese embassy, the city was attacked, taken, and razed to the ground by a Crotonese army led by the prize fighter, Milo, in person. The Crathis River was diverted to engulf the ruins, and the very site was lost for many centuries. Not until 1968 did archaeologists identify it under twenty-three feet of topsoil; excavations, carried on since then, have uncovered rests of habitations and some fragments of temple decorations. The silting-up of harbors, malaria, and the tramp of Roman legions finished off what had been a magnificent civilization. By 200 B.C., Magna Graecia had expired.

GROTESQUE. A word with a surprising etymology. Grotesques are painted decorations of a fantastic type, often combined with stucco work, whose function is entirely ornamental. They are characterized by a profusion of diverse subjects, capriciously arranged to form a single composition. Grotesque designs were popular in ancient Rome where—liberally applied to walls and ceilings, often on a white, red, black, or yellow background—they turned rooms into entertaining picture books. Their rediscovery during the Renaissance provided a new stimulus to painters, who promptly imitated them. When, about 1480, some Romans penetrated into buried rooms on Oppius, the hill facing the Colosseum, torches revealed ceilings and walls covered with intricate designs. Having descended through the surface ruins of the Baths of Trajan, the discoverers believed that they had entered subterranean caves or grottoes (*grotte* in Italian) and bestowed the name *grottesche* (sing. *grottesca*) on the curious ornaments. (*Grotta* itself derives from the Greek *kryptein* ["to hide, conceal, or bury in the earth"]—surviving in crypt, crypto-, and Apocrypha.) The "grottoes" turned out to be the Golden House of Nero (54–68), disused after his death and buried by the emperor Trajan (98–117) under his Baths. And although several other Roman ruins were found to have grotesques, the Golden House remained the major source of inspiration for Italian painters, who came to copy the designs. Pliny the Elder (c. 23–79), in his *Natural History,* remembers their creator, Famulus or Fabullus, as a dignified and rather fussy man who wore a toga even while he worked, worked but a few hours a day, and painted a *Minerva* that looked at you no matter where you stood. Much of the decor of the "grottoes" has since deteriorated or completely disappeared. Among the mass of graffiti left by visitors is that of Pinturicchio (c. 1454–1513), whose contract (1502) for the Piccolomini fresco cycle in the cathedral of Siena contains the first known mention of "grotesques," and whose ceiling (New York, Metropolitan) echoes the "Golden Vault" of one of Nero's state rooms. Another signature still legible is that of Giovanni da Udine (1487–1564), Raphael's pupil, who created Italy's best-known grotesques, under his master's supervision, in the Loggias of the Vatican (1517–19). To the unhurried viewer of grotesques—"these calculated freaks," as Edgar Wind calls them in *Pagan Mysteries in the Renaissance*—a world of fancy opens up. A typical arrangement consists of an ornate vase from which rich scrolls of foliage ramble upward to engulf a variety of tiny images culled from nature's animal and vegetable kingdoms, or bizarre figments of imagination, all interlaced in such a way as to form a busy little universe. Among fruits and flowers, we glimpse such fabled creatures as harpies, griffins, centaurs, and sphinxes living in harmony with crabs, bats, peacocks, swans, butterflies, monkeys, giraffes, and elephants. Nymphs ride on rams. Winged putti dance a jig. And framed medallions, painted or in delicately molded stucco, represent figures human or divine. Anything goes, and in this utter freedom lies the significance of the grotesque. Artists, bound by rules of logic in their serious works, let their imagination roam in these lightheaded fantasies through which their whimsey could escape. The adjective "grotesque" entered the English language in the seventeenth century.

————◆————

HOLY ROMAN EMPIRE (800–1806). A grandiose concept resting on a shaky base. Much of the time, no more than an unstable union between Germany and Northern Italy.

It was sprung on the world on Christmas Day, 800, when Pope Leo III, whose predecessor had relied on Frankish military aid, unexpectedly crowned Charlemagne, the Frankish king, "emperor" at St. Peter's in Rome. It was the Church that took the initiative in setting up this empire, whose purpose was to fuse all Christendom into one body. (Rom. 12: 5: "So we, being many, are one body in Christ.") The political idea was to replace Europe's incipient anarchy with a law-and-order structure borrowed from the old (27 B.C.–A.D. 476) Roman Empire. The word "holy" was added by the German emperor Frederick I, Barbarossa, in 1157, to emphasize that he held secular dominion directly under God. The popes continued to claim the right to choose and crown the emperors, most of whom belonged to the great dynasties of Germany. Otto I was crowned in 962, and many date the empire from that year. But though Pope Gregory VII (1073–85) called the pope "the Sun," the emperor, "the Moon," this bold configuration did not work. Far from content to be mere vassals of the pontiff, emperors quarreled and warred with Rome (especially over their authority to nominate bishops—the tedious investiture controversy); led armies into Italy to assert their claims to secular rule in that country; formed anti-papal alliances and were, in turn, the victims of papal excommunication. At its height, about 1200, the empire comprised the major part of Europe, but it never was a political entity. Its historic value lies in the fact that it pursued the ideal of a united Europe and kept alive old Roman legal concepts. Charles V, ruler of Germany, the Netherlands, and Spain, was the last emperor to be crowned by the pope (1530). Toward its end, the empire—then little more than a federation of German princes—was but a shadow of its former self, said to be neither holy, nor Roman, nor an empire. It fell under the hammer blows of Napoleon, and the last emperor, Francis II, resigned the hollow title, to remain emperor of Austria.

---◄◆►---

H O L Y   Y E A R . An event full of spiritual meaning for Catholic Christianity, and a boon to Roman innkeepers, souvenir peddlers, and pickpockets, it comes every twenty-five years: in '00, '25, '50, and '75. Originally intended to commemorate the birth of Christ every hundred years, the jubilee was first celebrated in 1300 under Pope Boniface VIII as a substitute for the Crusades (1096–1270), which had carried with them special indulgences—remissions of punishment for sins- -for the participants. With Moslem-ruled Jerusalem inaccessible to Christians, Rome, the "New Jerusalem," a goal of Christian salvation-seekers since the late sixth century, thus became Christendom's chief pilgrimage center. (A man who had made the pilgrimage to Rome was known as a *Romeo.*) The one-hundred-year interval, never observed, was soon reduced to fifty, then to thirty-three years, for the span of Jesus' life. The present quarter-century rhythm was decreed in 1470 by the Venetian Pope Paul II. A Holy Year begins on Christmas Eve, with the ceremonial opening of the normally walled-up Holy Door (on the extreme right of the façade of St. Peter's) by the pope flanked by the cardinal penitentiary. The door remains open during the next twelve months for the benefit of pilgrims, to be closed again, by the pope, at Christmas of the following year. The Holy Year Indulgence is plenary, meaning remission of all temporal punishment for past sins. Prerequisites for obtaining the full spiritual benefits of the pilgrimage may change occasionally. But, generally speaking, the pilgrim must be genuinely repentant, receive Communion and the sacrament of penance, say prayers for the pope, and visit one of Rome's four major basilicas (the duty to visit all four having been abolished in order to save time, as well as to avoid an aggravation of Rome's traffic problem). Each Holy Year adds a large number of pilgrims to Rome's annual tourist invasion. Precise statistics are not available. With hostels and hotels packed to capacity, many pilgrims sleep in nearby towns, visiting Rome during the day. In 1975, the last Holy Year, the number of bona fide pilgrims was estimated at more than one million. A Holy, or Supersabbatical, Year was known to ancient Jewry. Marking the passage of seven sabbatical years, each of them terminating a seven-year period, it was celebrated every fifty years and announced by the sound of a trumpet (*yobel* in Hebrew, originally a ram's horn—hence, "jubilee"). During it, Hebrew slaves had to be liberated, land wrongfully taken from its owners had to be restored, and sowing and reaping were—at least in theory—forbidden (Lev. 25: 8–17).

H U M A N I S M. From the Latin *studia humanitatis,* a term used with reference to a liberal education stressing the study of the Greek and Latin classics as a means to the perfection of the human being. It is applied, particularly, to an intellectual movement dominating Italian culture, roughly, between 1400 and the 1520s, and nourishing—sometimes directing—the Renaissance in art, to which it is inseparably linked. The first cultural current since the Middle Ages evolving outside, and independently of, the Church—though many leading churchmen adhered to it —it did much to transform the God-centered medieval image of the world into the man-oriented outlook of the Renaissance. The heralds of humanism were Petrarch (1304–74) and his friend Boccaccio (1313–75). From 1400 onward, Italy led Europe in an unfolding of the human spirit. Not since the days of Periclean Athens, in the fifth century B.C., had there been so large, so fruitful, a gathering of questioning minds. Adventurous Italian scholars, bent on salvaging lost literary treasures, journeyed to the Near East, especially to Greek-speaking Constantinople, to fill their valises with manuscripts of classics heretofore unknown in Italy. A Sicilian, Giovanni Aurispa (c. 1369–1459), who traveled east in 1414, brought home 238 rare manuscripts, among them works by Pindar, Aeschylus,

Sophocles, and Plato. Francesco Filelfo (1398–1481), who had been a professor at Padua at the age of eighteen, went to Constantinople in 1419 as secretary to the Venetian consul there, learned Greek, ran several diplomatic errands for the Byzantine emperor, and returned, some six years later, with more than forty precious manuscripts. He spent the rest of his life teaching Greek, Latin, and classical literature in various Italian cities. For about thirty years, the center of his manifold activities was the court of Milan, where, on his arrival, Duke Filippo Maria Visconti placed a diamond ring on his finger. At the same time, Greek scholars came to Italy, where they were warmly welcomed, to teach their language and their literature to an eager generation of Italian students. Manuel Chrysoloras (c. 1350–1415), who arrived in Italy in 1393 to solicit, on behalf of the Byzantine emperor, aid against the advancing Turks, was persuaded by the early humanist, Coluccio Salutati (1331–1406), to settle in Florence and teach Greek. He translated Plato's *Republic* into Latin and wrote the first Greek grammar to be printed (in 1471) in Western Europe. The Greek theologian, John (later Basil) Bessarion (c. 1400–72), was sent to Italy to attend the Council of 1438–39 held in Ferrara and Florence, which tried to reconcile the Eastern and Western Churches. He converted to Catholicism, was made a cardinal by Pope Eugene IV, translated Aristotle's *Metaphysics,* and donated his splendid collection of Greek manuscripts to the Venetian Republic, where it became the nucleus of one of Italy's most important public libraries, the Biblioteca Marciana. (Byzantine scholars finding asylum in Italy after the fall of Constantinople to the Turks in 1453 were, on the whole, mediocre intellects.) Elated by the unexpectedly rich Eastern loot, Italian literati now began to ransack their own cobwebbed monastery libraries, and often those of other European countries. Results were equally rewarding. The Tuscan, Giovanni Francesco Poggio Bracciolini (1380–1459), a pupil of Chrysoloras, sifted the shelves of German, Swiss, French, and Italian monasteries and came up with important works by Cicero, as well as Frontinus's treatise on aqueducts. Among Poggio's own works is a book on the *Misery of the Human Condition.* He served as a papal secretary and ended his days as chancellor of the Republic of Florence —a post in which he was preceded by another outstanding humanist, Leonardo Bruni (1370–1444), translator of Greek classics and author of the first scholarly history of Florence. As soon as a rare manuscript had been secured, it was copied and recopied, often by the humanists themselves. Though humanism profited, to some extent, from Johann Gutenberg's mid-fifteenth-century invention of movable type, facilitating the dissemination of texts through printed books, it remained a select establishment. (Federigo da Montefeltro, duke of Urbino [1444–82], maintained a palace staff of more than thirty copyist-calligraphers and would not tolerate a printed book in his library.) Humanists commanded high fees as tutors, lecturers, translators, and letter writers; the princely courts of Italy competed for their services. But their true home was Florence, where Cosimo the Elder de' Medici (1389–1464) had founded the Platonic Academy as a forum for classical studies. Among them were Marsilio Ficino (1433–99), the first translator into Latin of Plato's complete works, a translation in universal use until the eighteenth century; Politian (Angelo Poliziano, 1454–94), the leading classical scholar of his time, accomplished poet, translator of the *Iliad*, and tutor of Lorenzo the Magnificent's children; and Giovanni Pico della Mirandola (1463–94). In the bucolic setting of the Medici Villa at Careggi, in the Tuscan countryside, humanists contrived their own philosophy, an uneasy compromise between paganism and the Word of Christ—the Neoplatonism of the Renaissance. From about 1450 onward, the movement's center of gravity was Rome. Under a succession of humanist popes, such as Nicholas V (1447–55), patron of Leon Battista Alberti and founder of the Vatican Library, scores of humanist intellectuals were employed in the Apostolic chancery. Humanism did have its seedy side—some of its best-known representatives were erratic, obscene, vainglorious, and cantankerous, and quarreled viciously with rivals. Though almost all of them wrote poetry and prose, few left behind great literary works. They did not have to. Their foremost interest was antiquarian, and their undying merit lies in their literary discoveries, their learned commentaries and translations. And though the roots of humanism reach back into medieval soil—Dante himself (1265–1321) was one of its precursors—its reckless exaltation of the individual, making man the measure of all things, speeded the breakup of the collective, theocratical society of the Middle Ages. From

Italy, the movement spread through Europe. In Hungary, then Central Europe's mightiest kingdom, King Matthias Corvinus (1440–90), aided by Italian humanists, built up one of the finest libraries of the age. At his death, Lorenzo the Magnificent, who had tried to keep up with Corvinus's generosity, observed, "Now their [the humanists'] wages will at last come down!" In the north, Erasmus of Rotterdam (c. 1466–1536), who taught Greek at Cambridge, England, and published a critical edition of the New Testament in Greek and Latin, was humanism's torchbearer.

INTARSIA. No sooner had the fine art of perspective been invented (by Filippo Brunelleschi) than it started showing off. A natural vehicle for its refinements was the woodwork decoration called intarsia—a Florence specialty, in which flat, cutout pieces of varicolored wood are inlaid (*tarsiare*, "to in lay")—jigsaw-puzzle fashion into a wooden background to produce a picture. Throughout most of the fifteenth century, intarsia work was in demand for choir stalls, sacristy furniture, and doors. Favorites were trompe-l'oeil views through open windows upon townscapes, imaginary architecture, cupboards with doors ajar revealing various objects on their shelves, allegorical figures placed in niches, and cleverly composed still lives with books, skulls, geometrical bodies, and musical instruments— even musical notes—in fanciful foreshortenings. Intarsia artists took pride in displaying the individual leaves of casually opened books and the broken strings of a viola. Among surviving specimens are the exquisite panels in the doors of Raphael's Stanza della Segnatura in the Vatican by Fra Giovanni da Verona (1457–1525), a member of the white-robed Olivetan branch of the Benedictines. Some of Fra Giovanni's most sophisticated intarsias are in the order's mother house, the Monastery of Monte Oliveto Maggiore, situated in a desert patch of Tuscany. More of his panels—still lives, architectural views, and animals—are in the Olivetan Church of S. Maria in Organo in his birthplace, Verona. What may be Italy's best-known intarsias are those in the private study (*studiolo*) of Duke Federigo da Montefeltro in Urbino; sometimes credited to designs by Botticelli, they probably come from the Florence workshop of the architect Baccio Pontelli (1450–95). Intarsias ascribed to Pontelli and the Sienese painter, sculptor, architect, and engineer, Francesco di Giorgio Martini (1439–1502), from the ducal study at Gubbio (an Umbrian town ruled by the Montefeltro), are in the Metropolitan Museum of Art in New York.

JEWS. Italians are not racists. What hostility they had shown to Jews before the days of Fascism and World War II stemmed mainly from the claim that, as a people, the Jews were responsible for the death of Christ. Colonies of Jewish merchants existed in various parts of Italy during the second century B.C. Julius Caesar took the Jews under his protection, and they are said to have wept most bitterly over his body after his assassination, in Rome, in 44 B.C. We know from inscriptions that there were synagogues in Rome in the first century A.D., and Europe's oldest surviving (ruined) synagogue in Ostia, Rome's ancient seaport, built in the first and enlarged during the next two centuries, points to the presence of a prosperous Jewish community there. Throughout the Middle Ages, Italy's Jews experienced periods of tolerance and oppression, depending on the ruling pontiff and the spirit of the times. In the twelfth century, we hear of some two hundred wealthy Jewish families in Rome, of an academy of Hebrew studies, good relations between Jews and Gentiles, and of one "young, handsome, intelligent, and cultured" Jew, named Jechiel, serving as administrator of Pope Alexander III's (1159–81) household and finances. Yet, in the following century, Pope Innocent III (1198–1216) refers to them as "the perfidious Hebrews who, because of their guilt, are destined for eternal slavery." Jews now had to wear a dis-

tinguishing badge—usually a yellow circle sewn to their garment
—to prevent their mingling with Christians and were forbidden
to appear in public on Good Friday and Easter. The expulsion
of the Jews from Spain in 1492 sent many of them to Italy,
where they set up in business and trade; the port city of Livorno
(Leghorn) prospered thanks to them. Several other cities welcomed them as merchants and moneylenders; for though the
ancient church injunction against Christians charging interest
("usury") was already loopholed, it was still on the books—
and Jews were exempted. (Even in periods of severe repression,
Jewish moneylending could never be stamped out; it simply
went underground. Princes and prelates, often clandestinely, remained their borrowers.) The Counter Reformation ushered in
a period of deep anguish for the Jews. Pope Paul IV, a Neapolitan fanatic, who, in his own words, "would burn his father at
the stake if he were a heretic," reactivated the old office of the
Inquisition, which henceforth proceeded cruelly against suspected heretics. Torture was authorized. Many were burned at
the stake. And though the Jews stood outside the struggle between Catholic and Protestant that caused this massive persecution, the Church considered them, more than ever, enemies. In
1556, all Roman Jews were herded into the ghetto, a low-lying,
malarial district consisting of a few blocks of narrow houses by
the Tiber. (A ghetto had existed in Venice since 1516; the word
is of uncertain origin.) The gates were closed at night, and the
unfortunate inhabitants, when venturing out during the day to
ply their officially permitted trade of rags or old iron, had to
wear yellow caps (for men) or yellow veils (for women). Paul
was disliked by Christians as well as Jews. Riots were set off by
his death in 1559. The people stormed the Inquisition building,
burning the files and manhandling the staff, and smashed Paul's
statue on the Capitol—but not before a Jew had crowned it with
his yellow cap. While Jews were treated relatively leniently in
Medici-ruled Tuscany and Este-ruled Ferrara, their life in Rome
—where they sat, so to speak, at the pope's doorstep—was full
of humiliations. At one time or another, they were forced to
listen, on certain days, to proselytizing sermons in a church; to
decorate, for papal coronations, the Arch of Titus, which com-
memorates Rome's capture of Jerusalem and the destruction of
the Temple in 70 A.D.; to run foot races down the Corso, Rome's

main thoroughfare, during Carnival, to the merriment of spectators. And though Pope Pius IX, in 1847, had briefly opened up the ghetto, razing its walls, chains soon replaced the gates. It wasn't until Italy's unification in 1870 that the ghetto was, at last, abolished, and Jews became citizens with full rights in the Italian kingdom. Today, out of about 40,000 Jews in Italy, 13,000 live in Rome.

LAOCOÖN. A celebrated marble sculpture, in the Vatican, carved, probably in the first century B.C. or A.D., by three Rhodian sculptors, Hagesander (or Agesander) and his two sons, Polydorus and Athenodorus. It was famous in antiquity. Pliny the Elder (A.D. 23–79), in his *Natural History* (XXXVI, 37), calls it "superior to any painting or sculpture." He states, erroneously, that it was carved from a single block of marble, while it was actually made of at least four blocks, closely fitted together. Lost to sight for many centuries, it caused a stir when it was found, in 1506, beneath a Roman vineyard in the area of Nero's Golden House. Michelangelo, not waiting for it to be moved, hastened to see it, as did other artists then in Rome. Pope Julius II bought it from the owner of the grounds for an annual pension and placed it in his collection. The group of three nude figures, pyramidally arranged, shows a father and two sons, entwined by two huge snakes. It illustrates an incident occurring in the Trojan War not mentioned in Homer's *Iliad,* whose principal source is the post-Homeric *Iliu Persis* ("the Sack of Troy"), an epic probably composed about 700 B.C., and reflected in a number of Greek vase paintings. Sophocles wrote a tragedy, *Laocoön* (lost). The Roman poet Virgil (70–19 B.C.) gave the episode its classic form in the *Aeneid.* It introduces the final act of the ten-year-long siege of Troy by a Greek expeditionary force. The Greeks have withdrawn in their ships to the nearby island of Tenedos, feigning a complete abandonment of the wearying enterprise. They have left behind an enormous wooden horse, whose belly holds the best of Hellas' heroes, among them Odysseus. The happy Trojans, taking it for a precious votive offering, are about to drag it into the city, when Laocoön, a priest (of Apollo or Poseidon), comes running from the citadel to warn them that this can only be a typical Greek ruse. To prove his point, he thrusts his spear into the horse's flank, but fails to get more than a hollow sound. At this, the Trojans pull down part of their wall and draw the horse inside with much rejoicing to station it on their Acropolis. While this is happening, Laocoön, assisted by his sons, prepares to sacrifice a bull at an altar on the beach when two gigantic sea serpents come rushing through the surf, beating it with their hideous coils, holding their blood-red-crested heads aloft. Sent by Athena, presumably as a punishment for the priest's warning, they make straight for his two young sons, then for the father as he attempts to rescue them. In a moment, the trio is caught. In the marble group, we witness the event at the razor's edge of action, when the three naked bodies still struggle desperately to escape. The moment of suspense is brilliantly depicted. We do not know whether or not they will be crushed to death; according to one version of the story, the older son (on Laocoön's left) eventually frees himself, and his position makes this not unlikely. (Virgil does not describe the end.) Laocoön's taut, muscular torso—indeed, the group in its totality—is a masterpiece of Hellenistic art. Michelangelo was profoundly impressed by it, and there are echoes of it in some of the athletic nudes of the Sistine Ceiling as well as in his marble *Slaves*. As Laocoön's right arm was missing, several attempts were made to restore it, but all of the replacements were attached in an ungainly, raised position. It was in this false guise that the Laocoön group was viewed by generations of admirers—until, one day in 1905, a German art dealer, Ludwig Pollak, found the missing arm in a Rome stonemason's shop. It has since been substituted for the former restoration, enormously improving the harmony of the group. Its spell has lasted through the centuries. Titian owned a cast of the statue, and used the figure of the father for a *Risen Christ* he painted in 1520–22 (Brescia, Ss. Nazaro e Celso). Napoleon transported the Laocoön to Paris to display it at the Louvre. The German playwright and critic, Gotthold Lessing (1729–81), in his influential essay, *Laokoon* (1766), uses the work to define the limitations of poetry and the visual arts. While Virgil describes Laocoön as "bellowing to heaven like a wounded bull that has broken loose from the sacrificial altar, shaking off the ax," the sculptors show no horrid and distorting outcry, but a sigh of agony that does not interfere with the Greek ideal of dignity and beauty—a discrepancy already noted by Winckelmann. Lord Byron strikes a similar note: "turning to the Vatican, go see Laocoön's torture dignifying pain." Goethe, in his essay on Laocoön, suggests standing well back from the group and rapidly closing and opening one's eyes a few times to see the group "in motion."

LEONARDO da Vinci (1452–1519). Painter, sculptor, architect, physicist, engineer. Born in Vinci near Florence, the illegitimate (later adopted) son of a notary and a peasant girl. Had he created nothing but the *Last Supper* and the *Mona Lisa,* his reputation would rest on solid ground. Having studied painting and bronze casting under Andrea del Verrocchio (who is said to have thrown away his brushes when seeing the beautiful angel the youth had painted into his *Baptism* [Florence, Uffizi]), he worked in Florence under Medici patronage. Later, Duke Ludovico Sforza of Milan ("the Moor"), then one of Europe's most powerful rulers, employed him as a military and hydraulic engineer. He served as an architect on Milan's cathedral; made a colossal clay model of a bronze horse for the tomb of Ludovico's father, Francesco (the equestrian monument was never completed); and organized flamboyant pageants. The blue-eyed, golden-bearded, impeccably dressed artist, who often improvised songs, accompanying himself on a silver lyre shaped like a horse's head, became the star of the Moor's court. Aged about forty-two, he began painting the *Last Supper* for the Convent of Santa Maria delle Grazie in Milan. It took three years to create the more than thirty-foot-long mural, which catches the moment just after Christ has said, "One of you shall betray me," and depicts the startled reactions of the twelve fishermen and artisans of Galilee. A young nobleman had been the model for his Jesus. But he had trouble with his Judas and searched prisons and foul neighborhoods for a sufficiently repulsive character—only to give the traitor, in the end, a rather human face, marked only by a shadow. Leonardo was rewarded with a vineyard by the grateful duke. But, in order to avoid the speed demanded by fresco painting, he had experimented with a new technique, painting on dry rather than wet plaster, and the mural soon was an unsightly mass of scales and bubbles. It has been doctored by not always competent restorers ever since, and what we see today is but the ghost of a great masterpiece. It was not until about ten years later that Leonardo, probably in Florence, was to paint the portrait of a beautiful young woman, perhaps the wife of one Francesco del Giocondo, known to us as *Mona Lisa* (now in the Louvre, Paris). Few other paintings have stirred man's imagination so profoundly as this likeness of a seated lady fixing us with an enigmatic smile—a smile that was kept flickering, so legend has it, by flutists and comedians during the sittings. Walter Pater, in his famous essay on Leonardo, calls her strange presence "expressive of what in the ways of a thousand years men had come to desire. . . . It is a beauty wrought out from within upon the flesh, the deposit . . . of strange thoughts and fantastic reveries and exquisite passions." But Leonardo did not think of himself primarily as an artist. His notes and drawings, of which he left at least a trunkful—some 6,600 pages are accounted for—reveal him as an earnest scientist who could apply his talent with as much dedication to cogged wheels as to the human figure. For Ludovico, and later for Cesare Borgia, he designed fortifications and implements of war, such as a multibarreled gun and a tank propelled by foot soldiers moving inside an armored mantle. He may be the inventor of breach-loading, the Bailey Bridge, the submarine. Whether any of this formidable hardware was executed at the time and used in action is not known. Most of the 800-odd contraptions he designed are meant to make man's labor easier. They include machines for spinning silk, for sharpening needles, for grinding meat; clocks, cranes, an air conditioner. He was the first to look at flight with scientific eyes. He thought up a helicopter that would never work, and a parachute that might. But he had to make do with nature's power—wind, water, muscle, gravity—and was forever thwarted by the lack of a prime mover such as electricity. It was the universal law he tried to capture. Why can owls see at night? he wondered. What makes the womb conceive? Why does water splash? "All weights desire to fall toward the center of the earth by the shortest path," he wrote. Spending nights dissecting corpses—eerie business, he confessed—he left us drawings of the heart and fetus, unprecedented in the annals of medical research. But while his rational approach to nature's hidden forces put him ahead of his time, it is doubtful whether Leonardo furthered science or advanced material progress. What makes his scientific studies fascinating is that they sprang from the brain that gave us *Mona Lisa*. There emerges a perplexing figure who conjured up strange, evanescent worlds. The fact that he wrote mirror-script, from right to left—now recognized as a result of his left-handedness—tended to reinforce his reputation as a wizard. He had received no formal education, studied mathematics and Latin as an adult, and claimed, at one time, to have squared the circle. Much of his life was spent in the pursuit of the unfindable. Only about a dozen of his paintings have survived; others—such as a marvelous *Leda*—are known through copies. The object of universal wonder, a legendary figure in his age, he spent the last two years of his life at the manor house of Cloux, in France's smiling Loire Valley, "chief painter, engineer, and architect" to King Francis I.

LIPPI, FRA FILIPPO (c. 1406–69). How difficult it was to follow in Masaccio's footsteps is shown by the curious case of this Florentine butcher's son who, orphaned as a child, was placed as a boarder with the Carmelite friars of S. Maria del Carmine. There he took his first vows at the age of fifteen—and there he later copied Masaccio's frescoes. The latter's influence is visible in the ponderous figures of Lippi's early work. But, drifting away from Masaccio's plastic approach, he soon lapsed into the linear style, to which he added a dreamy lyricism that accounts for his great popularity, both during his lifetime and again in the nineteenth century. He is the hero of a series of unmonkish escapades caused by an indomitable appetite for play and sex. Vasari reports that, on a boat ride with some friends, Lippi was captured by marauding Saracens and sold as a slave in Barbary, where he sketched his master, in his Moorish costume, so perfectly that he was freed and taken back to Naples. Be that as it may, Lippi returned to Florence, where Cosimo the Elder de' Medici commissioned him to execute a fresco in his palace, locking him in so he would stay until the job was finished. When Lippi let himself down from the window with a rope and was found frolicking in town, Cosimo, content he had not broken any bones, allowed him to finish at his pleasure. Employed to execute some paintings in a convent at Prato (outside Florence), Filippo fell in love with a nun, Lucrezia Buti, abducted her, and had a son, Filippino, of later fame. Although Pope Pius II offered both of them dispensations from their vows, they are not known to have married, and Filippo remained a rake. Nevertheless, he was called *Fra,* for "friar," all his life and concentrated on religious subjects. His paintings express, along with a sincere devotion, a wry humor, turning angels into pixies and monks into clowns. His best works, such as his frescoes of the *Birth of St. John the Baptist* and the *Funeral of St. Stephen* in Prato cathedral, are distinguished by a delicate color scheme and a flowing elegance of line—characteristics he was to pass on to his pupil, Botticelli. Lippi's influence lives on in the art of the far less creative Domenico Ghirlandaio (1449–94)—briefly the teacher of Michelangelo—whose frescoes, in Florence's Church of S. Maria Novella and elsewhere, prove him a virtuoso of the form, if not of the substance, of the Renaissance. Filippo's son, Filippino (1457–1504), completed, rather feebly, Masaccio's fresco cycle in the Brancacci Chapel. As a painter in his own right, he continued in his father's groove, shading off into Mannerism.

—————— ◆ ——————

M A C H I A V E L L I, Niccolò (1469–1527). Political theorist and patriot, whose name has long been linked with political cunning and deceit. "Am I politic?" asks the host of the Garter Inn in Shakespeare's *Merry Wives of Windsor;* "Am I subtle? Am I a Machiavel?" Thomas Jefferson identified him with "the mean, wicked, and cowardly cunning of the cabinets." Frederick the Great of Prussia (1712–86) wrote his own *Antimachiavel.* Machiavelli's notoriety is based on a slender booklet, *Il Principe* (*The Prince*), published after his death (though pirated in his lifetime), in which he advises rulers on how to govern. "A ruler must emulate the fox and the lion," he writes, "for the lion cannot avoid traps, and the fox cannot fight off the wolves. He must be a fox to beware of traps and a lion to scare off the wolves. . . . A prudent ruler does not have to keep faith when that would be to his disadvantage. . . . If men were all good, this would not be good advice. But as they are bad, and won't keep their faith with you, it follows that you do not have to keep faith with them. . . . But it is necessary to disguise one's conduct, and to be a good actor and dissembler." Still, "if your people hate you, all your fortresses won't save you." The third child of an impecunious country squire and lawyer, Machiavelli said of himself, "I learned to do without before I learned to do with." Of medium height, delicate of limb, he looked much like a bird, and a tough bird at that. In 1498, aged twentynine, he was named second chancellor of Florence, which, having driven out the Medici, was a free republic. As head of the second chancery—one of two government departments staffed by civil servants—and in his additional capacity as secretary to the watchdog committee of the Ten of Liberty and Peace (Dieci di Libertà e Pace), he had a voice in the affairs of state. His memos, penned in his third-floor office in the Palazzo Vecchio—the town hall—drew attention to his discernment and powers of observation. The city fathers sent him on some thirty diplomatic missions, four of them to France. The Holy Roman emperor, Maximilian, who had demanded a huge sum from Florence as a military contribution, was thunderstruck when Machiavelli, on behalf of the republic, offered less than one-tenth. "Who *is* this fellow?" he asked his aides—and agreed to Machiavelli's terms. But the successful "Secretary of Florence," as he styled himself, was poorly paid, and, in one of his reports, he threatened to sell his horse and return on foot. His inconspicuous appearance was an asset on missions in which the line between diplomacy and spying was not too clearly drawn. He importuned anyone for information and thought nothing of standing by the roadside and counting the pack mules in a hostile force. His most important mission took him to the camp of Cesare Borgia, son of Pope Alexander VI, who, on his rampage of conquest, was operating uncomfortably close to Florence. Machiavelli fastened himself to the potential foe, accompanying him from one fallen fortress to the next, observing closely, and the two men, in many conversations during leisure hours, conceived a fancy for each other. "This lord is splendid and magnificent," Machiavelli reported home. (To the relief of Florence, Cesare's dominion collapsed before he could attack the city.) During a war with Pisa, Machiavelli proposed raising a militia which would replace the customary mercenary force led by a condottiere. Told to go ahead, he recruited sturdy peasant sons from the valleys around Florence and built up a well-disciplined army which he accompanied in the field. When, having taken part in a skirmish, he was ordered to the rear, he demurred, in writing: "If I had wanted to avoid exposure, I would have stayed home." After an almost bloodless victory, he marched into Pisa with his men. In 1512, the Medici returned after eighteen years of exile, and Machiavelli's fortunes changed abruptly. Arrested as a prominent republican, he was tortured, and lay in shackles, beset by lice "as big as butterflies," until an amnesty restored him to liberty. Out of work and dejected, he withdrew, with wife and children, to his small farm near Florence. Bitterly, he observed, "I cannot talk of silk, or wool, or gains and losses—I must keep silent or talk politics!" He spent his days chatting with woodcutters, visiting bird traps, reading Dante or Petrarch, playing tricktrack at the inn, and writing. Among his literary works are a book on the *Art of War* and a comedy about a love potion,

La Mandragola (*The Mandrake*), which is still playing to full houses. He longed for employment in his native Florence, the city he loved "more than [his] soul." The *Prince* was written as a plea to the Medici, already ruling the Papal States, through Leo X (Giovanni de' Medici), and most of Tuscany, to drive the hated foreigners from Italian soil and thus create an Italian nation. "May Italy, at last, find her savior! I cannot describe with how much love he would be welcomed in all those regions that have suffered from foreign invasions. . . . This barbarous foreign invasion stinks to heaven. May your illustrious family take up the task with all the courage and the hope inspired by a just cause, so that our fatherland may rise." Machiavelli had been asked to join the Noon Club, a group of cultured men who met periodically in the garden of a Florence merchant. There, under spreading trees, he read his manuscripts to the assembled members. Still, their applause could not make up for the loss of his active life. "Isn't there anyone," he wrote to his friend Francesco Vettori, the Florentine ambassador in Rome, "who remembers my services and believes that I can be useful? I can't go on like this much longer, rotting away in idleness." In the end, the Medici remembered him, but did so without grace; for modest pay, he was to write the history of Florence. Clearly, his deep commitment to the cause of the republic disqualified him from an influential post. Here lay the final irony of Machiavelli's fate. When, after the Sack of Rome, in 1527, the Medici were expelled once more, and, with the revival of the Florentine republic, the secretaryship fell vacant, he was not asked to take up his old desk on the third floor. Had he not eaten the bread of the Medici? To the lifelong observer of the human comedy, the play was over. He died, presumably of stomach ulcers, a month after the resurrection of the people's state. "The greatest honor men may enjoy," he had written, "is honor granted them by their own fatherland. And the greatest good one might do, and the most pleasing to God, is the good one does to one's fatherland. No man can glory so much in his actions as those who have reformed republics and kingdoms with laws and institutions." Modern historians consider Machiavelli one of the earliest Italian patriots, who dreamt the dream of a united Italy, and the first scientific student of the game of power politics. His tomb in S. Croce, resting place of the city's famous sons, bears the inscription, "So great a name no praise can hallow."

MANNERISM. A term characterizing an artistic development prevalent in Italy (and spreading from there to other parts of Europe) roughly between 1520 and 1600. It may be negatively defined as "neither Renaissance nor Baroque." Its major traits in painting (it also affected sculpture and architecture), are complex compositions, melodramatic gestures, and a preference for elongated, contorted human figures. A strong note of erotic freakishness creeps in from time to time. While Mannerism is wholly Italian, it often echoes the "Gothic" angularity of woodcuts and engravings by Albrecht Dürer (1471–1528), which circulated widely throughout Italy. Restless, self-conscious, with a neurotic edge to it, Mannerism brought to painting a snobbish element which made it art for the connoisseur. Many Mannerist works are of disturbing beauty; others seem contrived and mediocre. Because true Mannerism is not easy to pin down, the term has been used in an ever wider sense, and is sometimes applied to Michelangelo himself, in whose late works symptoms of Mannerism may be readily discerned. The term *maniériste* was first used (in 1662) by a French architectural theorist, Fréart de Chambray, to deprecate the pictorial output of such sixteenth-century artists as Giorgio Vasari (1511–74) and his fellow painters who were placing *maniera* ("style") above the contents of their art, attempting virtuosity for its own sake. It was enlarged upon by German art historians of the 1920s, who sensed an affinity between Mannerism and the Expressionism of their own time. Among leading Mannerists was Jacopo da Pontormo (1494–1557), whose esoteric *Deposition* in Florence's Church of S. Felicita displays the tense imbalance so typical of Mannerist design. Pontormo was a man of pleasing ways, but he dressed like a pauper, abhorred crowds, could not bear any mention of death, led a solitary life, and slept in a room whose only means of access was a ladder which he drew up after him. His pupil, Agnolo Bronzino (1503–72), another prominent member of the group, whose portraits are of a brittle elegance, was court painter to Grand Duke Cosimo I de' Medici in Florence. A third, Francesco Mazzola, "Il Parmigianino" (1503–40)—whose *Madonna with the Long Neck* (Florence, Uffizi) is one of Mannerism's most successful works—changed gradually, according to Vasari, from a smooth worldling into a bearded, unkempt, almost savage man, strange and mournful. Giulio Romano (c. 1499–1546), Mannerist painter and architect, was introduced by Baldassare Castiglione to Duke Federigo II, ruler of Mantua, where he built the Palazzo del Te, the ducal pleasure residence, decorating it with illusionistic frescoes in which the influences of his teacher, Raphael, and of Michelangelo are detectable. Giovanni Battista Rosso, "Rosso Fiorentino" (1495–1540), and Francesco Primaticcio (c. 1504–70), both exponents of the Mannerist movement, exported it to France in 1530–32, where they were among the founders of the Fontainebleau school of painting, making a lasting impact on French art. Mannerism conquered many parts of Europe, including Germany and Holland. It never dominated Venice, where Titian's sovereignty remained unshakable, but traces of it may be found in Tintoretto. If one calls Tintoretto's follower, El Greco (1541–1614), a "Mannerist"— as many art historians do—then Mannerism surely reached its zenith in Spain, where that Cretan-born artist spent the last thirty-seven years of his life. In Italy itself it never grew strong roots; the tidal wave of the Baroque swept it away.

MANTEGNA, Andrea (1431–1506). Painter and engraver, one of the leading North Italian artists. To many, he is an "acquired taste"—his figures often have a "stony" look, as Vasari was the first to note. Born near Piazzola (northwest of Padua), the son of a carpenter, Mantegna was apprenticed to Francesco Squarcione, Paduan painter and antiquary. Seat of an important university and a center of humanistic studies, the rich and learned city instilled in him a lifelong taste for classicism. Among older masters who influenced his style was Donatello, in Padua from 1443 to 1453. Though Andrea's first large-scale work, a fresco cycle for Padua's Eremitani church, was almost totally destroyed by an aerial bomb in 1944, its partial reconstruction conveys a fair idea of the excellence of the original. In 1459, he reluctantly accepted the position of court painter to Ludovico Gonzaga, marquis of Mantua, trading his cherished freedom for dependence and security. His duties included painting small Madonnas on canvas to be rolled up and shipped to the marquis's friends as wedding gifts, devising decorations for feasts and pageants, and designing costumes for the stage. In 1474, he completed the fresco of the Gonzaga family in the palace at Mantua, in which its individual members and their attendants are shown seated, standing, conversing, or simply wrapped in their own thoughts. (The rather stout Barbara of Brandenburg, Ludovico's German wife, sits like an intruder among these polished Latins.) The chamber's painted ceiling is a piece of illusionism often imitated since—a circular balcony open to the sky with various figures bending over the balustrade to look down at us. Mantegna's art is saturated with the spirit of idealized antiquity. Many of his paintings are replete with meticulously executed Roman columns, arches, statues, bas-reliefs, and medallions. He has a predilection for backgrounds of odd geological formations, such as stratified rocks, and unlikely cliffs whose overhanging tops seem at the point of dropping off. A master of perspective, he excels in bold foreshortenings and spacious architectural settings. Much of his work, including a painted chapel in the Vatican, long since pulled down, is lost. Among survivors are the altarpiece of S. Zeno at Verona, with its somber Madonna, one of the prime religious paintings of mid-fifteenth-century Italy, and the much damaged *Triumph of Caesar* at Hampton Court near London, a deft emulation of Roman relief work. The house in which he and his family lived in Mantua, with its circular courtyard, is probably of his design. Quarrelsome, easily offended, Mantegna was involved in many feuds and lawsuits, but treated with immense respect at the Gonzaga court. The bronze portrait gracing his tomb at S. Andrea, attributed to himself, shows a stubborn head, with long, unruly hair, a broad nose, a firm jaw—and the expression of a troubled personality.

M A N U T I U S , Aldus—Latinized form of Aldo (for Teobaldo) Manuzio, "Aldo" for short—(1449–1515). Humanist, publisher, founder of the Aldine Press. Born in Bassiano (near Rome), Aldo was six years old when Johann Gutenberg, north of the Alps, published the Western world's first book printed with movable type, the Gutenberg Bible. German printers soon migrated to Italy and set up presses. The first book printed in Italy was Cicero's *De oratore,* published in 1465 at Subiaco by Sweynheym and Pannartz. Aldo resolved to use the new process to present the world with the entire range of Greek classics, heretofore known mainly from unreliable manuscripts (though there already had been a few crude printed editions, including Homer's *Odyssey* and *Iliad* published in Florence in 1488). Aldo's ambitious plan envisaged both completeness and perfection. Through his friend Giovanni Pico della Mirandola, whose interest in foreign languages he shared, he raised money for a printing press. Settling (1490) in Venice, where printing was already well established, and where Greek refugees were looking for work, he engaged Greek scholars and compositors, boarding them in his house where only Greek was spoken. The books he began to publish were distinguished by their critically edited texts, based on the best available manuscripts, and the clarity and beauty of their typeface, designed by ranking artists. He was the first to use Italics, derived by humanist Niccolò Niccoli (1363–1437) from the cursive script of scholars. And while he did not invent the small book format, he was the first to issue low-priced pocket books, making up for the meager profit by printing editions of a thousand copies, rather than of the customary 100 to 250. He gradually added Latin and Italian authors to his list. His output, which includes some thirty first editions, reaches from Plato, Aristotle, and Euripides to Virgil, Horace, and Catullus; from Petrarch and St. Catherine of Siena to Bembo and Politian. His 1502 edition of Dante first displays his famous ensign, the dolphin draped around an anchor. In 1508, while he was turning out the second, enlarged edition of Erasmus' *Adages,* or *Proverbs,* which was to become one of the most widely quoted books, Aldo read proof at one end of the workshop while the Dutchman, then northern Europe's reigning intellectual, corrected his manuscript at the other. Aldo's most celebrated book is the *Hypnerotomachia,* or *Dream of Poliphilus* (1499), an arcane allegory by an unknown humanist, perhaps Francesco Colonna, a Dominican friar. Illustrated by an anonymous artist, it is a volume dear to bibliophiles for its rarity and beauty and to psychologists for the riddle of its symbols. Paolo Manuzio, Aldo's third son, an accomplished classicist, managed the Aldine Press before going to Rome as printer to the papal court; *his* son, Aldo the Younger, was the last of the line to run the press which had turned out a total of some one thousand editions, making Venice a focal point of European humanism.

MARBLE—from the Greek *marmairein* ("to glitter")—is limestone transformed by the earth's heat and pressure into a medium-hard, crystalline rock, cold to the touch, that will yield willingly to the sculptor's chisel, take a brilliant polish, and last almost forever. It is found in many countries and exists in a wide range of colors and designs. There are rich reds and blacks, deep green, and tender lilac. There's precious, rare *Giallo Antico* ("old yellow"). There are marbles as lively as Joseph's coat, displaying many kinds of foreign matter mixed in with the original limestone mass. There's a silver green called *Cipollino,* from the Italian *cipolla* ("onion"). And there's *Arabesco,* distinguished by what looks like Arabic script on a white background. As a building stone, marble was first used on a large scale by Pericles, who built Athens' Parthenon temple entirely of white marble from nearby Mt. Pentelikon (438 B.C.). In Rome, Augustus is said to have boasted that he had found a city of brick and was leaving it one of marble. Imperial Rome imported a wide variety of exotic marbles, blocks of which have been salvaged from the Tiber mud. Today's building trade uses marble largely as an economic facing stone, sometimes less than an inch thick. As a sculptor's material, marble came into use five thousand years ago when Greeks from the Cycladic Islands carved it into idols. In Italy, where every city child grows up in a setting of marble statues, fountains, churches, palaces, and porticoes, and where marble floors and stairs are common, the stone is intimately linked with the Carrara region of the Apuan Alps, between Genoa and Pisa. Here was the hunting ground of Michelangelo, who visited the quarries at least eight times, contracting for the "live white without veins or fractures" that was the matrix of his unborn works. He even toyed with the idea of carving an entire marble mountain into a colossus, to serve as a beacon for storm-tossed mariners. Although Carrara marble lacks the crunch and high translucency of the Greek island whites, its tiny interlocking crystals make it a compliant carving stone—and the supply is virtually inexhaustible. Its ivory-hued patina often gives it an uncanny resemblance to warm human flesh. Bernini's *Abduction of Proserpina* (Rome, Borghese), showing Pluto's brawny hand clutching the lady's silken thigh, makes the most of this resemblance.

MATILDA OF CANOSSA (c. 1046–1115). Countess of Tuscany, known as the "Great Countess," female protagonist of a crisis that shook Europe. Her great-grandfather, grandfather, and father had enlarged the family's small county (Canossa lies between Parma and Modena) until it formed a domain covering much of northern Italy. Inheriting the dukedom in 1076, after the murder of her father, the death of her elder sister and brother, and the loss of her husband, Godfrey the Hunchback (all in that same year), Matilda was a solitary ruler, endowed with exceptional moral strength. She had no children. Her isolation was mitigated by a family tradition of close ties to the papacy. It happened that one of the most eminent figures of the Middle Ages, a Tuscan monk named Hildebrand, ascended the papal throne in 1073 as Gregory VII (1073–85). Their alliance was to prove decisive in the drama that now opened. Gregory's program encompassed a purge of the wayward clergy (many priests were married), the centralization of the Church in the pope's hands, and the supremacy of the papacy over all worldly power. In order to enforce the last-named point, he issued a decree forbidding the sale of bishoprics and the appointment of bishops by kings and princes—the so-called lay investiture. This bold abrogation was a direct threat to rulers who, having absorbed the higher clergy into the feudal system, drew large revenues from sales of ecclesiastical tenures and owed much of their power to the fealty of bishops with lands and armies of their own. Among those who rejected it offhand were William the Conqueror of England (1027–87) and Henry IV of Germany (1050–1106). The latter—an able leader and fine soldier—reacted violently to the pope's decree. He, too, ruled by the grace of God! In a stern letter, he called on Gregory to resign. When Henry refused a summons to appear in Rome, the pontiff excommunicated him and released his German subjects from their allegiance, starting the historic conflict between crown and tiara. Gregory's action divided Germany. A council was to be held in Augsburg in February 1077 to depose the king. Faced with this threat, Henry decided to submit. Crossing the Alps during the particularly severe winter of 1076, he made for Canossa, where Gregory was stopping on his way to Augsburg as Matilda's guest. For three freezing January days, he waited in the castle grounds, dressed in a penitent's rough garb—tradition adds that he stood barefoot in the snow—before the gate creaked open and the pontiff gave the kneeling ruler absolution. Both men are said to have wept during the act—which settled nothing. Their clashing interests brought on new warfare and a new excommunication. In a show of force, King Henry marched on Rome and, after three long sieges, entered the city in 1083. An obedient antipope, Clement III, crowned him Holy Roman emperor at St. Peter's, while Gregory fumed in the nearby papal fortress of Castel S. Angelo. He was eventually liberated by his Norman ally, Duke Robert Guiscard of southern Italy (c. 1015–85), whose troops subjected Rome to burning, killing, and plundering for days, while Henry prudently withdrew. The pope, chastened and sick, departed with his rescuers, and died in Salerno in 1085. His last words were "I have loved justice and hated iniquity, therefore I die in exile." Having reformed the Church and set in motion its separation from the feudal system, he is justly called the father of the modern papacy. Henry did not enjoy his triumph long. Much of his remaining life was spent in skirmishes with his rebellious sons. Matilda, who survived both emperor and pope, was none the happier for it. Politically weakened, she married, in an attempt to mend her fortunes, an adolescent princeling of the House of Este—who soon fled her overbearing presence. The luckless lady, who had donated her remaining lands to the Holy See—thus broadening the base of the popes' secular dominion—died, aged about seventy, near Mantua. In recognition of her gift, she was reburied in St. Peter's in 1634. As for the castle of Canossa, it was destroyed in 1255 by the people of nearby Reggio, and there is little to remind us of the encounter of three stubborn characters.

MEDICI. A family of Florentine bankers—ex-farmers from the Mugello Valley north of Florence—which, from the fourteenth century onward, produced a number of outstanding individuals: rulers of Florence, dukes and grand dukes of Tuscany, a batch of cardinals, three popes (Leo X, Clement VII, and Leo XI), and two queens of France. The Medici are remembered largely for their patronage of arts and letters which, for more than a century, made Florence the cultural capital of Italy, less so for their abolition of civil rights, suppression of the 250-year-old Florentine republic, oppressive taxes, and tortures practiced in their dungeons. Accumulating wealth through commerce and moneylending (with the same disregard as that of other Christian bankers for the Church's injunction against usury), they gradually went into the wool, silk-cloth, and spice trades, bought tracts of real estate, and set up branches in London, Bruges, Lyons, and Seville. Having climbed to power as champions of the "little people"—in 1378, they sponsored the rising of the *ciompi*, the poorest of the city's wool workers —the early Medici packed the republic's governing bodies with their men, building up a political machine through which they controlled communal affairs. The established merchant aristocracy—the Strozzi, Albizzi, and Pazzi, among others—looked at them at first as upstarts, later as dangerous rivals. Cosimo the Elder (1389-1464), who had inherited a major fortune from his father Giovanni, banker to the pope, multiplied it prodigiously. Through his domination of the city's executive council, the *Balìa*, he emerged as Florence's de facto ruler, earning the honorific *Pater patriae* ("Father of his Country"). When the jealous elite succeeded in having him banished from the city, he simply took his business with him, operated out of Venice, and was ruefully recalled by nearly bankrupt Florence. Like his father, who had financed the building of the Old Sacristy of S. Lorenzo by Brunelleschi, Cosimo the Elder promoted the arts. His name is closely linked with that of Donatello, and he entrusted the Florentine architect Michelozzo Michelozzi (1396–1472) with the building of the Palazzo Medici, the rebuilding of the Convent of S. Marco (made famous by Fra Angelico and its prior Savonarola), and the creation of two Medici villas. He commissioned Benozzo Gozzoli to paint the frescoes of the *Journey of the Magi*. Alberti, Luca della Robbia, and Fra Angelico were his protégés. He founded the Platonic Academy, sponsored a number of humanists, and encouraged the study of Greek. His son Piero liked to pore over books, in the words of a contemporary, as if they were made of gold, and indulged the Medici squirrel instinct by collecting antique gems, jewelry, vases, precious marbles, and manuscripts of Greek and Latin classics. The family, astutely avoiding the odor of dictatorship, was still content with the title of Magnifico Signore, not uncommon for leading citizens in other republics. It was under Lorenzo il Magnifico (1449–92), Cosimo's grandson, that Florence and the Medici attained their brightest luster. Lorenzo, strong in body, was cursed with an ugly, simian, sallow face, with squinting eyes, a protruding chin, and a flat, misshapen nose. Like many members of the dynasty, he suffered from gout. Still, he was open-minded and of cheerful disposition, loved hunting parties, held his own at the discussions of the Platonic Academy, and was a better-than-mediocre poet. His taste in arts and letters made him Italy's arbiter of culture. He married an Orsini, but remained a roving lover. Reigning at home with a light hand, he strove, by way of alliances and warfare, to enlarge his territory, using no less a military genius than Federigo da Montefeltro as his condottiere. Meanwhile, Florence grew rich and beautiful. Churches and palaces, outshining one another in their architectural perfection, rose in streets and squares. A diadem of villas ringed the city. Weddings and jousts were celebrated with imaginative splendor. Greek scholars lectured at the university. Leonardo da Vinci, Botticelli, Michelangelo, and the learned Politian were part of the Medicean circle. In city politics, the Magnifico still championed the people (whose civil rights he had virtually nullified), rather than the aristocracy. Nor did he neglect the family business, making the Medici, by way of shrewd financial operations, one of Europe's leading money clans. The Medici's rise rankled with the old merchant families, whom Lorenzo, through his influence with the administration, tried to undo with arbitrary taxes. Among them were the Pazzi—the noble family for whom Brunelleschi had built the Pazzi Chapel—presided over by the respected Jacopo Pazzi in Florence, while his nephew, Francesco, ran the Pazzi bank in Rome. Medici-Pazzi rivalry came to a head when Pope Sixtus IV wanted to buy for his nephew, Cardinal Girolamo Riario, the lordship of strategic Imola, some sixty miles northeast of Florence. Lorenzo, who also had his eye on Imola, tried to prevent the purchase by refusing to finance it, whereupon the angered Pope switched his banking business to the Pazzi, who were only too glad to advance the needed sum. Cardinal Riario, fearing Lorenzo's continuing designs on Imola, now leagued with Francesco Pazzi in a plot to murder both Lorenzo and his trusted brother Giuliano. The twin blow, they were sure, would extirpate the Medici. They had no trouble persuading Francesco Salviati, archbishop of Pisa, who hated Lorenzo, and other malcontents, to join the conspiracy. The papal condottiere, Gian Battista da Montesecco, agreed to kill Lorenzo; but when the plotters wanted the murder done in the cathedral, where they were sure of finding the brothers together, he backed out—bloodshed was one thing; sacrilege, another! A substitute was hurriedly enlisted. At mass on Sunday, 26 April 1478, during the elevation of the Host, two would-be assassins leapt at Lorenzo, wounding him slightly, but bungled the job when Lorenzo drew his dagger and escaped into the sacristy, barring the door. Francesco dei Pazzi, however, so furiously stabbed away at Giuliano, whom a fellow conspirator had already floored, that he gashed himself severely in the thigh. Giuliano was dead. Lorenzo lived. The plot had failed. When Jacopo dei Pazzi, like a specter, rode through the town, hollowly calling on the people to revolt, the response was hostile. Vengeance was swift and merciless. Most of the conspirators were caught and tossed alive from the upper windows of the town hall (Palazzo Vecchio) to the mob below, which tore them to pieces, littering the streets with their severed limbs. Others, among them Francesco dei Pazzi and Archbishop Salviati (in full regalia), were hanged from the Palazzo windows. The God-fearing Montesecco was decapitated. Jacopo, captured while fleeing, was brought back and hanged. His body, unwanted in the family tomb, was thrown into the swollen Arno. Before Lorenzo died, he had the satisfaction of seeing his second son, Giovanni (the future Leo X), created a cardinal at the age of fourteen. Legend has it that Savonarola himself—soon to rule Florence until his execution in 1498—came to his deathbed to administer the last sacraments, but when he demanded the restitution of Florence's old freedom, Lorenzo turned to the wall and died unblessed. He was succeeded by his first-born son, Piero ("the Fatuous"). Years of turbulence followed. With French and Spanish armies on the move and strategic Tuscany a pawn in the struggle for European domination, the Medici were twice expelled (1494 to 1512 and 1527 to 1530) by the Florentines —ever republican at heart—and had to be restored to power, first by papal, then by imperial, troops. Both times, they started their new rule with a wave of arrests and torture. Henceforth, they reigned as despots. Alessandro, officially the great-grandson of Lorenzo the Magnificent, but, most likely, an illegitimate son of Pope Clement VII, himself the illegitimate son of Lorenzo's murdered brother, Giuliano, was made a duke by the emperor Charles V, whose illegitimate daughter, Margaret of Austria, he married. (His sister, Caterina, known as Catherine de Médicis, married King Henry II of France. Another Medici heiress, Maria, married Henry IV of France in 1600.) Greedy and profligate, Alessandro was murdered by a distant relative and boon companion, Lorenzino (killed by hired assassins eleven years later). Medici rule now shifted to the family's junior branch. Duke Cosimo I, a descendant of the younger brother of Cosimo the Elder, and son of the brave condottiere Giovanni delle Bande Nere ("of the black bands," or companies, thus called for their black armor), stepped into the dukedom. In 1569, he was invested as grand duke of Tuscany by Pope Pius V. He proved a rather able monarch, promoted prosperity in town and country, but brutally starved independent Siena into vassalage. The dynasty held on for nearly two more centuries, mingling its blood with that of Europe's ruling houses, mostly from north of the Alps, and, in spite of an occasional flash of the old Medici fire, fizzled in humorless debauchery. Noteworthy among the last of the grand dukes, admirably portrayed in Harold Acton's *The Last Medici,* was the ever so pious Cosimo III (1642–1723), whose frivolous, eccentric wife, Marguérite Louise, a cousin of Louis XIV of France, was entertained on her arrival with chariot races and horseback ballets, and allotted a generous allowance. But Florence, to her French taste, seemed strait-laced and barbaric. She quarreled with her husband, flaunted all protocol, and, having given him two children, fled to Paris, where she comported herself as a merry widow. Cosimo, left alone, trembling at the thought of her return, spent fortunes on banquets, became interested in botany, and began persecuting Jews, intellectuals, and suspected heretics. He squeezed the farmers dry with taxes. His son, Gian Gastone (1671–1737), who was persuaded to marry a horsy countess from Bohemia, drank heavily, grew immensely fat, and, at his last public appearance, vomited out of his carriage window. Yet, this caricature of an absolute monarch was ahead of his times in separating church and state, stopping the persecution of Jews, choosing his advisers for their qualifications, and abolishing capital punishment. The last male member of the House of Medici, Gian Gastone was survived by a widowed sister, Anna Maria Louisa (1667–1743), who, having married the Elector Palatine, John William of Neuburg, was known as the Electress. At home in the ornate, enormous Pitti

Palace, she queened it with unsmiling dignity—sleeping in a bed-chamber furnished in solid silver, driving to church in a carriage drawn by eight horses, receiving visitors standing under a black canopy. Meanwhile, the European powers, not knowing what to do with orphaned Tuscany, handed it to the dukes of Lorraine, and the Electress, in her will, left the world's greatest art collection to the future rulers, stipulating that it be kept in Florence, and be accessible to the public of all countries. And that, as one sums up the merits of the dynasty, remains the most conspicuous. Without the Medici, there would be no *Spring* by Botticelli; no *Dawn* and *Dusk,* no *Day* and *Night,* by Michelangelo.

MICHELANGELO BUONARROTI (1475–1564). Sculptor, painter, architect, poet. Italy's supreme artist, and the tragic hero of the Renaissance. His works include the sculptures of *David, Moses,* and the St. Peter's *Pietà;* the frescoes of the Sistine Chapel ceiling; and the dome of St. Peter's. Born of an ancient Florentine family in Caprese, Tuscany, where his father served as mayor at the time, he was briefly apprenticed to the Ghirlandaio workshop in Florence. According to Vasari, he moved from there to the Medici Garden, Florence's informal art academy, where young men steeped themselves in the spirit of antiquity with the aid of ancient sculptures the Medici had brought together, and where he learned to draw and sculpt in imitation of the classical style. (Recently, the existence of this academic garden has been called into doubt.) Spotted as a budding genius by Lorenzo the Magnificent, who lodged him in his palace and treated him "like a son," he was swiftly drawn into the circle of humanists and artists enlivening the court. Aged twenty-one, he arrived in Rome—already, under papal tutelage, the hub of Italy's artistic action. Sponsored by a discerning art collector, Jacopo Galli, for whose garden he sculpted the nude marble *Bacchus,* a tipsy young god (Florence, Bargello), he obtained, from the French cardinal Jean de Bilhères de Lagraulas, a commission for a marble *Pietà*—the Virgin with the dead Christ—that was to be "the best marble statue in Rome." When it was installed in (the old) St. Peter's in 1499, the serene beauty of the youthful mother, the anatomical precision of Christ's body, and the grace and majesty of the whole composition left Rome agape. Having heard visitors attribute the work to another sculptor, Michelangelo, legend says, stole into the church at night and, by the light of a candle, engraved his name on the Virgin's mantle strap. It remains his only signed work. A celebrity before he was thirty, he returned to Florence, where there was no want of commissions. His outstanding work of the period is the 13.5-foot-high naked *David,* looking out for the enemy with confident defiance. Carved from a block of white marble spoiled by another sculptor, the famous statue is all virility and classical perfection. A committee, including Leonardo da Vinci, Botticelli, and Piero di Cosimo, recommended that it be placed at the entrance to the Palazzo Vecchio, the city hall—perhaps as an expression of the citizens' spirit of independence. It stood there until its removal, in 1873, to the Accademia Museum and was replaced by a copy in 1910. In 1505, acknowledged as the country's leading sculptor, Michelangelo was invited to Rome by Pope Julius II (1503–13), and there ensued the fateful meeting of two irascible and headstrong personalities who were to irritate and stimulate each other for the next eight years. The pope, thirty-two years older than the artist, commanded him to create a tomb for himself, to be placed in the center of the new St. Peter's (soon to rise) as a perpetual astonishment to Christendom. Michelangelo spent eight months in the marble quarries of Carrara selecting flawless blocks for the gigantic monument, which was to comprise some forty statues. Julius eagerly followed the work-in-progress. Then, one spring morning in 1506, Michelangelo—aware that the pope's interest had shifted to the new basilica to be erected by his enemy, Bramante—got on a horse and rushed off to Florence, where he plunged back into his local projects as if nothing had happened. Julius bethought himself. On a campaign of military conquest in the north, which he himself directed, he asked the sulking artist to join him in Bologna, promising safe conduct. When Michelangelo arrived, the erratic Julius, forgetting both his tomb and the new basilica, commissioned him to make an outsized seated bronze statue of himself, to be placed over the main door of Bologna cathedral. Michelangelo knew nothing about bronze, and the work had to be cast twice. It was to live only four years. In 1511, the people of Bologna rose against papal rule and smashed the statue; the pieces were used by Duke Alfonso d'Este to cast a cannon, dubbed "Julia" in mock honor of Pope Julius, on whose troops it fired. Meanwhile, Michelangelo had been entrusted by the pope with a bigger project than he had ever undertaken—the fresco decoration of the ceiling of the Sistine Chapel (built by Julius's uncle, Pope Sixtus IV) in the Vatican. In vain did he point out that he was a sculptor, not a painter. He had already done some paintings and manifested his extraordinary talent as a draftsman in the (lost) cartoon, or drawing, of the nude bathers for a fresco of the *Battle of Cascina*, to be painted in the Great Council Chamber of Florence's Palazzo Vecchio, but never executed. There was no doubt in anybody's mind that he was as great a painter as he was a sculptor. But, for him, the four years he spent painting the 5,600-square-foot ceiling, with a handful of young Florentine assistants as his only company, meant physical and mental suffering. He had to learn the demanding technique of fresco painting from the beginning and almost gave up in despair when some of the area already finished broke out into moldy patches—which were, however, quickly removed. (Devised nearly 4,000 years ago, the technique requires special skill and experience. The artist applies pigments diluted with water to a wet wall already marked with the contours of the future picture. He must work fast, as the paint will turn to dust if applied to a dry surface. Once absorbed, the paint sets with the plaster and becomes part of the wall. Colors change during the drying process—another pitfall to look out for.) He had to do his painting with his head raised and his eyes screwed up, while the wet paint trickled onto his scraggly beard. For months thereafter, he could not read anything except by holding it above his head. His letters of the time complain of fatigue, and he asked his father to pray for him. Often too tired to undress at night, he slept with his boots on. The impatient pope sometimes climbed up to the swaying scaffold (which Michelangelo had rested on a high ledge) to watch him work and hurry him along. On one occasion, he struck the artist with his cane in a fit of temper. The surface of the ceiling

—until then a blue field of stars—with its supporting spandrels
was to be filled with a pictorial presentation of the Creation and
man's beginnings on earth. Having divided the long vault, by
way of a painted architectural framework, into nine main panels,
Michelangelo started at the "wrong" end, opposite the altar, with
the stories of Noah and the Flood. Finding the figures he had
painted too small to be seen properly from the ground, sixty-
eight feet below, he switched, for the rest, to a larger, simpler
scale. As we read the ceiling from its altar end, following
Genesis, we see God floating in space, with his eyes closed, dividing light from darkness; next, calling forth the heavenly
bodies, he is streaking through the skies so rapidly that we perceive him twice; next, he creates dry land, and with it, animals
and plants. The fourth panel is one of the most popular paintings in Italian art: the *Creation of Adam,* wherein God is an
ageless Apollonian figure, propelled by cosmic energies, wrapped
in a cloud of heavenly beings, while Adam, clothed in beauty,
seems to awaken from a dreamless sleep as he receives the spark
of life from God's extended finger. "So God created man in his
own image." No one had ever been able to depict, as Michelangelo had done here, the first flutter of a human heart. Eve rises
from the sleeping Adam's rib in the next panel, and the Fall
abruptly brings the story down to earth. The Flood and Noah's
drunkenness conclude the cycle. Ever the sculptor, Michelangelo
gives his figures a roundness that seems to burst the boundaries
of two-dimensional art. Read backward, the ceiling shows the
human soul, stemming from God and captive here below, returning to the divine spirit. The program may have sprung from
the collective brain of a humanist committee. He painted it, and
his imaginative power animates each composition. Around the ceiling's edge, twelve colossal figures—Hebrew prophets and pagan
sibyls, all of them heralds of Christ's coming—ponder man's
fate. Old Testament scenes, ancestors of Christ, and twenty beautiful nude youths (many of them recalling classical prototypes)
bring the ceiling's population to three hundred figures. "All the
world hastened from every part to view it," records Vasari, "and
they remained amazed and speechless." Did Julius know his days
were numbered when he drove Michelangelo to hurry? He died
less than four months after the work was finished and was
eventually buried in the tomb of his uncle, Sixtus IV, beneath

St. Peter's. Still, his heirs insisted on a tomb by Michelangelo. The latter, signing contract after contract for its execution, suspending work and returning with a vengeance, spent a good part of the next thirty years on it. Among the statues he sculpted for the monument are the *Victory* (Florence, Palazzo Vecchio); the first two *Slaves,* or *Captives,* nearly finished (Paris, Louvre); four unfinished *Captives,* which seem to struggle with every one of their muscles to free themselves from the raw marble (Florence, Accademia); and *Moses,* whose "anger waxes hot" as he sees his people worship the golden calf. (Moses' horns, his attribute for centuries, result from a misreading of Exodus 34:30, "the skin of his face shone"—the Hebrew word *qaran* ["shine"] being akin to *qeren* ["horn"].) When the empty monument, in 1545, was finally put up in Rome's S. Pietro in Vincoli (St. Peter in Chains), this statue, planned as a mere corner figure, was made its center and framed by lesser figures sculpted by disciples (*Leah* and *Rachel* are largely by Michelangelo himself). It was a pathetic comedown from the original design and a cause of much heartbreak for its maker. Michelangelo now became the (somewhat unreliable) pet of the Medici popes, Leo X and Clement VII, and their Florentine relatives. After wasting considerable time designing a complicated marble façade for their family church, S. Lorenzo, Florence, which was never executed, he received two major commissions—the Laurentian Library, whose vestibule, with its staircase of *pietra serena,* the dark-gray Tuscan stone (he had wanted it done in nut wood), is one of the most perfect spaces created in the late Renaissance, and the New Sacristy of S. Lorenzo. The latter, a square room with sober gray and white architecture, houses the celebrated Medici tombs. Again, the final product is but a shadow of the original project, which envisaged a single, free-standing monument entombing Lorenzo the Magnificent, his brother Giuliano, and two lesser relatives—Giuliano, duke of Nemours, and Lorenzo, duke of Urbino, the dedicatee of Machiavelli's *Prince.* The sixteenth-century arrangement (though not supervised by Michelangelo), with the tombs of the two dukes facing each other across the central space, could hardly be surpassed for harmony and balance. (The Magnificent and his brother are buried in an inconspicuous tomb, set against the entrance wall and topped by a Madonna and two saints after designs by Michelangelo.) The dukes represent Thought (Lorenzo) and Action (Giuliano). They are not portraits; "a thousand years from now," said Michelangelo, "no one will know what they looked like." Of special beauty are the four nude figures reclining on the sarcophagi beneath them: *Night* and *Day* on Giuliano's tomb, *Dawn* and *Dusk* on Lorenzo's. *Dawn,* a mature, strong-limbed woman in the process of waking up, is perhaps Michelangelo's highest sculptural achievement. But we are entering a murky period in his life. When, after the Sack of Rome in 1527, Florence expelled the unpopular Medici and set up a republic, Michelangelo was appointed procurator general of the city walls and charged with designing new fortifications that would withstand the expected assault of Imperial troops and thus prevent another "sack." But, as the enemy arrived and laid siege to the city, his spirits sank. In the grip of panic that revealed a deep streak of anxiety in him (and that manifested itself repeatedly), he fled to Venice. Begged to return by the republic, he did come back. But Florence fell by treason, and when the Medici were reinstated with Imperial backing, heads rolled and tortured screams were heard from the Bargello dungeons in a grim settling of accounts. Michelangelo, whose name was on the list of militant republicans, went into hiding until pardoned by the Medici, who needed him. He worked on the tombs again—so hard, in fact, that he nearly ruined his health, and Clement VII had to order him to take a rest. Then, in another unaccountable move, he rode off to Rome at the end of 1533, leaving the Medici Chapel a shambles, with the statues strewn haphazardly about the floor. (In 1975, a series of wonderful charcoal sketches, among them an almost photographically exact head of Laocoön done from memory, was found in a closed-off space beneath the chapel—the most important Michelangelo discovery in modern times.) He was not to return to Florence. The new pope, Paul III (Farnese), greeted him with the words, "I've been looking forward to employing you for thirty years!" and called on him in his modest dwelling, attended by ten cardinals—a rare distinction for a private citizen. One of his first commissions was the fresco painting of the *Last Judgment* on the wall behind the altar of the Sistine Chapel, whose ceiling he had completed twenty-one years before. The task was to absorb him for five years. Before he could begin, he had to destroy some previous paintings, among them two of his own lunette groups of the *Ancestors of Christ*. In the enormous fresco (48 x 44 ft), the ageing master conjured up a fantasy of swirling shapes that, for sheer impact, has no parallel. Against a background utterly devoid of decor—a glimpse into limitless space—about 400 human figures seem to revolve around their Judge. The blessed rise on Christ's right; the damned, on his left, tumble headlong into lower depths—sped on their way by a fierce Charon with a stroke of his huge oar (an image taken from Dante's *Inferno*). Here no longer reigns the Platonic freedom of the Sistine Ceiling, but a grim mood of reform—soon to erupt into the Counter Reformation. On this Day of Wrath, Christ smites the sinners with a terrifying gesture of finality. Michelangelo, himself by now all somber introspection, painted his own face on the stripped-off skin of St. Bartholomew, seen below Christ. On hearing the pope's master of ceremonies pronounce the painting, with its explicit glimpses of anatomy, "fit for a brothel or a tavern," Vasari says, he painted him into Hell; Pope Paul, asked to make Michelangelo remove the likeness, replied that he might pray a person out of Purgatory, but not out of Hell. Michelangelo was still alive when Pope Paul IV, promoter of the Inquisition, ordered the painter Daniele da Volterra—who was to go down in history as *Braghettone* ("pants maker")—to cover the most obvious exposures with bits of garments. A fresco of the *Fall of the Rebellious Angels,* which Michelangelo had been commissioned to paint on the opposite wall, was never executed. Paul III kept spurring him to more creative ventures. Aged seventy-five, he completed two large frescoes in the Vatican's Pauline Chapel, the *Conversion of St. Paul* and the head-down *Crucifixion of St. Peter.* In them, he found a radically new pictorial language, disdaining the beauty, color, and perspective of the Renaissance, and bordering on the Mannerist. He would not touch the brush again. Returning, on Paul's request, to architecture, he worked on the Farnese family palace, the grandest sixteenth-century palace in Rome (today the French embassy), which Antonio da Sangallo the Younger (1483–1546) had begun. Michelangelo designed the splendid cornice, the central balcony with its large coat of arms, and portions of the courtyard. Charged with the rearrangement of the untidy Capitol Square, Rome's civic center for many centuries, he faced the central (Senatorial) palace with an imposing double-ramped stairway, gave the palace on the right (Conservators) a High Renaissance façade, and, with uncanny ingenuity, projected a new palace (Capitoline Museum) with an identical façade across from it, set at the same oblique angle. He thus obtained a well-defined, symmetrical space, a room rather than a piazza—one of Europe's most studied bits of urban planning. In its center he placed, on the pope's orders and against his own will, the equestrian statue of the emperor Marcus Aurelius (161–180)—moved hither from the Lateran Square—which had survived the Middle Ages' greed for bronze because it was believed to represent the Christian emperor, Constantine. During his active life, Michelangelo served seven popes, all eager for the best of his art. For Pius IV (1559–65) he designed the basic features of Porta Pia, one of Rome's city gates, built, for scenic effect, with its decorative face toward the city—a novelty. And, with a sure eye for the subtleties of inner space, he transformed a section of the Baths of Diocletian into a church—S. Maria degli Angeli ("of the Angels")—without detracting from its Imperial vaults. The peak of his architectural career, however, was his lifetime appointment by Paul III, in 1546, as chief architect of St. Peter's, a much-coveted position left vacant by Sangallo's death. Michelangelo revolutionized the new basilica's basic plan, discarding Sangallo's concept of a Latin cross church in favor of Bramante's original Greek cross. (His design was eventually changed again into a Latin cross, whose long nave can accommodate more worshipers facing the main altar.) Making use of Bramante's reinvention of ancient Rome's "malleable" concrete-filled brick walls, he visualized a flowing inner space of striking unity, defined by a smooth skin of travertine. His most conspicuous contribution is the cupola, whose 142-foot (approx.) diameter is slightly shorter than that of Brunelleschi's Florence dome, its predecessor by about one hundred years. But while the Florence dome still has a Gothic accent, Michelangelo's creation, with its twin-columned buttresses and elegant windows, reflects the idiom of the High Renaissance. He retained Brunelleschi's idea of a double dome—one climbs the stairway to the top between the inner and the outer shell. The cupola was finished after Michelangelo's death by Giacomo della Porta (1533–1602), who gave it a somewhat steeper profile than the hemisphere of the original design. (Its height, to the top of the cross, is 435 feet.) The artist, who during his long life poured forth this unbelievable number of peerless works, was a stocky man, a rustic at first sight, whose nose had been bashed in by a rival's fist in his youth. Only the delicate hands, the darkly glowing eyes, and a bitter mouth, betrayed the divine madness within. Though he is thought to have had passionate love affairs as a young man, he was, in the word's deepest sense, alone—consumed by a voracious genius, racked with inner tensions. Courted by high society, he was instinctively drawn to simple people, such as his stonecutter, Topolino ("little mouse"), and his loyal servant, Urbino, who, by his death, he said, taught him to die without regret, and for whose wife and children he provided for the rest of his life. He lived modestly, even shabbily, and did not mind discomfort. During his work on Julius II's statue in Bologna, he shared a bed with three assistants. Later, while visiting Ferrara, he was invited by Duke Alfonso d'Este to lodge in his palace, but declined, preferring a poor inn. Many of his letters are addressed to his numerous family—he was the second of five sons—that had come to depend on him for money, houses, and advice. He tells his nephew, Leonardo, to find himself a good wife and not to marry for money; when he does marry, Michelangelo sends the bride two rings, one with a diamond and one with a ruby. Of the beans, cheeses, and wines his family sent him from Tuscany, he often presented some to Pope Paul III, with whom he was on terms of familiarity—on one occasion, six flasks of Trebbiano wine, and a basket of pears "which the Pope thought excellent." He himself ate and drank sparingly and, in his old age, took but one frugal meal at the end of the day. Young artists could depend on him for counsel, or for a sketch to help them with a painting. Having been put up in the house of a rich Florentine exile, Roberto Strozzi, during two illnesses, he gave him the two nearly finished *Slaves,* worth a king's ransom. (Strozzi later presented them to King Francis I of France, and they changed hands several times before they wound up in the Louvre.) But he was quick to take offense. Hearing a pompous fellow whom Duke Alfonso had sent from Ferrara to collect the painting of *Leda with the Swan,* which he had commissioned, refer to it as a "trifle" (*una poca cosa*), he gave the painting to his poor assistant, Antonio Mini, who took it to France. (The lost master-

piece is known from several copies.) Among the few who penetrated the invisible wall he had set up around himself was Tommaso Cavalieri, a handsome, sensitive young aristocrat and art
collector, for whom he had a deep affection. Of Michelangelo's
300-odd surviving poems, some of the loveliest are addressed to
the widowed Vittoria Colonna, the light and solace of his autumn
years. A member of Rome's most distinguished family, a woman
of great learning and a poetess, she gave Michelangelo the fem-
inine affection that was wanting in his life, and he, in turn, saw
in her the personification of the highest spiritual ideal. They
often sat together in a garden on the Quirinal Hill, discussing
art and religion. Both had been thrown into a crisis of conscience
by the Reformation, and she had joined a group of intellectuals
believing in salvation by faith—a position close to that taken by
Martin Luther—but withdrew from it in fear of the Inquisition.
Michelangelo made a drawing of a *Pietà* for her (Boston, Gardner), as well as one of *Christ Crucified,* showing the Savior alive
and suffering (London, British Museum). When Vittoria had
died, in 1547, he said that he regretted having only kissed her
hand, rather than her face, when she lay close to death. Probably
the most famous citizen of Italy in his old age, he was overwhelmed with commissions that he would or could not execute,
among them requests from the king of Portugal and Queen
Catherine de Médicis of France. Lectures were given about him.
A medal was cast in his honor. In the midst of so much worldly
noise, Michelangelo was silent. He had no thought, he said, "in
which Death was not sculpted." Alone, working mostly at night,
he concentrated on the three marble *Pietàs*—none of them finished—which show the long and stony road he had traveled since,
as a hopeful twenty-three-year-old, he had carved his first *Pietà.*
These sculptures (now in Florence, Opera del Duomo and Accademia, and in Milan's Castello Sforzesco) are art interiorized—
upright, gaunt, tormented, and almost Gothic in their figuration.
He labored on one of them (Milan) until six days before his
death. He died at home, aged nearly eighty-nine, in the presence
of a few friends and assistants, a servant, and two doctors. He had
wished to be laid to rest in Florence; but as the Romans would
have liked to keep him, his casket was secretly conveyed there,
disguised as merchandise. His tomb in S. Croce, Florence's Pantheon, is near the cenotaph of Dante, his compatriot. Vittoria

Colonna had voiced what many felt when she told him, "Those who know you value your person even more highly than your works."

NEOCLASSICISM. A style that ruled the visual arts roughly between 1780 and 1850. Primarily the result of a revolt against Baroque exuberance, it coincided with the "Age of Reason" that favored sobriety and purity of form. It owed much of its popularity to the excavations of Pompeii and Herculaneum—the Roman towns in southern Italy buried by the eruption of Mt. Vesuvius in A.D. 79—whose antiquities generated a preoccupation with ancient art. Although Neoclassicism swept all Europe and parts of the United States, its headquarters was Rome, the meeting place and study center of artists from many countries. Unlike the Renaissance, whose rediscovery of classical antiquity drew on every human resource, the neoclassical "revival" was largely an anemic imitation of Greco-Roman forms. For all its mediocrity, it did have the guidance of a first-rate mind—Johann Joachim Winckelmann (1717–68), the son of a Lutheran cobbler, who started his career as a librarian to a German count and perished at the hands of an Italian cook. Bookish, well-versed in Greek and Latin, he was also something of a social climber. A chance encounter with a papal nuncio led to a job as a librarian in Rome, where he arrived in 1755, having converted to Catholicism the year before. He had already broken new ground with an essay on the emulation of Greek art, in which he presented the latter's "noble simplicity and quiet grandeur" as the product of an ideal society which, he explained, combined a love of beauty with the pursuit of physical and mental health. His rosy concept of Greek culture was to tint the aesthetics of his own and of succeeding generations. "Good taste was born under Greek skies" he wrote. In Italy, he felt at home among cypresses and marble statues. He was befriended by Anton Raffael Mengs (1728–79), one of the most successful painters of his time and, like himself, a neoclassicist. Studying Rome's collections of antiquities and journeying south to view the newly found art treasures of Herculaneum and Pompeii, he confirmed his conviction that the path to greatness lay in the imitation of the Greeks. His learning and his good Italian secured him entry into high society. He was engaged as secretary and adviser by Cardinal Alessandro Albani (1692–1779), the nephew of Pope Clement XI, and an avid art collector, whose Roman villa, decorated with Mengs's ceiling painting of Parnassus, was built to house his treasures. As a final accolade, Winckelmann received in 1763 a papal appointment as director of antiquities. His work included playing guide to visiting dignitaries—many of whom went home as neoclassicists. His reputation was buttressed by an *Open Letter on the Finds of Herculaneum* in which he exposed the irresponsible way in which the excavations were carried out under the auspices of Naples's foolish and tyrannical Bourbon king, Ferdinand IV (1751–1825). The diggers were prisoners of war, so tightly chained together that they could hardly move. There was no proper cataloguing, murals were cut from their walls, and many objects were destroyed or stolen. What was kept was often clumsily restored and placed in the local museums, or shipped abroad as royal presents. Grave injury was being done to culture. The *Letter,* read with keen attention throughout Europe, was of considerable consequence. International opinion soon forced Naples to change its procedure, and excavations henceforth were entrusted to competent scholars—Winckelmann had become the father of modern archaeology. In 1763–64, his major work, the *History of Ancient Art,* made him the first systematic art historian and established art history as an independent science. And although taste has radically changed since then, its influence persists. Drawing on his multifarious knowledge, the author traced the cycle of Greek creativeness from its archaic phase through the "lofty" (or classical) and the merely beautiful to imitative decadence. Much of the educated world, henceforth, considered him the final authority on art. But, standing on the pinnacle of fame, Winckelmann seemed to undergo a change of personality. Passing up a chance to travel to Greece, which would have meant the ultimate fulfillment of his dreams (his acquaintance with Greek art was almost wholly based on Roman copies), he suddenly decided to revisit Germany. Accompanied by an Italian sculptor, he left Rome on 10 April 1768. As they crossed the Alps, he grew more and more morose and finally abandoned his companion at Vienna to return to Rome. On June first, he arrived by mail coach at the Austrian port of Trieste. Finding no ship ready to sail for Italy, he made friends with one Francesco Arcangeli, an unemployed cook occupying the hotel room next to his own. They regularly dined together and went for walks, and "Signor Giovanni," as Winckelmann chose to call himself, became so trusting that he showed Arcangeli some gold and silver medals given him, he said, by the Empress Maria Theresa when he called on her in Vienna. The confidence was his undoing. On June eighth, his neighbor entered Winckelmann's room, as he often did, and, walking up to his friend who was seated with his back to him, threw a noose around his neck. Half-strangled, Winckelmann jumped up, and, during the ensuing struggle, Arcangeli stabbed him with a knife he had bought for the purpose—then fled without taking the time to grab the medals. Bleeding profusely from five wounds, the victim with his dying breath told those who crowded around him who had done the deed. Arcangeli was caught, tried, sentenced, and cruelly put to death on the piazza in front of the hotel. Such, with some questions never answered, was the end of this original thinker, who had called "the love of art" the guiding passion of his life. Soon afterward, the neoclassical fashion he had so eagerly promoted found its chief exponent in the sculptor Antonio Canova (1757–1822), whom his contemporaries thought worthy of comparison with the ancient Greek masters. Among his works, remarkable for technical perfection, are mythological figures, monumental tombs, and idealized portraits. He made two colossal marble statues of Napoleon in the nude—one of which, captured by the duke of Wellington, is at Apsley House in London. He represented Napoleon's sister, Paolina Borghese, seminude, as "Victorious Venus" (Rome, Borghese). After Napoleon's fall, Canova was named papal commissioner for the repatriation of the five hundred cartloads of works of art Bonaparte had removed from Italy to Paris. The sculptor had filled in some of the gaps himself, and three of his frigid statues still grace the Vatican's Belvedere. Canova is buried in his birthplace, Possagno (near Venice), in a neoclassical temple of his own design. His work was continued by Bertel Thorvaldsen (1770–1844), the son of an Icelandic woodcarver, whose "Grecian" sculptures made him one of the most admired artists of his day—and who is the hero of Hans Christian Andersen's fairy tale, *The Ugly Duckling.* Neoclassicism breathed new life into the Vatican collections. Clement XIV (1769–74), patron of Mengs and Piranesi, purchased many ancient sculptures, and Pius VII (1800–23) created, with Canova's help, the Vatican's 230-foot-long *Braccio Nuovo* ("New Wing"); lining it with Roman statues. As an art, neoclassicism was an artificial, often sentimental, version of an antiquity whose spirit totally escaped it. Perhaps its major contribution was Winckelmann's suggestion that we look at art within its social and historical context.

❖

NERO, Claudius Caesar (A.D. 54–68), Roman Emperor. The bugaboo of Roman history; the "Antichrist" to Christians. Placed on the throne by a palace conspiracy at the age of seventeen, Nero was a direct descendant of Augustus, who had set up the empire in 27 B.C., and nephew of the emperor Caligula, who had murdered and tortured hundreds for pleasure. Ruling a realm that stretched from the Atlantic to the Caspian Sea, he was at once its highest administrator, judge, and priest. Having started his reign humanely—he shrank from signing death warrants—he soon revealed himself as one of the most fiendish creatures ever to disgrace a throne. He killed his mother, Agrippina the Younger, and the first two of his three wives. He forced his friend and close adviser, the philosopher Seneca, to cut his wrists. Sniffing treason everywhere, he turned a room of his palace into a one-man tribunal, where he condemned, out of hand, senators, army officers, and members of the old ruling class, many of whom were instantly beheaded. After the great fire of Rome in A.D. 64, rumor asserted that Nero had started it in order to clear ground for a new palace. Some claimed they had seen him strum his lyre on a tower high above the sea of flames. The allegations were probably false—Nero had ably directed the fire-fighting, and opened public buildings and his garden to the homeless. Still, he needed a scapegoat and hit on the defenseless Christians, a friendless, secretive community consisting largely of poor people, slaves, and foreigners. Hundreds of them were picked up on the charge of "hatred of the human race." "Nero persecuted the so-called Christians with extraordinary cruelty," writes the Roman historian Tacitus. "Christ, for whom they were named, had been put to death under Tiberius. . . . The confessed members of the sect were now arrested. . . . Derision marked their end. Some were dressed in animal skins and torn to death by dogs. Others were fastened to crosses and set aflame to serve as torches. Nero held this spectacle in his private circus, mingling with the crowd dressed as a charioteer. . . . In spite of the victims' guilt, there arose a feeling of pity, as the public sensed that they were being killed to gratify the savage instincts of one individual." Nero might have been a better man had he been a professional artist or sportsman. He was an able painter, sculptor, and poet. He had a fine singing voice and often performed on the stage, to thundering applause. He drove his own racing chariot in Rome's Circus Maximus, and at games in Greece. He brought the first polar bear to Rome, was the first to use a speechwriter, the first to envisage cutting a canal through the Isthmus of Corinth, a task accomplished in 1893. He went to picnics accompanied by one thousand carriages drawn by silver-shod mules. In his "Golden House" where dining-room ceilings slid back to admit a rain of roses—he played with toy chariots or padded aimlessly around in dressing gown and slippers, a bull-necked, pot-bellied, spindle-legged goblin. He was assailed by horrid nightmares and haunted by the bloody specter of his murdered mother. Toward the end of his ignoble reign, the treasury was empty, the army's pay was overdue, no friends were left. Hatred spread through the realm, rebellion seethed in Rome, and his legions started marching on the capital. The senate, no longer cowed, sentenced him to death by flogging. Nero, disguised, got on a horse and, with the last handful of retainers, rode to the lonely country place of a former household slave. Unable to kill himself, he put a dagger in his secretary's hand and guided it across his throat seconds before an armed detachment arrived to seize him. "What an artist dies with me," was one of his last sayings.

THE NORMANS. Nietzsche's "magnificent blond beast" comes to mind as one surveys the Norman caper in south Italy. The sons of Viking pirates ("Northmen") who emerged from Scandinavian mists to penetrate deep into continental Europe—up the Rhine, up the Seine, into Russia—they were, by A.D. 900, firmly entrenched in what is still called Normandy, in northern France. They became Christians and governed as a warrior caste. Their inbred courage, their spirit of adventure, their recklessness and taste for plunder, combined with population pressure to lead them on to further conquests. Even before William, illegitimate son of Robert "the Devil" of Normandy, set sail for Britain in 1066, bands of bellicose Normans—most of them younger sons of landed nobles—had cast a predatory eye on rich and sunny southern lands. In 1003, some forty Norman knights, returning from a pilgrimage to the Holy Land, stopped off in southern Italy, then fragmented into weak principalities, and played a part in local warfare that proved them so superior in military skill that they were asked to stay on as mercenaries. They were soon joined by Normans from the French homeland. They rode big horses, built stout castles, wore heavy armor, carried a broad sword, and moved with terrifying speed. Their flair for adaptation to local customs and their talent for administration soon propelled them into power. The sons of Tancred, Baron of Hauteville, distinguished themselves by outstanding valor and considerable cunning. In 1043, the eldest, William Bras-de-Fer ("Iron Arm") set himself up as count of Apulia. His brilliant step-brother, Robert Guiscard—"the Weasel"—(c. 1015–85), added new conquests in Saracen-ruled Sicily and Calabria. After a decisive battle in which 4,000 Normans, almost all cavalry, routed a papal force of 30,000 come to push them out of Italy, the conquerors were acknowledged as protectors and nominal vassals of the Church. In 1059, the Weasel was installed as duke of Apulia and Calabria. In 1071, his younger brother, Roger I, became count of Sicily, much of which was taken with a force of one hundred knights. When, in 1130, Roger's half-Italian son, Roger II, perhaps the greatest and the most enlightened of the Hauteville lords, had himself crowned king of Sicily in Palermo, that fertile island became the redoubt of the Norman realm and one of the most powerful and richest countries in all Europe. Reigning as a thin military upper class, the Normans exercised admirable racial and religious tolerance. Although the state religion was Roman Catholicism, Greek-Orthodox monasteries multiplied, the large Moslem population prayed in its mosques, Greeks and Jews worshiped and worked freely. Cotton and sugar cane were planted. Silk was produced. Orange and lemon groves turned Sicily into the garden it is today. Palermo, the capital, became a busy clearing house for Mediterranean commerce. Roger himself spoke Greek and Arabic besides his native Norman-French, the court language. He lived more like a sultan than a Christian king. His food, served on golden plate, was prepared by Arab cooks. He kept a harem. His prime minister was styled emir. His subjects prostrated themselves before him. The arts and sciences flourished. Roger reared the cathedral of Cefalù; the mosaics there and in his palace chapel at Palermo were probably made by local craftsmen trained by Byzantines. The romances of Roland, Charlemagne's legendary paladin, imported by French minstrels, remain, today, the stock-in-trade of the traditional Sicilian puppet show. The safe possession of all southern Italy did not prevent the Normans from following their natural bent for waging war. They constantly harassed the Byzantine Empire. They took Malta and colonized much of North Africa. They played a leading part in the Crusades. The Weasel's eldest son, Bohemund (c. 1059–1111), passed over in the line of succession, became the family's rogue male. He joined the First Crusade and quickly rose to be its unofficial captain. Matching the heretofore little-known Turkish tactics blow by blow, he captured, by a typically Norman combination of trickery and daring, biblical Antioch, and made himself its ruler—only to be crushed by the overwhelming forces of Byzantium and Islam and to suffer three years' harsh imprisonment in a Turkish mountain fortress until an Armenian ally ransomed him. Back in Europe, hailed as a hero, he wooed and married the daughter of Philip I, the half-Russian king of France. In a new war against Byzantium, he ended up defeated. The line of Norman counts he sired became extinct with Bohemund VII, count of Tripoli (now in Lebanon), in 1287. The first Bohemund lies buried in a marble tomb at Canosa in Apulia, a domed Byzantine-Romanesque-Arab structure epitomizing Norman taste. The Hautevilles had become the equals of the mightiest of monarchs. In 1186, Roger II's daughter, Constance, married no less a prince than Henry (VI), son of the Holy Roman emperor, Frederick Barbarossa. Henry assumed the royal crown of Sicily in 1194, and, with the coming of age of his part-Norman son, Frederick II, the story of the southern kingdom becomes the story of the House of Hohenstaufen. The Norman heritage survived in many aspects of its culture. There still are families in southern Italy that pride themselves on their —somewhat diluted—Norman blood.

NUDITY IN ART. The cult of the naked human body as an ideal of beauty is innate to the Mediterranean world. It pervades its visual arts. Early in the fifth century B.C., the Greeks evolved the classic concept of the human form that mirrored the harmonious oneness of mind and body, the "good and beautiful" (*kalos kai agathos*). The naked human body was sculpted (most Greek paintings are lost) to surpass, rather than copy, nature. The fifth-century B.C. sculptor Polyclitos prescribed the rigorous proportion of seven-and-a-half heads to a figure. Phidias, the master sculptor of the Parthenon, portrayed gods in the nude or seminude, presenting them as superheroes. Such was the legacy Greece left to Rome. Shiploads of Greek originals and replicas arrived in Rome during the early empire, to be snapped up by rich collectors; others were copied, over and over again, by sculptors in Rome itself, many of them

Greek immigrants. Plenty of artifacts must have lain around when, a millennium later, Italian artists were seeking a way back to classical antiquity. Moreover, triumphal arches, sarcophagi, and cameos displaying nudes had never been lost to sight. The Renaissance revival of the nude was aided by such archaeological discoveries as the Belvedere Apollo (a Roman copy of a lost Greek statue found before 1500) and the Laocoön found in 1506 (both in the Vatican); and by the new science of anatomy, which imparted realism to the classic norm, changing it in the process. The Florentine initiators of true Renaissance sculpture, especially Donatello, created nudes that were ideal, not idealized, bodies; instead of merely copying antiquity, as they set out to do, they were in fact launching an artistic revolution. With the emplacement of Michelangelo's 13.5-foot marble *David* on Florence's Piazza della Signoria in 1504, the Renaissance male nude was solidly established. Even before that time, Venus had entered the artistic orbit. We do not know what sea change this rustic deity of the kitchen garden, native to Italy, had undergone before she was identified with Aphrodite, the Greek goddess of love, and had the brightest planet named for her. She had her temple on the Capitol since 215 B.C., and Julius Caesar claimed descent from her. By then, she had already two identities, one representing youthful love and beauty, the other, *Venus Genetrix,* maternity. This ambiguity became a doctrine of the Renaissance, which took from Plato's *Banquet* the distinction between a celestial and a natural, or earthly, Venus, often thought of as twins. Greek sculptors had left, in originals or replicas, a variety of Venus types, among them *Venus Pudica* (the "modest one"), of which the "Capitoline" and "Medici"— both ancient copies—are the best-known examples. Botticelli, painting his *Birth of Venus* in 1486, well before the above statues were discovered, must have known other versions of the shy one, for he adopts her posture (shielding breasts and pubes with her hands) in the first great Venus figure of the Renaissance. Here, a chaste, youthful body, freed from all mathematically fixed proportions, throbbing with life, sails toward us on a large shell, speeded by friendly breezes—a poem as much as a picture. Her almost melancholy little head—the head of a Madonna, as Kenneth Clark (*The Nude*) has pointed out—identifies her as celestial. But nudity itself, to Renaissance philosophy, can be an aspect of divinity. Titian's celebrated painting known to us as *Sacred and Profane Love* (Rome, Borghese) shows two women —one richly dressed (terrestrial), the other nude (divine)— and hints that they are twins, for the same model evidently posed for both. While many masters, notably Michelangelo, continued to keep their nudes in the spiritual realm, others delighted in their carnal aspect. Some of Titian's full-blown, voluptuously reclining Venuses are hardly the celestial type. And there is little doubt that countless Danaës, Ledas, Dianas—and, surely, St. Sebastians—were put on canvas for their flesh appeal, which never lessens their artistic splendor. ("All flesh is not the same flesh . . ." says St. Paul. "There are also celestial bodies, and bodies terrestrial: but the glory of the celestial is one, and the glory of the terrestrial is another" [1 Cor. 15: 39–40].) The Counter Reformation frowned on nudity in all religious art and in all holy places, relegating it to pious scenes of martyrdom and Crucifixions. Not only did Pope Paul IV have "pants" painted on the naked figures in Michelangelo's *Last Judgment* in the Sistine Chapel while the artist was still living, but Clement VIII (1592–1605) was with difficulty dissuaded from scraping the entire fresco off the wall. And Innocent X (1644–55) had a little shirt put on a Jesus child in a Madonna by Guercino. Still, nudity was not outlawed in secular and private settings, and naked gods and goddesses continued to cavort in palaces and villas, while the forbidden fruit was smuggled back into churches in the suggestive guise of seminudes during the High Baroque. When, in the eighteenth and nineteenth centuries, the nude was seized upon by the Neoclassicists, it had become a disembodied body, lifeless and sugary, an imitation of an antiquity that never was—neither terrestrial nor celestial.

OBELISKS. Rome has the largest number of obelisks of any city—thirteen. What is this all about? The obelisk—a free-standing, four-sided, monolithic pillar, tapering toward the top and, as a rule, inscribed with hieroglyphs—is basically a fetish. Though obelisks existed in Babylonia as early as the third millennium B.C., they are primarily associated with Egypt. The sixth-century B.C. prophet Jeremiah (43:13) predicted that King Nebuchadnezzar "shall break the obelisks . . . of Egypt" (translated "images" in the *King James Bible,* but more correctly rendered "obelisks" in the *Jerusalem Bible;* the Hebrew word, *massebah,* means a free-standing cultic stone). We call them by their Greek name, *obeliskos,* derived from *obelos* or *obolos* (meaning "skewer" or "nail"). Most Egyptian obelisks are carved out of the mottled pink granite quarried at Aswan, where one unfinished shaft can still be seen embedded in the mother rock. They probably were emblems of the Sun-god, Ra, and may have been designed to resemble sunrays. Their pyramid-shaped tops were covered with sun-reflecting electrum, a natural alloy of gold and silver. Obelisks proliferated at Heliopolis ("Sun City") outside modern Cairo, where they guarded the great temple of the Sun-god or stood like sentries by the tombs of kings. They also served, usually in pairs, as memorials of the thirtieth anniversary of a ruler's accession. When the Romans conquered Egypt in the first century B.C., they were impressed with these skillfully wrought spikes, which to them seemed worthy of adorning their own capital. Rome eventually collected more than forty specimens, many of which, today, lie buried under streets and palaces. Special ships were built to ferry obelisks across the Mediterranean, and Pliny the Elder (c. A.D. 23–79) tells us in his *Natural History* (XXXVI, 15, 16) how these ungainly vessels, "the most extraordinary things ever seen at sea," drew curious crowds on their arrival. Sailing up the Tiber, still navigable at the time, they discharged their cargo three miles below Rome, whence it was hauled, no doubt by oxcarts, along the highway and in through the city gate. The emperor Augustus (27 B.C.–A.D. 14) was the first to bring obelisks to Rome. He placed one of them, dating back to Ramses II (thirteenth century B.C.), in the Circus Maximus, where the seventy-eight-foot shaft eventually toppled over. In 1589, Pope Sixtus V, who had already moved three obelisks as part of his great urban planning and beautification project, re-erected it in its present position in Piazza del Popolo, where executions used to be held near its base. Augustus's other import is the sixth-century B.C. obelisk of the Pharaoh Psammeticus I, which served as the style of a sun dial in the Campo Marzio until it was moved, in 1792, to its present site in front of the Italian parliament. (Rests of the dial itself, in travertine and bronze, were excavated at the original site in 1980.) Both obelisks were taken from Heliopolis. Rome's oldest, tallest obelisk, erected by Thutmose IV at Thebes in the fifteenth century B.C., was earmarked by the emperor Constantine for shipment to Constantinople, but sent to Rome, after his death in A.D. 337, by his son, Constantius II. The indefatigable Sixtus V transferred it from the Circus Maximus, where a fire had fractured it, to a spot near the Lateran Palace. Its height, without the base, is an impressive 105 feet, making it the tallest one known. The obelisk with the most interesting story is the uninscribed—hence undatable—eighty-three-foot-high granite shaft from Heliopolis in Piazza S. Pietro. Placed by the emperor Caligula (A.D. 37–41) in his private circus on Vatican Hill (later known as Nero's Circus, where many Christians were martyred), this obelisk had remained upright throughout the Middle Ages. A golden urn on top, since replaced by the bronze arms of the Chigi family, enclosing a Christian relic, was thought to contain the ashes of Julius Caesar. It was the first of the four obelisks moved by Pope Sixtus, who entrusted the tricky operation (1586) to his architect, Domenico Fontana. Nine hundred men, 140 horses, and forty-four windlasses were employed. Absolute silence, on pain of death, was commanded, so that Fontana's orders could be heard by all. Suddenly, when the obelisk was half-way up, a sailor from Bordighera, Bresca by name, saw that the ropes were giving way under the strain. *"Dai de l'aiga ae corde!"* "Give water to the ropes!" he shouted, in Genoese dialect. Water arrived in the nick of time, the fibers tightened, and all went well. As a reward, Bordighera was granted the privilege of supplying palm fronds to St. Peter's every Palm Sunday. The obelisk topping Bernini's Four Rivers Fountain in Piazza Navona is a Roman imitation, fabricated under Domitian (A.D. 81–96). Other Imperial fakes are the obelisk on top of the Spanish Steps, and the one in the Pincian Gardens, ordered by Hadrian (117–138) in Egypt for the tomb of his handsome young favorite, Antinous, whose name is inscribed on it. The small sixth-century B.C. Egyptian obelisk carried by an elephant, in front of the Church of S. Maria sopra Minerva, a monument designed by Bernini, symbolizes strength supporting wisdom—as prefigured in the *Hypnerotomachia,* published by Aldo Manuzio in 1499. In modern times, Egypt has sent abroad some obelisks as gifts, among them the two fifteenth-century B.C. "Cleopatra's Needles," one of which stands on London's Thames Embankment, the other, in New York City's Central Park.

OPERA. Italians are in love with music and, in particular, with the human voice. Opera is an Italian product, and it arrived in other countries labeled "Made in Italy." For centuries, foreign composers based their operas on Italian texts, and Italian singers and musicians dominated the operatic stage in European capitals. Far more than a play set to music, opera is a potent brew of action, decor, songs, and orchestral music. It has generated its own world—a world of sulky prima donnas, implacable impresarios, dressing room intrigues, claques, and bouquets. Its roots—if we exclude Greek drama with its sung choruses—reach back into the late Renaissance. In 1597, a group of scholarly Florentines performed an embryonic opera called *Daphne,* whose score is lost, and the idea of sung drama captured princely courts. Italy's big and little rulers, among them the Farnese, the Gonzaga, and the Medici, installed spacious private theaters in their palaces, and music enlivened every play. The works of Claudio Monteverdi (1567–1643) mark the transition from a princely pastime to a public entertainment. In his hands, opera emerged from its experimental, fragmentary phase into a solid and cohesive entity, fusing music and text in such a way as to convey the moods and the development of each character. He got his start as a string player at the court of Vincenzo I, duke of Mantua, and, always at his master's call, accompanied him on long journeys to Hungary and Flanders, distracting him during leisure hours. In 1613, already widowed, he became music master at St. Mark's in Venice, a post that gave him both the freedom and the prestige needed to realize his talents to their full extent. His operas, among them *Orfeo, Arianna* (largely lost), and *L'incoronazione* ("Coronation") *di Poppea* (written when he was seventy-four and had joined the priesthood), are true lyric dramas, whose emotional passages, such as Arianna's Lament, moved audiences to tears. It was, perhaps, no mere coincidence that the first public opera house opened in Venice in 1637, to be followed in short order by five others. The lagoon city thus became the home of opera, with its productions at their best during the carnival. Opera soon caught on in other cities, and Naples, then Milan, took over as the country's operatic capitals. A night at the opera, in the eighteenth century, was hardly the ritual it is today. Hot meals were served in boxes rented for the season, chitchat and games went on during performances—hushed, maybe, for an aria —and candles allowed visitors to read the text while it was being sung. Meanwhile, opera as an art form had to cope with a peculiar problem. As the composer distributed his parts, women were needed for alto and soprano voices. Women were banned, however, for the sake of prudery, from appearing on the stage, as they were banned from singing in most churches. The answer to the prohibition was castration—practiced, from about 1650 onward, for the purpose of obtaining a high singing voice. The operation had to be performed before puberty began to thicken a boy's vocal cords. It consisted of a primitive vasectomy and was done under a rudimentary anesthesia. Though the Church officially frowned on the practice, threatening surgeons with excommunication, hundreds of castrati sang in church choirs, including the papal chapel choir. Most of the boys came from poor families in southern Italy and were trained in well-run conservatories. No stigma or derision was attached to them. Nor did the operation, which resulted in sterility, effect a loss of manhood. As the young men grew up, they were much in demand as lovers, since intercourse with them was safe. Many of them married. The carefully trained alto voice, combined with the lung power of a fully-grown male body, yielded astonishing results. Castrati may well have possessed the greatest voices ever heard, producing tones beyond the range of female sopranos and excelling in coloratura. Expected to improvise, they might deliver the same aria differently every night. During much of the eighteenth century, as many as two out of three male Italian singers were castrati. (It was not until the social changes of the Napoleonic age that women finally replaced their impersonators—from whom they inherited the cult of the capricious diva.) The most renowned male prima donna was Carlo Broschi, known as Farinelli (1705–82), who made his stage debut aged sixteen in an opera whose libretto ("booklet," or text) was written by young Metastasio, originally Pietro Trapassi (1698–1782), with whom he formed a lifelong friendship. An acrobat of the high registers, as well as an accomplished actor and a winning personality, Farinelli earned resounding plaudits and immense fees wherever he appeared. After triumphant European tours, he was invited to the court of the morose king Philip V of Spain, for whom he sang every evening for nine years the same four songs, gradually lightening his melancholia and even getting him to shave. Farinelli spent his free time raising thoroughbred horses and designing irrigation schemes. After retiring to Italy (where he knew Casanova) he died respected and rich in his villa outside Bologna. His friend, the librettist Metastasio—the two addressed each other as "Dear Twin"—knew equally good fortune. The son of a grocer, he was apprenticed to a goldsmith, but preferred standing at street corners extemporizing poetry. A rich and learned jurist, Gian Vincenzo Gravina, struck by the child's unusual talent, took him into his house, gave him an education, made him his heir, and hellenized his name. The boy wrote his first play at fourteen and, after Gravina's death, moved to Naples, where he was pampered by high society. A famous lady singer (a rare bird at the time), Marianna Bulgarelli ("La Romanina"), fell in love with him, introduced him to the world of music, and persuaded him to write lyric tragedies, which, set to music by various composers, were performed with success. In 1730, he accepted a call from the emperor of Austria, Charles VI, who made him poet laureate to his court. In Vienna, where he was to die fifty-two years later, Metastasio became Europe's most sought-after operatic dramatist. A facile and prolific poet, he turned out librettos of polished verse that melted into music. His twenty-seven major opera scripts, conservative in taste, contained just enough tension and emotion, just the right dose of passion and anxiety, to make them irresistible to both musicians and the public. Set to music by a swarm of plot-hungry composers, they went around the world, some of them set as often as sixty times. Mozart's *La Clemenza di Tito* (1791), requiring a castrato in the cast, was the seventh setting of that libretto from Metastasio's hand. His undeniable dramatic talent earned him, on his death, the absurd byname of "Italic Sophocles." Over the years, Italian opera brought forth a galaxy of famous names, among them Alessandro Scarlatti (1659–1725), composer of 115 operas; Giovanni Paisiello (1741–1816); Gioacchino Rossini (1792–1868); Gaetano Donizetti (1797–1848—*Lucia di Lammermoor*); Vincenzo Bellini (1801–35—*Norma*); and Giacomo Puccini (1858–1924—*La Bohème, Tosca, Madame Butterfly*).

At the same time, the glory of composers was frequently eclipsed by that of individual singers—sopranos like Giuditta Pasta (1798–1865) and Adelina Patti (1843–1919); tenors like Enrico Caruso (1873–1921) and Beniamino Gigli (1890–1957)—for whom composers would write special arias, or whole operas. Italian opera reached its apex with Giuseppe Verdi (1813–1901), its outstanding master, who wrote his first symphony at the age of fifteen and his last opera at seventy-nine. He was both an artist and a national figure—a living emblem of Italy's successful struggle for unity and freedom. As the neatly dressed old gentleman, sporting thick mustaches and a trim white beard, ambled back and forth between La Scala and the Grand Hotel e Milan, well known as a musicians' rendezvous, the Milanese saluted him. The son of a poor innkeeper in the village of Le Roncole in the Po plain, not far from the great fiddlemakers' center of Cremona, the boy became the protégé of a music-loving merchant, who helped him study music in Milan and later gave him his winsome, sixteen-year-old daughter's hand in marriage. She died a few years later after the death of their two children. Verdi's first opera, *Oberto, conte di San Bonifacio,* produced at La Scala in 1839, was a moderate success, but his next work, *Il finto Stanislao* (1840), failed miserably and closed after one performance. Crushed by his misfortunes, Verdi decided never to touch opera again. One day, the impresario of La Scala casually handed him a libretto based on the life of King Nebuchadnezzar II, scourge of Israel. Despondently, the young man tossed it on his table, and it fell open at the chorus of the captive Jews, lamenting by the waters of Babylon: *Va pensiero sull'ali dorate* ("Go, my thought, on gilded wings!") When Verdi's eye lit on it, he went to work. The resulting opera, *Nabucco* (1842), was a triumph. An attractive member of the cast, Giuseppina

Strepponi, became his mistress and, seventeen years later, his second wife. (The opera was performed at the reopening of La Scala in 1946, after wartime damage had been repaired.) Verdi was now unstoppable. His twenty-six operas are of uneven quality, but most of them reflect his genius both as a dramatist and a musician. Never before had opera been so popular a medium, so beloved an entertainment. To this day, his tunes, even amidst the splendor of La Scala, may be accompanied by a soft humming on the part of helpless devotees. Verdi's strength lies in fast-moving, often violent, action, which, swept along by the broad river of his music, speaks straight to our emotions. The human drama was his element, and it is not for nothing that he chose Shakespearean themes for three of his operas—*Macbeth, Otello, Falstaff.* But Verdi conveyed something else to his Milanese public: the passionate desire to be rid of Austrian tyranny, and to see a united Italy rise from the divided and oppressed peninsula. Much of his rousing music, underlining an ambiguous text, smacked of rebellion. His chorus of the captive Jews was promptly understood as the lament of captive Italy. The chorus of medieval knights in his *La Battuglia di Legnano,* swearing to free Italy from the German invaders, caused a near riot. His *Rigoletto* (1851), with its attempt on a king's life, barely squeezed through the Austrian censorship. And the setting of *Un Ballo in Maschera,* based on the murder of King Gustavus III of Sweden, had to be shifted, for security reasons, from Stockholm to Boston, Mass.! When the public discovered that Verdi's name formed an acrostic for the national aspiration, which centered on the person of Victor Emmanuel, ruler of Piedmont and Sardinia (who later did become united Italy's first king), the shout of *Verdi! Verdi!* turned into a battlecry: *Vittorio Emanuele Re* ("king") *d'Italia!* Verdi's perennials include *Il Trovatore* (1853), *La Traviata* (1853), *La Forza del Destino* (1862). When the khedive (viceroy) of Egypt commissioned him to write a festive opera for the inauguration of the Suez Canal, Verdi chose an Egyptian plot and outlined the libretto. A splendid opera house was built in Cairo for the occasion, complete with curtained boxes for the ladies of the harem. But Franco-Prussian tension and the ensuing war delayed the project; and when the empress Eugénie of France inaugurated the Canal in 1869, she had to return to Paris without *Celeste Aïda* ("Heavenly Aïda") ringing in her ears. *Aïda* opened at Cairo in 1871. Its exotic atmosphere, its spectacular mass scenes, the tragic story of its starcrossed lovers, and, above all, the dynamism of its music, showed Verdi at the height of his creative powers. *Aïda* has remained one of the major hits in the Italian repertoire. When the dream of Italian unity was realized, at last, Verdi was elected to the chamber of deputies, but took no further interest in politics and declined a title of nobility. In 1874, he wrote a Requiem for his close friend and fellow patriot, the novelist Alessandro Manzoni, author of *I promessi sposi* (*The Betrothed*). The ageing Verdi spent much time tending his model farm, Sant'Agata, near his birthplace, where he took an interest in the welfare of his two hundred workers and their families. After Giuseppina's death, in 1897, he settled in Milan, looking in on La Scala whenever possible. He died, aged eighty-eight, at the Grand Hotel, having left most of his fortune to a home for retired musicians which he had founded. At his state funeral, the mourners broke spontaneously into the chorus, "Go, my thought, on gilded wings." Today, the grand tradition of Italian opera is linked to—among many other theaters—four proud old houses. Milan's august Teatro alla Scala ("La Scala"), still the world's leading operatic stage, is known for its bejeweled gala openings, and for the long line of composers whose works it first produced. Inaugurated in 1778, it is named for the Church of S. Maria della Scala which formerly occupied the site, and which was named, in turn, for the della Scala family, medieval lords of Verona. The Teatro S. Carlo, at Naples, originally built in 1737, and since remodeled and restored, shares La Scala's fame. Venice's La Fenice ("Phoenix"), opened in 1792 and rebuilt after a fire, remains one of the world's most elegant theaters, a center of Venetian social life. Parma's lovely neoclassical Teatro Regio is noted, above all, for its fastidious public—rightly or wrongly, Parma opera buffs consider themselves infallible judges of the human voice, and their reaction can make or break a singer's reputation.

———————◀◆▶———————

P A G A N I N I , Niccolò (1782–1840). The leading violinist of his generation. He created a sensation with his first solo
violin concert at the age of nine and went from that success to
ever greater conquests, becoming a popular idol and a legend in
the process. A hard worker, who could spend ten hours at a time
trying to master a single passage, Paganini wrote compositions
so difficult that only he could play them. Among his surviving
works are Twenty-Four Caprices for the unaccompanied violin,
illustrating his unorthodox technique. His novel ways of finger-
ing and tuning—his bag of tricks included playing an entire
number only on the fourth string—made audiences rave. Fellow
artists—Schumann, Chopin, Liszt and later Brahms and Rach-
maninov—payed tribute to him by basing piano compositions on
his themes. The Austrian emperor appointed him court virtuoso.
The pope awarded him the Order of the Golden Spur. His weird,
pied-piper's spell gave him a demoniac aura, which was reinforced by his skeletal frame, his long dark hair, his pale, feline
face. His passion for gambling often drove him into debt—he
once had to pawn his violin. In his twenties, he lived with an
aristocratic lady in Tuscany. Later, we find him in carnivalesque
Venice in the company of a ballerina, Antonia Bianchi, with
whom he had a son, Achillino. He and Antonia separated in
1828 because of her—probably well-founded—jealousy. Paganini's most resounding triumphs came in his late forties when
he set off wave after wave of bravos in the theaters and concert
halls of Vienna, Paris, London. Hats, perfumes, boots, gloves,
dishes were named for him. His playing, technically perfect,
broadened the range of the violin, giving it a new dimension.
Many called it "divine," though at least one dissenting critic
compared it to the "mewlings of an expiring cat." His British
concert tour of 1831–32 yielded a fortune, enabling him to buy
a villa near Parma. The crash of the Casino Paganini in Paris,

four years later, in which he was financially involved, did not ruin him, but impaired both his fortune and his health. He died at Nice, having spent his last hours improvising—more beautifully than ever, said those who were present. He bequeathed his favorite fiddle—a "Joseph," made by Giuseppe Guarneri—to Genoa, his home town, where it is kept in the sixteenth-century town hall.

THE PAPACY. The bishop of Rome is known as the pope. As such, he is the spiritual head of the Roman Catholic Church, with a membership of 540 million out of the world's 950 million Christians, and the secular ruler of Vatican City. His claim to spiritual primacy rests on Christ's words to Peter, "Thou art Peter, and upon this rock I will build my church. . . . And I will give unto thee the keys of the kingdom of heaven" (Matt. 16: 18–19). Catholic doctrine applies this saying to Peter's successors, that is, each pope. That Peter, the fisherman of Galilee and "Prince of Apostles," came to Rome is neither proved nor seriously contested. An oblique reference to his presence and martyrdom in Rome is contained in a letter written by St. Clement, bishop of Rome, about A.D. 96, and St. Irenaeus, a second-century bishop of Lyons, refers to Peter and Paul as founders of the Roman Church and initiators of the papal succession. Although some archaeologists believe they have found Peter's tomb beneath St. Peter's basilica in Rome, the Church has not pronounced itself officially on this matter. The Church at Rome, then the capital of the Roman empire, asserted its primacy at an early date. St. Clement intervened in a dispute dividing Christians at Corinth. Pope Victor I (189–199) already regarded himself as head of Christendom, using his rank to discipline other Christian communities and to lay down doctrinal rules. From the fifth century onward, the popes have used the designation Pontifex Maximus ("Highest Priest"), the title of the chief religious officer in pagan Rome. While in the early centuries the general, or ecumenical, council of the world's bishops was held to take precedence over the popes and was occasionally convoked by a worldly authority, such as the Byzantine emperor, modern Catholic opinion tends to aver that only the pope can call a council and must confirm its decisions in order to give them validity. The First Vatican Council, in 1870, decreed the infallibility—or inability to err—of the pope when defining matters of faith or morals *ex cathedra,* that is, "from the chair" of St. Peter. The pope's spiritual supremacy has long been complemented by his secular rule over certain territories. The claim to such possessions was first asserted in the "Donation of Constantine," a document in which the first Christian Roman emperor (306–337) granted to the popes perpetual dominion over Italy and "the Western regions." Probably concocted by papal jurists in the eighth century, it was exposed as a forgery by the Renaissance scholar Lorenzo Valla in 1440. King Pepin of the Franks (c. 714–68), father of Charlemagne, however, handed to the popes the "exarchate" of Ravenna, formerly owned by the emperor of Byzantium, thus setting up a sovereign papal state. This patrimony waxed and waned with the fortunes of papal armies, covering at one time much of Italy. In 1861, all papal lands except for Rome itself were absorbed into the new Italian nation. In 1870, Rome too was lost, and the pope constituted himself a "prisoner" in the Vatican, the chief papal residence since the end of the "Babylonian Exile" of the papacy in Avignon, France (1309–77). Today, no longer a "prisoner" thanks to a concordat (1929) with the Italian Government, the pope remains sovereign ruler of Vatican City, a territory of 0.17 square mile in Rome, with its own postal service, prison, and diplomatic corps. On the death of a pope, his "fisherman's ring" is smashed, and a new pope—traditionally, but not necessarily, a cardinal—is elected by the world's cardinals convening in conclave (from the Latin *clavis,* "key," because they are locked in). That the conclave was not always the dignified affair it is today is illustrated by a passage in the memoirs of the great humanist, Aeneas Sylvius Piccolomini (1405–64), on the Conclave of 1458, from which he emerged as Pius II. Several of the eighteen participating cardinals, he records, "begged, promised, threatened," and some, "shamelessly casting aside all decency, pleaded their own causes." Large bribes were offered, and a clique of voters met in the latrines where they agreed on a French candidate—who later, as teller of the ballots, was caught cheating. At one point, two cardinals attempted to hustle Cardinal Prospero Colonna out of the room in order to prevent his voting. When it was clear that Aeneas Sylvius had the majority, his seventeen rivals knelt before him, acknowledging that he was chosen by the Holy Ghost. (Pius, immortalized by the fresco cycle by Pinturicchio in Siena cathedral, was to enjoy the pontificate for six years. He was a poet, cosmographer, and nature lover, who often traveled in a gilt sedan chair through the countryside, and held consistories in shady groves. He founded the University of Basel and transformed his Tuscan birthplace into the Renaissance city of Pienza, named for him.) To this day, conclaves are unpredictable; even though this or that cardinal may be considered *papabile* ("likely to be made pope"), it is said in Rome that "he who goes into the conclave pope comes out a cardinal." It was customary in medieval times and during the Renaissance for the rabble to plunder the house of the winning candidate—he would have no further use for it! Cardinals are created for life by the reigning pope. Innocent IV (1243–54) invented the red hat for cardinals, and Boniface VIII (1294–1303) clothed them with royal purple (actually crimson red) in token of the fact that they were "Princes of the Church." Cardinals resident in Rome form the Curia, or papal court, with "congregations" functioning under the pope's absolute authority, like the departments of a secular government. There have been good and evil popes, several antipopes, and, at times, three simultaneous claimants to the Chair of Peter. The youngest pope on record is Benedict IX (1032–45), a profligate boy elected at the age of fifteen, who is said to have sold his office to his godfather, who became Pope Gregory VI. The once widely believed tale of Joan, the female pope who reigned dressed as a man and died after giving birth during a procession, has long been shown to be a medieval hoax. But though the Holy See did have its share of scandal, and people frequently suffered from its oppression, it often played the leading role in the defense of Western civilization, and its contribution to Italian culture is inestimable. Not only did the popes themselves create one of the world's great libraries and art collections, but their much maligned nepotism, by showering church revenues upon some favorite nephew (Lat.

nepos), spawned a brood of princely dynasties that vied with one another in sponsoring the arts. Some of Italy's finest churches, palaces, villas, gardens, thoroughfares, fountains, and piazzas were commissioned by popes and their ambitious kin.

PERSPECTIVE. The notion of forcing a three-dimensional reality onto a plane is patently absurd. Yet, the mirror does it; photography does it; and it lies at the root of painting, whose purpose was, for many centuries, the imitation of reality. Cave dwellers drawing a herd of buffalo knew that a distant beast, to our eye, seems smaller than a near one. A child drawing a treelined road running off into the distance knows that the trees move closer to one another as they recede. Fifth-century B.C. Greek stage designers used perspective to give the illusion of depth to their stage sets. And the first-century B.C. Roman architect, Vitruvius, has left us fragmentary writings which show that he had worked out a rudimentary system of perspective. Roman artists may have followed his guidelines in painting the complex architectural fantasies of Pompeii. Whatever the ancients knew about perspective was forgotten during the Middle Ages. Efforts of medieval painters to impart depth and volume to their pictures were sustained by intuition and experience rather than by logic. It remained for the Renaissance, forever striving for accurate knowledge, to elevate perspective into a science and search for rules that would create the mathematically unassailable illusion of space. Filippo Brunelleschi (1377–1446), the Florentine architect and sculptor, is credited with having discovered (before 1420) the vanishing point, key to all perspective presentation. He did not put his findings into writing, but his two lost panel paintings of Florentine cityscapes, probably history's first pictures based on accurate perspective, astonished those who saw them: *el proprio vero* ("the real thing!"). Some fifteen years later, Leon Battista Alberti (1404–72) publicized this new discovery in his treatise *Della pittura* (*On*

Painting). A picture, he explained, is not merely a surface decked with pigment, stopping the eye, but a *window* set across our field of vision. Not what is on the picture, but what is behind it, matters. The place and size the distant object assumes on the window pane will be its place and size in the picture. The basis for this doctrine was the proposition that parallel lines (like those two rows of trees), running away from us, meet at a point located in infinity, and that infinity begins at the horizon, a real or imaginary "horizontal" line crossing the picture surface. All straight lines running "into" the picture at a right angle to its surface converge, and *vanish* at a single point on the horizon. This vanishing point, to which the viewer's eye is automatically drawn, may be located in the center of the horizon, or to its right or left. (In Leonardo da Vinci's *Last Supper,* it is in the center of Christ's forehead.) Before starting to paint, the artist draws straight lines—"orthogonals"—on the blank picture surface, which converge in the vanishing point, as well as crosslines as an aid to putting objects in their proper place. And into this spider web he may paint any composition, confident that it will look "real." All painted objects not parallel to the picture surface will be distorted, or foreshortened, to fit into his construction, diminishing in size in proportion to their distance from the viewer's eye, while distances between them shrink accordingly. The result will be a unified, organic picture space, wherein all objects occupy their natural position. Alberti called this *costruzione legittima* (scientifically correct construction), in contrast to mere guesswork. No sooner had his theory been published than it became the almost obsessive preoccupation of artists. Once in command of the new science, they could paint anything—landscapes, streets lined with a variety of houses, interiors of any shape, people coming and going—without risk of error. Perspective was to them the philosopher's stone assuring its possessor of true knowledge. By the time of Alberti's death, Florence alone had more than a dozen teachers of perspective. One painter who "went off his head with love of perspective," in the words of John Ruskin, was Paolo Uccello (1397–1475). He'd spend much of the night working out the foreshortenings for his paintings, and when his wife, Tommasa, called him to bed, reply, "Oh, what a sweet thing—*che dolce cosa*—is this perspective!" Cosimo Rosselli (1439–1507) painted an octangular table, properly foreshortened, into his *Last Supper* fresco in the Sistine Chapel, a fact mentioned with appreciation by Vasari. And Mantegna (1431–1506) painted a dead Christ lying on his back, with the soles of his feet toward the viewer—a piece of bravado showing how *costruzione legittima* can cope with the most baffling problem (Milan, Brera). Albrecht Dürer, the German painter and engraver (1471–1528), during one of his Italian sojourns made a special trip to Bologna "out of love for the secret art of perspective," which, he hoped, someone would teach him there. Piero della Francesca (c. 1410/20–92), called "the poet of perspective," not only experimented in his pictures with high and low horizons and with more than one vanishing point in the same painting, but wrote a manual on perspective—*De prospectiva pingendi*—in which he applied his knowledge of geometry to the solution of specific problems in the realm of *costruzione legittima*. Being the perfect means to "fool the eye," in Brunelleschi's words, perspective has been playfully employed to do just that. Bramante (1444–1514), short of space in rebuilding the Church of S. Satiro in Milan, provided it with a fake apse, consisting of a cunningly articulated stucco decoration simulating depth. Borromini (1599–1667) constructed a thirty-foot colonnade in the garden of Palazzo Spada (Rome), whose columns rapidly diminish as they recede from the viewer looking down its length, making it seem much longer than it is and thereby aggrandizing, to the trusting eye, the tiny statue at its end. This architectural caprice is thought to have given Bernini (1598–1680) the idea for his Scala Regia ("Royal Stairway") in the Vatican which, thanks to a combination of perspective tricks, looks far more "royal" than its tight dimensions warrant. "The least defective thing I've ever done," the master called it. In the Baroque, Bologna became the capital of illusionistic perspective, whose practitioners traveled through Europe decorating walls and ceilings with their eye-deceiving fancies, designing stage sets, and erecting theaters. Outstanding among them were four generations —ten artists—of the Bibiena family, whose drawings greatly stimulated Piranesi (1720–78) and whose influence on stage design remains decisive to this day. Their best known work is the court opera house in Bayreuth (Bavaria), built for Wilhelmine, sister of Frederick the Great of Prussia, by Giuseppe Bibiena and his son Carlo in 1745–48.

PETRARCH (Francesco Petrarca, 1304–74). Poet and proto-humanist. Born in Arezzo (Tuscany), the child was taken by his father, a Florentine exile, to Carpentras, near Avignon. He studied law at Montpellier and Bologna, and spent part of his twenties at the papal court in Avignon, partaking of its profane pleasures, deepening his knowledge of the Latin classics, and writing verse. One April day in 1327, in the Church of St. Clare, he first saw Laura, the golden-haired girl who was to be the chief source of inspiration for his art. Nothing is known about her identity, but there is little doubt that she existed. She is the central figure of his *Rime,* a collection of 366 lyric poems, including 317 sonnets, composed during Laura's life and after her death, and dwelling on the poet's joys and sorrows. One of them pictures Laura on a spring day, seated under a tree by a clear stream:

> Da' be' rami scendea
> (Dolce nella memoria)
> Una pioggia di fior sovra 'l suo grembo;
> Ed ella si sedea
> Umile in tanta gloria,
> Coverta già dell'amoroso nembo.
> Qual fior cadea sul lembo,
> Qual su le trecce bionde,
> Ch'oro forbito e perle
> Eran quel dì a vederle;
> Qual si posava in terra, e qual su l'onde;
> Qual con un vago errore
> Girando, parea dir, "qui regna Amore."

From the branches there fell
—Sweet memory!—a rain of blossoms into her lap
While she sat humbly in such glory,
Letting herself be covered by the amorous shower.
This flower landed on her skirt, that on her blond tresses

Which looked that day like burnished gold and pearls.
This fell onto the ground, that on the waves,
And one, twisting charmingly as it drifted down,
Seemed to say, "here reigns Love."

Much of Petrarch's life was spent in moving from place to place. Among his patrons were some of the grand families of Italy— the Colonna, with whom he broke over his admiration for their enemy, Cola di Rienzo; the Carrara, lords of Padua; and the Visconti, tyrants of Milan, who sent him on diplomatic errands to Venice, Prague, and Paris. Periods of intense activity alternated with quiet retreats. During repeated sojourns in the sylvan wilderness of the Vaucluse (east of Avignon), he meditated on religious questions and wrote poetry and prose. A Latin treatise, *De vita solitaria* (*On Solitary Life*), extols the moral profit of loneliness. In a celebrated letter to a theologian friend, Petrarch describes his ascent, in 1336, of 6275-foot Mt. Ventoux, from whose top he could see the Mediterranean surf beating against the coast, several days' journey to the south. Mountain climbing was not the fashion then, and Petrarch viewed his feat as a symbolic gesture, enabling him to face—if not to solve—the dualism of his character. How to reconcile pleasures of the flesh and of the spirit? Pure heights and somber valleys? For many years, he carried on his person a small copy of St. Augustine's *Confessions,* and he may well have prayed, with the great Doctor of the Church (A.D. 354-430), "Lord, give me chastity—but not just yet, not yet!" (Two illegitimate children, Giovanni and Francesca, were born to him by an unknown mother in 1337 and 1343 respectively.) Petrarch's first visit to Rome, in 1337, was a turning point. Here was the former capital of the world, now a mere symbol of a glorious past. With growing fervor, he dedicated himself to the study of classical antiquity. He is thought to have been the first collector of Roman coins, whose portraits and inscriptions were precious clues to history. During subsequent visits to the city, he "read" its ruins, trying to determine their age and their significance. In his relentless hunt for manuscripts, he found, in the cathedral library of Verona, Cicero's letters to his friend and publisher, Atticus, with their intimate glimpses of life in republican Rome —one of the most important literary discoveries of the age.

(Petrarch remained a Latinist to the end, having, to his regret, not mastered Greek.) His *Africa,* in Latin hexameters, tries to recapture the flavor of Rome's bitter and victorious struggle against Hannibal of Carthage in the third century B.C. On 8 April 1341, upon his own initiative—the quest for fame, he admitted, was one of his vices—he was crowned with laurel as his country's leading poet on the Capitol in Rome. After the ceremony, he placed his wreath upon St. Peter's presumed tomb, a gesture underlining his desire to harmonize Christian and pagan cultures. The plague of 1348 brought deep unhappiness. Laura was among the victims. So were many of his friends. "Oh Brother, Brother, Brother!" he writes to his only brother, Gherardo, a Carthusian monk, who remained alone, with only a dog for company, in his plague-ravaged monastery. "What can I say? Where can I turn? Sorrow and fear are everywhere. Wish I had never been born. Where are our friends? Where their familiar faces, their cheering talk? Oh, happy people of the future, who will consider our suffering mere fiction!" By 1350— the year in which he met Boccaccio—he finally renounced the distractions of this world, and, turning down an offer of a chair at the newly founded University of Florence, returned to the solitude of the Vaucluse. There, among murmuring waters and whispering trees, he edited much of his lifework. A perfectionist, he corrected and revised both prose and verse with extreme self-discipline, aiming at simplicity and elegance. His final work, *Trionfi* (*Triumphs*), composed, like Dante's *Divine Comedy,* in *terza rima* ("triple rhyme"), is in the form of a dream, or vision, wherein humanity advances by slow stages toward God. In 1362, the Republic of Venice presented Petrarch with a comfortable house overlooking the wide Canale di San Marco. His daughter, Francesca, with her husband and their little daughter, moved in with him, and he worked happily—settled, it seemed, for life. But, having been insulted by four young blades who publicly charged him with ignorance, he left for Padua. Henceforth, he divided his time between that learned city and his country house in nearby Arquà—today Arquà Petrarca—in the Euganean Hills, with its quiet garden and its delightful view. He was a figure of European stature. "Frdaunceys Petrark, the laureat poete," Chaucer calls him. Distinguished visitors coming to see him were received with regal gravity. Princes entrusted him with diplomatic missions. Struck by a heart attack on one such journey, he died at Arquà—according to tradition, he was found with his head resting on a tome of Virgil.

PICO DELLA MIRANDOLA, Count Giovanni (1463–94). Humanist. Son of the lord of Mirandola, a fortified town near Ferrara. One of the most attractive, and most complex, figures of the Renaissance, young Pico spent much of his life as a wandering scholar. He studied philosophy and canon law, collected books in Italy and France, and became a paragon of learning. His memory was phenomenal. Although the story that he knew twenty-two languages has been discredited, he probably had a good command of Hebrew, Arabic, and Chaldean, besides Greek and Latin. His chief accomplishment is his oration on the *Dignity of Man,* in which he maintained that the individual is responsible for his own destiny and free to shape it within God's created world. The speech—a basic contribution to humanist thinking—was to be given at a learned gathering in Rome in 1487, which Pico had intended as a setting for the exposition of 900 scholarly arguments, or theses, drawn largely from non-Christian sources. They show him deeply enmeshed in the pseudo-science of astrology and in the mysteries of the Cabala—an occult Hebrew teaching which saw in the words and numbers of the biblical text a hidden meaning, often predicting future events. Both trends—astrology and Cabala—formed a strong undercurrent of magic in the Renaissance. One of his theses, which circulated in printed form, postulated that magic formulae proved the divinity of Christ. The Vatican could not believe its eyes. Pope Innocent VIII (1484–92)—sponsor of particularly cruel witch hunts by the German Inquisition—forbade the meeting. After examination by a special commission with Inquisitional powers in Rome, some of the theses were declared heretical. Pico escaped to France, where papal officers, armed with a warrant for his arrest, caught up with him. He was briefly imprisoned, but released upon French intervention, and given asylum in Florence by Lorenzo the Magnificent, himself receptive to occult science. In Florence, Pico became a prominent member of the Platonic Academy. But he was also drawn into the orbit of Savonarola and, under his influence, had a change of heart. In his *Disputationes adversus Astrologiam divinatricem* (*Disputations Against Astrological Divination*), he condemned the magic aspects of astrology not merely on religious grounds, but, in particular, because they transformed man's God-given sovereignty over himself and over nature into a slavish dependence on the stars. Stars, after all, were real bodies, not pagan deities lifted into the skies. The work aroused great interest and gave rise to bitter controversy among humanists, who saw Savonarola's grim intolerance behind it. Before he died, Pico, on the Magnificent's intercession, was formally forgiven by Pope Alexander VI (Borgia), who liked a bit of magic himself.

PIERO DELLA FRANCESCA (c. 1410/20–1492). Painter, mathematician. Neglected for centuries by art historians and the public, Piero is now acknowledged as one of the key figures of the fifteenth century. Numerous visitors to Italy make "pilgrimages" to Sansepolcro (his birthplace), Arezzo, Monterchi, and Urbino to see some of his works. Many of his pictures, among them a self-portrait, are lost; but all of the nearly twenty surviving paintings are masterpieces, bearing the stamp of his highly individual genius. His life seems bereft of drama. The eldest son of a shoemaker, he may have been drawn toward painting by the beautiful vistas of the upper Tiber valley where he grew up. He was probably apprenticed to Domenico Veneziano in Florence, where he is known to have worked under him on the (lost) frescoes in the church of San Egidio. Piero was deeply attached to Sansepolcro where he had his house, his relatives, and friends (there is no record of a marriage), and where he served intermittently on the town council. His powerful *Resurrection of Christ* at Sansepolcro, perhaps his earliest known work, shows that he had closely studied Masaccio's statuesque figures and formed his own pictorial language. There is a farmyard air about this fresco, with the dead background of a north Italian winter promising a spring of resurrection, and Christ himself, so vigorously rising from his tomb, looking (in the words of art historian Roberto Longhi) like a grim tenant farmer. As Piero's fame spread, the charitable Brotherhood of Mercy—Misericordia—commissioned him to paint an altarpiece of the *Madonna of Mercy,* who takes mankind under her protective mantle (Sansepolcro). It was to be finished in three years, but you could not hurry Piero, who painted slowly and deliberately, often deserting a work-in-progress for a while to turn his hand to something else, driving his clients to despair. His father had to promise the impatient brethren to refund the sum they had advanced unless his dilatory son "sat down and worked on the picture all through Lent." Piero's talent soon caught the eye of Federigo da Montefeltro, duke of Urbino. Piero went back and forth between both cities, forty-five miles apart, becoming an important figure at Federigo's court, where he met Leon Battista Alberti and Luciano Laurana; the latter was then transforming the Duke's somber gothic castle into the Renaissance palace it is today. There, too, Piero saw Flemish paintings that had found their way across the Alps—the duke himself may have owned a Van Eyck—whose gemlike colors and meticulously painted details affected his own art. So did the Flemings' use of oil as a medium, little known in Italy where tempera painting, using egg as a binder, still prevailed. (Oil permits more subtle modeling.) Piero has left us souvenirs of Federigo—who had lost an eye and the bridge of his nose in a tournament: the portraits of the duke and his wife, Battista Sforza (Florence, Uffizi), painted in oil, and a *Madonna with Saints* (Milan, Brera) wherein the duke is portrayed kneeling in full armor. (The ostrich egg hanging in midair amidst the architecture of the background is an old symbol of life and resurrection.) For Federigo, Piero also created the mysterious *Flagellation of Christ,* probably intended for the ducal palace chapel. The event from which the painting takes its name is enacted in the far left background, while, in the right foreground, three male figures, whose identity has been the subject of much speculation, are engaged in "silent conversation." The real hero of this picture (Urbino, Castle) is Perspective, which here creates a depth not seen in other paintings of the time. Unfortunately, Piero's frescoes for the Este castle in Ferrara and for Pope Pius II's apartment in the Vatican are lost. But his lunette in Alberti's Malatesta Temple (*Tempio Malatestiano*) in Rimini, painted for the princely condottiere Sigismondo Malatesta, Federigo's bitter rival, is preserved. And so is, happily, much of his celebrated fresco cycle in the Church of San Francesco at Arezzo. Its subject, the *Finding of the Cross,* is taken from the *Golden Legend,* the medieval manual of saintly lives. Piero starts with the death of Adam—he and Eve are rendered with compassion for their old age—from whose grave grows a shoot of the Tree of Knowledge that will later yield the wood for the Lord's Cross. More than three hundred years after Christ's death and after many wonders the True Cross is discovered by St. Helena—whose son, Constantine the Great, in a pitched battle, is defeating the pagan emperor Maxentius. Among the cycle's personages are the statuesque figures of the queen of Sheba and her female retinue. Piero's labor, which occupied him for the better part of fifteen years, had a small epilogue. A religious confraternity, struck with the *Annunciation* of the frescoes, asked him to paint another Annunciation on a banner "as beautiful as possible." Piero obliged, working on it in a village to escape a pestilence then ravaging Sansepolcro; three delegates of the confraternity came in a one-horse cart to take delivery of the work (now lost). Piero's surviving lifework comprises several Saints; the *Hercules* (from his own house) in Boston's Gardner Museum; Madonnas (among them the sublime *Madonna del Parto*—"Pregnant Madonna"—in the graveyard chapel at Monterchi); and the *Baptism of Christ,* with its three impassive angels, in London's National Gallery. The unfinished *Nativity* (also in London), thought to have remained in Piero's family until little more than a century ago, may be his last painting. He was increasingly preoccupied with working out the problems of perspective, and his eyesight was failing. He died at Sansepolcro, leaving money and houses to his two brothers. Piero imparts to all his works a luminosity that seems to turn them into transcendental apparitions. With that, he gives us silence. A hush enfolds whatever happens in his pictures. Michelangelo borrowed his Eve for the Cumaean Sibyl on the Sistine ceiling. And the Venetian Renaissance is indebted to him for having been the first to capture the flow of living light—the light that was to be the touchstone of its painting. The manuscript of Piero's geometric treatise, *On the Five Regular Bodies*, was appropriated, on his death, by his friend, the mathematician Fra Luca Pacioli, who published it as if it were his own. Fra Luca has two other—less questionable—claims to fame. His work of 1494, on arithmetic, geometry, and proportions, contains the first systematic exposition of double entry bookkeeping, which had come into use spontaneously in the city-states of northern Italy; the earliest known double entry books were kept by Genoese merchants in 1340. Pacioli later wrote the first scientific treatise on the Golden Section, *De divina proportione* (*On the Divine Proportion*), a universal norm for the relationship of parts of a given unit to each other and to the whole that makes for aesthetic perfection. It has been used, since ancient times, in art and architecture—the Parthenon shows evidence of it—and to this day remains a basic tool of painters, builders, and industrial designers. It also occurs in plants, in animals, and in the human body—hence the *divine* proportion. The treatise, printed in Venice in 1509 with illustrations by Leonardo da Vinci, had considerable bearing on Renaissance art. A painting mysteriously signed, "Jaco.Bar." at Capodimonte, Naples, shows Pacioli instructing a young man in geometry; an icosahexadron, a crystal with twenty-six facets, painted in impeccable perspective, is suspended on Fra Luca's right.

PIERO DI COSIMO (c. 1461–1521). Florentine painter, author of some of the most haunting paintings of the Renaissance. He took his name from his teacher, Cosimo Rosselli, a relatively undistinguished artist, who, between 1481

and 1483, painted four biblical murals in the Sistine Chapel. Some of the work was executed by Piero, whose Roman sojourn in his master's company was his only absence from his native Florence. He specialized in mythological and allegorical themes. Both his choice of subjects and his style of painting were unusual. Art historian Erwin Panofsky (*Studies in Iconology*) speaks of a "strange lure emanating from Piero's pictures." Among his surviving creations is a bewitched series depicting man's slow rise from the Stone Age to civilization, which includes *The Discovery of Honey* at Worcester, Mass. (Worcester Art Museum), and *The Forest Fire* at Oxford (Ashmolean). His best known works are, probably, the *Death of Procris,* with its mourning faun and sorrowing dog (London, National Gallery), and *Mars and Venus,* showing these deities reclining against an idyllic landscape background (West Berlin, Dahlem). Vasari, who owned the latter work, gives a vivid account of this strange, troubled artist who, he avers, "lived like a wild beast," leaving his rooms unswept and letting his garden go to seed with unpruned trees and jungle-like growths covering the paths—explaining that nature should be left to nature. Piero had a reputation for arranging unusual pageants. Florentines long remembered his eerie Carnival procession, which featured a float drawn by pitch-black buffaloes and draped with black cloth, topped by a towering figure of Death holding a scythe. Tombs opened on the float whenever the procession halted, and, at a muffled trumpet blast, the "dead"—masked figures in black cloaks on which skeletons and death's heads were picked out in white—rose slowly from their coffins to chant dirges. Other "dead" mounted on "dead" horses rode before and behind, singing penitential psalms. Public spectacles such as this, Vasari assures us, were never matched by any other city. With advancing age, Piero concentrated on his work to the exclusion of everything else. Having once been a remarkable storyteller, who could elicit laughter from his listeners, he now refused to see anyone. Noises, such as the sound of bells, the voices of children, even a cough, exasperated him. During a thunderstorm, he would crouch in a corner, covering his head; but rain filled him with childlike pleasure. He lived exclusively on hard-boiled eggs, of which he would boil fifty at a time, and eat one whenever he felt hungry. He hated medicines and doctors, and envied those condemned to execution for their happy death in the fresh air.

P I R A N E S I, Giovanni Battista (1720–78). Etcher, architect, archaeologist, tastemaker. The contrast between his pleasing "views" (*vedute*) of Rome and his sinister interiors of imaginary prisons (*carceri*) makes him a Jekyll-Hyde figure. That he could balance these two worlds attests to the uniqueness of the man, who was to shape the taste of generations and who still dominates our own attitude to decaying ruins. His output was prodigious—more than a thousand etchings, and several treatises setting forth his highly personal views on art. Born at Mogliano (near Venice), the son of a stonemason, he was apprenticed to an architect, and studied stage design. His brother, a monk, taught him Latin. Aged twenty, he was hired as a draftsman by the Venetian ambassador to the papal court. A few years later, a master etcher and passionate antiquarian, he opened a printshop on Rome's main thoroughfare, the Corso. Reconnoitering crumbling temples, ducking into moldy tomb chambers, raising his eyes to the arches of Imperial aqueducts, he felt a sense of mission taking root in him. "When I first saw," he wrote, "the remnants of Rome's ancient buildings . . . wasting away under the ravages of time, or being broken up by greedy owners to be sold as building material, I decided to preserve them forever by means of my etchings." His major series, *Vedute di Roma,* was begun in his late twenties and grew to 135 plates during the next thirty years. (Each plate, under the hand press, yielded several hundred prints for individual sale.) Besides their high artistic value, these etchings form an invaluable inventory of eighteenth-century Rome. Field trips resulted in *vedute* of the Roman Campagna, and, later, of the sixth- and fifth-century B.C. Greek temples at Paestum, in southern Italy, then ignored by most tourists. As an archaeologist, Piranesi attended excavations and publicized the new discoveries of Etruscan art. He also found time to re-build, in one neoclassic stroke, the Roman church owned by the Order of the Knights of Malta; design handsome fireplaces; and decorate the English Café in Rome in the Egyptian taste—a gen-eration before that taste was popularized by Napoleon's return from Egypt. In 1752, he married Angela, a gardener's daughter. Raising a family, he moved to a spacious house on Via Sistina, then the haunt of foreign artists and rich "milords" on the Grand Tour of Europe. His printshop became a social center for educated foreigners, many of whom carried his etchings, and his fame, home with them. By the time he was forty, Piranesi was a European figure, better known abroad, especially in England, than in Italy. His conviction that one could "add new graces . . . to works of architecture" by combining a "profound study of nature . . . with that of ancient monuments" caught on. He was elected an Honorary Fellow of the Society of Anti-quaries of London, and through his friendship with the Scots ar-chitect, Robert Adam, to whom he dedicated one of his series of *vedute,* affected an entire phase of British architecture and deco-ration. Piranesi rarely bothered to prepare a careful sketch for an etching but, drawing on his uncanny memory for detail, used the needle to throw his final image straight onto the metal— talking to the copper plate while he worked. His "views" are often startlingly conceived, "taken" from an odd angle, favoring "crazy" perspectives, dramatizing the contrast between light and shade, and exaggerating depth, or height, or volume, so that the personages moving irresolutely through his ruins look like dressed-up insects. His buildings often ignore all laws of statics. "He has imagined scenes that would startle geometry," Horace Walpole said of him. This disregard for realism links the *vedute* with the *carceri.* Piranesi first created this perplexing series, comprising fourteen plates, when he was in his early twenties. He reworked them some fifteen years later, deepening the blacks, inserting some new, often cruel, touches, and adding two new plates. Deriving, outwardly, from his early studies of baroque stage design, these "prisons" are nightmares of im-mense, vertiginous interiors. Behind them we glimpse others and suspect still others, producing an impression of infinity from which escape is utterly excluded. Inside these vaults of permanent despair are stairways leading nowhere; bridges linking nothing; and lookouts, galleries, and balconies, arranged in such confusing ways as to deprive the inmate (or the viewer) of any notion of just where he stands. The whole is furnished with long ropes and cables, spiked instruments of torture, chains, pullies, giant wheels, and iron rings let into walls. Human beings—torturers, captives, spectators—people these spaces. The "why" and "wherefore" of this series eludes us.

P O L O , Marco (1254–1324). Venetian traveler, one of the first Europeans to visit Central Asia and the Far East, author of a famous travel book, *The Travels* (or, *The Book*) *of Marco Polo.* Traditional ideas of the fabulous East stem largely from his tale, which sounded so exaggerated to his contemporaries that he became known as "Mr. Million" (*Milione*). In fact, he was an acute observer and recorder. A pioneer of modern geography, the first to describe China and the trans-Asiatic trade routes, he caused Asia to rise from the mist of Western ignorance. Many places he named were not revisited by Westerners until the nineteenth century. His father and uncle, Niccolò and Matteo Polo, traders with Constantinople, had ventured as far as China before and returned with a message from the Great Khan to the pope, requesting missionaries to inform his people about Christianity. Seventeen-year-old Marco left Venice with the two older Polos in 1271, accompanied by two fainthearted friars—who soon turned back. East of the known Levant, they advanced along routes rarely trodden by Europeans, detouring unsafe areas, braving harsh weather (Marco was sick for nearly a year), traversing Persia, crossing the "Roof of the World"— whose name, Pamir, Marco was the first Westerner to mention. From there, they pushed on east through Turkestan, scaling mountain ranges, and crossing the Gobi Desert, to arrive after three years at the palace of Kublai—grandson of Genghis Khan, whose Mongol horsemen had conquered half the world. Founder of China's Yüan, or Mongol, dynasty (1260–1368), lord of an empire reaching from the China Seas to Poland, the hero of Coleridge's *Kubla Khan* did indeed build a "pleasure-dome" (his summer palace at Shangtu, or Xanadu, north of his capital near what is now Peking), and he did drink the "milk of Paradise" provided by his herd of 10,000 snow-white horses, fermented mare's milk being the Mongols' favorite liquor. Curious about the West, he received the Polos graciously and took a special liking to young Marco, who, after acquiring the ways (but not the language) of the country, became his trusted diplomat-at-large, while the senior Polos may have engaged in local trade. Kublai sent Marco on long journeys to his outlying provinces, and his minute reports on the character and customs of the people, their crops, their industries and commerce, induced the Khan to promote him to high official rank, possibly that of a provincial governor. Marco realized that he was facing a superior civilization. Here was an empire-wide communications system based on a network of fine, treelined roads, with relay stations spaced some thirty miles apart, each containing state rooms "fit for kings" and holding 400 swift horses ready for the use of dispatch riders. Here was the miracle of paper money, made legal tender by the Khan's red seal, which no one, at the risk of his life, dared refuse. Here was a capital through whose gates caravans laden with raw silk, drugs, spices, precious stones, and woven cloth entered every day from all parts of the realm. Ice cream, unknown in Europe, was sold in the streets. Feast days were marked by a procession of 5,000 elephants bearing gold-embroidered howdahs. Marco accompanied the Khan on bear hunts, with lions serving as hunting dogs. Besides the Khan's four empresses (each with a separate court of 4,000 attendants), Marco reports, concubines were selected for him from a place called Ungut, known for the beauty of its women. Picked by an official delegation, the girls were entrusted to the care of ladies of the court who observed them while they slept, making sure they did not snore, before being admitted to the Khan's chamber. After a stay of seventeen years, the Polos—whose prospects in case of the Khan's death appeared uncertain—made ready to leave. Kublai reluctantly parted with his guests, who, armed with a golden tablet of safe conduct and letters to the pope and European kings, sailed with a fleet conveying a young bride to the king of Persia. After many adventures and an epidemic that killed most of their men, and after finding that the Persian king had died (his son married the lady in his stead), the Polos struck out overland and finally arrived in Venice in 1295 by way of Trebizond and Constantinople. A fairly well-attested tradition says that they were dressed in rags, and that their relatives would not acknowledge them until they opened the seams of their soiled garments and spilled the priceless jewels that were the fruit of their twenty-four-year absence. Marco was later captured at sea by the Genoese, archenemies of Venice, and it was as a prisoner in Genoa that he dictated his book to a fellow captive who took it down in French. He died in Venice, survived by his wife and three daughters—Fantina, Bellela, and Moreta. Christopher Columbus studied and annotated Marco's book in preparation for his journey of discovery which, he believed, would take him to East Asia.

P R O P A G A N D A . The term, denoting the dissemination, with a purpose, of doctrines or ideas, derives from the Vatican's Sacred Congregation for the Propaganda of the Faith (*de propaganda fide*—"concerning the faith to be spread"), an offspring of the Counter Reformation. The Latin verb *propagare* (used here in its gerundive form), means to set out shoots from which new plants will grow, hence, to increase or perpetuate a species. It also came to mean "extend." *Propagator,* "Extender of (Roman) Boundaries," was an epithet of Jupiter, Rome's supreme god. The term seemed well adapted to the notion of spreading the Christian message, in fulfillment of Jesus' command (Matt. 28:19), "Go ye therefore and teach all nations, baptizing them . . ." In 1622, Pope Gregory XV created the Congregation for the purpose of propagating Christianity in heathen countries. Run by a committee of cardinals, like other Vatican congregations, or ministries, it is charged with the training of missionaries and the supervision of Roman Catholic missions throughout the world. Its headquarters, at the corner of Piazza di Spagna and Via di Propaganda, is one of Rome's most elegant baroque palaces, designed by both Bernini and Borromini. In the nonreligious sense, "propaganda," as a noun, came into English usage toward the middle of the nineteenth century.

RAPHAEL (Raffaello Santi or Sanzio, 1483–1520). Italian painter and architect, born in Urbino, where the Santi house still stands. Raphael is one of the most admirable and pleasure-giving painters of the Renaissance. As if to compensate for his brief life span, the gods seem to have showered on him all the blessings a mortal might desire—grace and good looks, a rare capacity for love and friendship, fame, health, and wealth. His father, Giovanni Santi, a respected painter, whom he lost when he was eleven, was his first teacher. For several years, Raphael was apprenticed to Pietro Perugino (1445/50–1523) in Perugia, imitating that master's limpid colors and staid compositions. His *Betrothal of the Virgin* (Milan, Brera), though borrowed from his teacher's *Consignment of the Keys to Peter* in the Sistine Chapel, demonstrates how far he had surpassed him. After a formative sojourn in Florence (1504–08), where he studied the works of Leonardo and Michelangelo, assimilating some of their pictorial idiom, he moved on to Rome, perhaps invited by his influential friend Bramante. Renaissance art was heading toward its culmination at the court of Julius II, and the young provincial was commissioned by the Pope—who had a flair for spotting genius—to fresco the walls of his new Vatican apartment. (Julius had decided to move upstairs from the old Borgia suite, jinxed by Alexander VI's demonic spirit.) Of the four rooms (*stanze*) Raphael was given charge of, the first we enter—the Stanza dell'Incendio, named for a fresco of a conflagration—and the last, decorated with scenes from the life of Emperor Constantine, were painted, for the most part, by assistants. But the two middle rooms, done almost wholly by Raphael himself, rank with the most important achievements of

High Renaissance art. He started with the Stanza della Segnatura ("Signature Room," actually Julius's private library) in 1508, the year in which Michelangelo began the Sistine ceiling, and it is likely that the "program," here as well as there, was dictated by Platonic-minded humanists, probably under Julius's guidance. The two main frescoes of the room are known as the *School of Athens* and the *Disputa*. The former represents, against a lofty architectural background in Bramante's style, a gathering of Greek philosophers dominated by Plato and Aristotle. The prominent foreground figure of Heraclitus, the "Weeping Philosopher," is an afterthought. Raphael had seen the portion of the Sistine ceiling that was unveiled in 1511, and the sixth-century B.C. pessimist not only bears the features of Michelangelo, but is dressed as a stonecutter and painted in frank imitation of Michelangelo's manner—another sample of Raphael's chameleonic versatility. The so called *Disputa* is no "dispute," but, in the opinion of most scholars, a twofold glorification of the Holy Sacrament, showing, above, the celestial Church (symbolized by Apostles, martyrs, and the Trinity), and, below, the Church on earth (formed by its saints and theologians). Besides these august compositions, the room contains the paganizing fresco of *Parnassus,* ruled by a fiddling Apollo, and, in the ceiling roundel just above it, *Poetry*—a sweet, winged maiden dressed in white and blue, ensconced amidst pink cloudlets, holding a lyre and a book, dreaming away with open eyes. The next room, named for the temple robber, Heliodorus (*Eliodoro*)— who, in the principal fresco, is chased from the temple by a mounted messenger of God—also contains the *Mass of Bolsena* with its group of handsome Swiss Guards officers, and the night piece of the *Liberation of Peter from Prison.* Raphael strewed his frescoes with portraits. Julius II and his successor, Leo X, are depicted several times. Among the theologians, we spot Savonarola, executed as a heretic some thirteen years before on orders of Alexander VI, and, among the philosophers, Leonardo (in the guise of Plato), and Bramante and Raphael as themselves. As the fresco cycle progressed, the painter was in such demand that he farmed out more and more work to assistants, who used his designs with a good deal of leeway, among them Giulio Romano (c. 1499–1546), the Mannerist architect and painter. (The Vatican Loggias, known as "Raphael's Bible," were decorated, during the last years of his life, by no fewer than eight members of his studio.) Even so, the speed and quantity of his production is incredible. Within a few years, he worked on banker Agostino Chigi's Rome Villa and his sepulchral chapel at S. Maria del Popolo. He supervised the decoration of the private loggia and bathroom in the Vatican apartment of Cardinal Bibbiena. He painted the great triple portrait—a symphony in red—of Leo X and two cardinals (Florence, Uffizi) and the small portrait—a symphony in gray and black—of his friend Castiglione (Paris, Louvre), which Rembrandt (1606–69) vainly tried to buy at auction. All of his portraits, among them the *Veiled Lady* (*La Donna Velata*), thought to have been his great love (Florence, Pitti), are psychological studies, probing the sitter's character beneath the finely finished features. Raphael's inner growth is strikingly reflected in his series of Madonnas, which so endeared him to nineteenth-century Europe and America, and which still form the basis of his worldwide popularity. During his brief Florence period, he painted seventeen of them, including Holy Familes, which pose a girl mother and her lively child in ever-varied attitudes, frequently with the boy Baptist as Christ's playmate. Many of them are outdoor pieces, suffused with sunlight and with glimpses of Tuscan landscape in the background. As Raphael matured, so did his Virgins. One of the loveliest is the *Alba Madonna* (Wash., D.C., National Gallery), the first he painted in Rome—a grave-faced mother, filled with premonitions as she plays, seated on the grass, with the two children. His two most famous Madonnas, the *Madonna della Seggiola*—"of the Chair"—(c. 1515; Florence, Pitti) and the *Sistine Madonna* (c. 1513; Dresden, Gemäldegalerie), mark the climax of the evolution of the Madonna image from its dim beginnings in Rome's Catacombs. The former, composed within a circle twenty-eight inches across, with a young peasant mother and her round-limbed, tightly-held baby gazing serenely at the viewer, has been a universal favorite for many generations. The latter, a large canvas (104 × 77 in.), confronts us with a tall, wind-blown Virgin of heavenly beauty, cradling a solemn-faced, two-year-old boy as she walks toward us over pale clouds between S. Barbara and S. Sixtus. (The latter bears the features of Julius II, who had just died when Raphael created this work

[1513/14], and his tiara-topped sarcophagus, supporting two enchanting putti, is seen below.) Raphael's last large painting, the powerful *Transfiguration* (Vatican), was, at his funeral, placed at the head of his bier. Raphael's ripest contribution to the Grand Manner of the Renaissance is the set of ten cartoons—preparatory paintings—for tapestries to be hung in the Sistine Chapel. Illustrating the lives of Peter and Paul, they present us with a race of heroes moving with the dignity of tragic actors. At least five of them are almost entirely by Raphael's hand, the rest being painted by assistants after his designs and often finished by himself. Superlatives are the *Miraculous Draught of Fishes,* the *Healing of the Lame Man, Paul Preaching in Athens.* Among their details is a squiggly catch of fish from the Sea of Galilee. The cartoons were sent to Brussels for weaving, and Raphael may have seen the finished tapestries, before he died, hanging on the lower walls of the Sistine Chapel. They were briefly pawned, for the value of their gold and silver threads, after Leo X's death. During the Sack of Rome (1527), Isabella d'Este had the good sense to take some of them north with her as she fled. At least two of the tapestries were captured by Barbary pirates who carried them to Tunis; sold to the doge of Venice, they turned up later in Constantinople and, in 1554, were returned to the pope by the duke of Montmorency, constable of France. Meanwhile, the rest of the series, minus some bits and pieces, had been repurchased by the Vatican, we do not know where. Having acquired European fame, the hangings were used, for centuries, to decorate the route of the Corpus Christi procession through Rome. Napoleon removed them to Paris, along with many other works by Raphael, including the *Transfiguration* and the *Madonna della Seggiola.* They are now in the Vatican Museum. As for Raphael's cartoons, seven of them—all that was left—were acquired, presumably from Genoese traders, by the future king Charles I of England in 1623, and are on loan from the Royal Collection in London's Victoria and Albert Museum. Art historian John Shearman, the expert on the subject, calls them "the greatest set of paintings in England." In 1514, a year before Raphael started work on the cartoons, Pope Leo X, upon Bramante's deathbed recommendation, appointed him chief architect of S. Peter's. Shortly afterwards, he bestowed on him the title of Superintendent of

Antiquities for Rome and its Surroundings, a position giving him responsibility for all excavations and newly found works of ancient art, and deepening his interest in antiquarian research. He employed draftsmen in the south of Italy who sent him plans and measurements of Greek and Roman structures. In a report to Leo, dated 1518, he came out strongly for the preservation of ancient monuments. Of Raphael's architectural works, little besides the Chigi Chapel has survived. His major project was Villa Madama on the slope of Monte Mario, then outside Rome, commissioned by Pope Clement VII when still a cardinal. Raphael planned a sprawling complex in the style of Nero's Golden House, a union of art, residence, and nature. Arranged around a circular court, it was to include a theater, a hippodrome, stables for two hundred horses, a running stream, vineyards, woods, terraced gardens, and a grand stairway leading down into the valley. The work was directed by Antonio da Sangallo the Younger. Nearly all he had built of it went up in smoke during the Sack of Rome, among the few surviving remnants being an elegant, tripartite garden loggia. Restored, the Villa, a shrunken image of Raphael's grandiose design, was acquired by "Madama" Margaret of Austria, the natural daughter of the emperor Charles V. It now belongs to the Italian government. In Rome, Raphael, during the last four years of his life, was the idol of the papal court. No artist ever had enjoyed such princely status. Made rich by his work, an intimate of humanists and savants, he went around with a jaunty retinue of some fifty adulators and assistants—a curious contrast to the *terribilità* (or "awesomeness") of Michelangelo, who walked alone. No love was lost between the two, inasmuch as Raphael was a protégé of Michelangelo's enemy, Bramante. Still, Raphael paid his respects to him with his Michelangelesque frescoes of *Isaiah* (Rome, S. Agostino) and the *Sibyls* (Rome, S. Maria della Pace), and was heard to say on several occasions that he was thankful for living in the days of Michelangelo. Raphael's numerous love affairs often made him divide his time between his work and the lady of the hour. He scribbled love poems on drawings for his *Disputa.* The idea of wedlock did not appeal to him, however, and when Cardinal Bibbiena virtually forced him into an engagement with his niece, Maria, Raphael did not hurry the marriage. He died, unwived, aged thirty-seven, probably of malaria. He was laid to rest, as he had wished, in the Pantheon, in an antique sarcophagus of Greek marble, bearing a Latin epitaph by his friend Pietro Bembo.

RENAISSANCE. This French term, meaning "rebirth," is thought to have been first applied by Honoré Balzac in his novel, *Le bal de sceau* (1829), to the period following the Middle Ages in Italian art. While it has long been understood as a spontaneous upwelling of the Italian genius, scholars now view it as a more complex phenomenon, the coming-to-a-head of a slow evolutionary process. However that may be, something now did happen after 1400, and whether it was an explosion, or a mere culmination, it is the Renaissance, with its abundance of masterpieces, that first comes to our mind when we think of Italian art. The sheer quantity of talent compressed in a mere century-and-a-half is staggering. It includes names that are familiar throughout civilization— Botticelli, Leonardo, Michelangelo, Raphael, Titian, Cellini. Without being too arbitrary, we might pinpoint the dawn of the Renaissance in sculpture by the competition, in 1401, for the bronze doors of the Florence baptistery, won by Lorenzo Ghiberti; in painting, by Masaccio's frescoes at S. Maria del Carmine in Florence, begun about 1425; and, in architecture, by Brunelleschi's portico of the Florence Foundlings' Home, designed in 1419. Although the surge of new artistic energies was stimulated by the study of Roman ruins, coins, gems, and sarcophagi, and reinforced by the salvaging of antique statues long buried in the soil, the age set its own style, in which the classical element was used, refined, absorbed. The discovery of correct perspective and the knowledge of anatomy (Giotto still based his anatomy on the writings of the Arab physician and philosopher Avicenna, c. 980–1037), introduced a new realism in art. And acceptance of the pagan side of humanism vastly enlarged the artist's range. The nude became a subject fit for presentation, and the same hand might turn out Madonnas and

Venuses—all of them bathed in the same beauty. A general rejoicing in the mastery of form was in the air. The all-round man, skilled in the visual arts, in poetry, music, science, engineering—typified by Leonardo—was a Renaissance ideal. Great masters gladly turned their hand to the arrangement of festivities, masquerades, pageants, and theatrical performances, creating fantasies not meant to outlast the day. This burst of artistic activity was facilitated (or made possible) by the patronage of wealthy families, guilds, and, in particular, the princely courts of Italy—Ferrara, Mantua, Milan, Urbino, Naples, among others—which kept artists going with commissions. Late in the fifteenth century, the hub of the Renaissance shifted from Medicean Florence, where it was born, to papal Rome, where erudite and worldly popes presided over the Grand Manner of the High Renaissance. The Sack of Rome of 1527 and the Counter Reformation unleashed by the Council of Trent (1545–63) put an end to the enchantment, whose evanescent glory is summed up in Politian's tender little verse:

> Quando la rosa ogni sua foglia spande,
> Quando è più bella, quando è più gradita,
> Allora è buona a metter in ghirlande,
> Prima che sua bellezza sia fuggita:
> Sicché, fanciulle, mentre è più fiorita,
> Cogliam la bella rosa del giardino.

> When the rose spreads each of her petals,
> When she is loveliest, when she is most pleasing,
> Then is the time to weave her into garlands,
> Before her beauty escapes.
> So, girls, when she is in full bloom,
> Let's pluck the lovely rose of the garden.

RIENZO, Cola di (1313–54). Tribune and dictator; hero of a bloody episode during the papacy's residence in Avignon, where it had taken refuge from the political chaos of Rome. Left without proper authority, half-ruined by decay, the Eternal City was a scene of desolation, enlivened only by the internecine fighting of the noble clans of the Colonna and Orsini. In this grim setting, the idealistic, handsome son of a poor tavern keeper dreamt of restoring Rome to its old splendor. In 1343, he went to Avignon as an envoy of the Roman people to plead with Pope Clement VI for the return of the papacy. His plea went unheeded, but Cola, during his long stay in Avignon, became friendly with Petrarch, who shared his patriotic fervor. Back in Rome, with the rank of papal notary, he launched a feverish one-man crusade for the city's resurrection. In street-corner orations, he stormed against the nobles (who had killed his younger brother) and dwelled on the story and significance of ancient monuments, making the glory of Imperial Rome rise from the ruins. His popularity encouraged him to call a people's assembly on the Capitol, where he made a rousing speech and was hailed as lord of the city; a second meeting gave him dictatorial status and he chose the ancient title of tribune. Thus empowered, he organized a militia, kept the nobles in check, and restored order. Petrarch wrote to congratulate him. Dressed in gold-fringed robes of silk, the tribune rode through Rome on a white charger, escorted by a bodyguard of one hundred lancers. On feast days, a band with silver drums and trumpets went before him, and the standard of the city was held above his head. He proceeded mercilessly against enemies of the state, who were, regardless of their rank, publicly executed on the Capitol, or thrown into prison. Aristocrats were driven from their fortress-palaces. New taxes brought in welcome revenue. Highways were safe again, and farmers could, once more, raise crops without fear of raiders. Rienzo next dispatched envoys bearing silvered rods to various Italian states and cities, asking them to send delegates to a parliament that would set up a national federation; among the few acceptances was one from Florence. But Cola's drive for total power had aroused the pope's suspicion and antagonized the nobles to the point where he was soon involved in civil war with them. His heavy taxes and his ostentation began to alienate the common people. When rioting broke out, Cola left Rome and lived two years with poor Franciscans ("Spirituals") in the wilderness of the Abruzzi. His reign had lasted barely seven months. He next went to Prague, where he proposed Rome's deliverance to the Holy Roman emperor, Charles IV—only to be treated as an outlaw and escorted as a prisoner to Avignon. Rather than punish him, however, Pope Innocent VI, eager to secure his hold on Italy, sent Rienzo to Rome as "senator," in the company of the papal legate, Cardinal Albornoz. Their mandate was the restoration of papal authority. Cola was received with jubilation by the fickle populace; but his despotic measures—largely stemming from his lack of funds—soon turned the tide of public favor. This time, he lasted just ten weeks. A furious mob attacked the Capitol, clamoring for his death. Cola tried to address the people from the balcony, but was shouted down. When an arrow hit his hand, he hurriedly withdrew, removed his armor, slipped on a beggar's cloak, cut off his beard, and smeared his face with dirt. As he tried to escape, mingling with the assailants who had battered in the gate, his gold bracelets and purple stockings gave him away. At first, they faced their captive in cold silence, while Cola tried to stare them down. But when one of them pricked him with his sword, the others pounced, and tore him limb from limb. For two days, his mutilated, headless body hung from a nearby house, until, on orders of his enemies, the Colonna, it was burned on a bed of thistles. Was Cola mad? No doubt, the sudden taste of power had alienated the taverner's son from reality. People believed that he was aided in his exploits by a familiar spirit, named Fiorone, whom he kept in a bronze mirror. He was a visionary, to be sure, and might have done well as a poet—he did write reputable rhyme. Still, there was method in his madness, and his fling was not without results. The tyranny of the nobles was, if not broken, drastically reduced. By 1364, Rome seemed sufficiently safe for Pope Urban V to visit the city and start rebuilding it, and, in 1377, Gregory XI, last of the French popes, persuaded by St. Catherine of Siena, finally re-established the papacy in Rome. Like Petrarch, Rienzo was the herald of an age about to dawn. Ferdinand Gregorovius, the German historian (1821–91), calls him "the prophet of the Latin Renaissance . . . whose grandiose ideas of the independence and unity of Italy . . . were sufficient to outshine his political blunders and save his memory from darkness." Lord Byron (1788–1824) immortalized him in verse. Richard Wagner (1813–83) composed an opera about him. Today, a modest statue of the tribune, dating from 1887, identifies the spot where he was put to death, on the slope of the Capitol.

ROMANESQUE, A term used since c. 1820 for a phase in the evolution of structural design, in particular for a robust architectural style distinguished by the use of such Roman elements as vaults and rounded arches. Origins and duration of the Romanesque are hard to fix—its Early Christian and Carolingian predecessors gradually blended into it. It prevailed in Italy roughly between 1000 and 1250. Romanesque churches (secular buildings are relatively rare) are remarkable for their compactness, the mystical mood of their interiors and their pleasing proportions. The fire hazard inherent in the timber ceilings of early specimens—usually an open arrangement of beams and struts under the rafters of a gable roof—led to experiments with stone vaults. "Barrel" or "tunnel" vaults, common in ancient Rome, were used, at first with caution, in low and narrow sections of the church, since they require complicated centering and heavy buttresses. Ribbed cross-vaulting, known in the Moslem East from about 900 onward, was adopted toward the end of the eleventh century, permitting building on a more ambitious scale. The long, wide ceiling of the nave was divided into a number of compartments—square or oblong—each of which was intersected by two diagonal stone ribs, forming an x, which served as a skeletal armature for the four billowing triangles between them. Centering was needed chiefly for the ribs themselves, and the light wooden forms could be moved from section to section. The drawback of this innovation, which gave both strength and beauty to the ceiling, was that the thrust, or pressure, of the heavy ribs called for massive piers rather than slim columns between nave and aisles. In many churches, piers and columns alternate, with the former underpinning the main pressure points. Thick outer walls, broken only by small windows and often reinforced by buttresses, do the rest. Hence, the robustness, the closed and heavy look, of Romanesque interiors. Italian Romanesque was pioneered in Lombardy, the region around Milan named for the Lombards, a Germanic people that invaded Italy in the sixth century, penetrated deep into the South, and maintained a kingdom in the North for nearly two hundred years. Well before 1000, the gifted and imaginative Lombards first developed Romanesque forms and constituted teams of itinerant masons whose skills were passed on from one generation to the next. Even long after the disappearance of the Lombard Kingdom and the absorption of its people, a migrant builder was called a "Lombard." One of Italy's most impressive Romanesque churches, perhaps the prototype, is the Basilica of St. Ambrose (S. Ambrogio) in Milan, built, for the most part, shortly after 1100, though sections of it are older; its "Monk Tower" dates from the ninth century. The most spectacular Romanesque complex is the "Square of Miracles" in Pisa, with its well-spaced ensemble of cathedral, baptistery, Camposanto, and leaning tower. The church, sheathed with white marble horizontally striped in dark green, was begun in 1063 and completed by 1200. The free-standing circular baptistery was begun in 1152. And the 184.5-foot tower (it started to lean while it was abuilding) dates back to 1174; its superimposed open marble arcades, like those of the cathedral façade, are a Lombard touch. This handsome "Pisan Romanesque" spread, with variations, to nearby Lucca and much of northern Italy, as well as to the South. Other Romanesque masterpieces are the Church of S. Miniato al Monte in Florence, whose noble white-and-green façade dominates the verdant hillside to the city's south, and the cathedrals of Modena and Parma. Regional differences in Italy are so pronounced that it is sometimes difficult to speak of a single "style" of architecture. The cathedrals of Apulia (spur and heel of the Italian boot)—Bitonto, Troia, Ruvo, Trani—and the grand pilgrimage church of S. Nicola at Bari, display strong local accents, in which Lombard, Byzantine, and Norman influences fuse with native fantasy. Typical of the Romanesque are the rose window above the entrance; the portal whose two columns rest on stone lions; and the campanile—bell tower, from *campana* ("bell")—square or cylindrical, free-standing or attached, which first appeared, it is thought, in the ninth century. (The Middle Ages were an age of towers. Forests of them, reared by individual families as a refuge and a symbol of prestige, formed the skylines of walled cities. Between 1000 and 1300, Florence had 150 towers; Bologna, 180; and San Gimignano [in Tuscany], 48—thirteen of which still stand.) Bits of sculpture, often grotesque, enliven capitals, pulpits, portals, and façades of Romanesque churches with a bewildering variety of shapes: human figures, some done with no regard for proportion or anatomy and shown in bizarre postures; fabled monsters; swirling foliage; and playful abstractions. One individual emerges from the anonymous mass of artisans—Benedetto Antelami (which may not have been his name, c. 1150–c. 1230), who is believed to have been of Lombard origin; spent some time in Provence, southeastern France, where he would have learned much from the profusion of local sculpture; and worked chiefly in Parma. He is credited with the design of the octagonal baptistery there and with much of the sculptural decor it contains His most interesting piece is the marble relief of *Christ's Deposition from the Cross* in the cathedral. North of the Alps, Romanesque was dethroned, about 1150, by Gothic, a style that would be structurally inconceivable without the cross-ribbed vault. Gothic builders combined it with the pointed arch and vast storied stained glass windows to achieve a virtually wall-less, fragile-looking, magically lit interior—braced from the outside by flying buttresses, a Gothic invention. In Italy, the Gothic style, imported probably by French Cistercians, was mainly used by the Franciscans and Dominicans. But Gothic never felt at home in Italy, and even the most celebrated Gothic structures, such as S. Maria Novella in Florence, look ponderous compared to the light, transcendental beauty of their French models.

SACK OF ROME. Rome has been captured and sacked several times, notably by the Visigoths in A.D. 410, and by the Vandals in A.D. 455. But *the* Sack of Rome (*Sacco di Roma*) refers to the catastrophe of 1527. A byplay of the rivalry between

Emperor Charles V and the French king, Francis I, it was brought on by a junction of Imperial (mainly Spanish) troops—which had defeated Francis at Pavia and captured Milan—and 12,000 unpaid Lutheran mercenaries whose aim was to seize Rome, strip it of gold and jewels, and "hang the pope." Ably captained by Charles de Bourbon, who had defected from the French to the Imperial side, this host of 40,000 rough-and-ready fortune hunters made its first assault on the sixth of May. The popular Bourbon was killed by a shot presumably fired by Benvenuto Cellini ("Ah, Notre Dame, je suis mort!"). Stung by his death, the attackers scaled the walls and swept into the ill-defended city, slaughtering the Swiss guards who resisted bravely. Pope Clement VII, irresolute nephew of Lorenzo the Magnificent, who had unwisely sided with the French, fled to the Vatican fortress, Castel Sant'Angelo, poorly accoutered for a siege. At midnight, the invaders broke ranks to wreak apocalyptic horror on the city. Houses and palaces were ransacked for valuables—rich furniture, silks, paintings, gold, pearls, precious stones—and systematically burned down. People were set upon and, under savage torture, forced to betray their hidden treasures. Women of every age were raped and killed. Nuns were violated in their convents. Noble ladies were dragged naked through the streets. Horses were stabled in churches. Soldiers and prostitutes feasted at altars, drinking from golden chalices. A priest was told to give communion to a kneeling ass, and killed when he refused. Tombs were pried open in a mad treasure hunt. At dawn, 6,000 corpses littered the streets. Some Romans were able to buy their lives with gold. Others committed suicide. The orgy of destruction raged, unchecked, for a whole week. Many had fled, others were hiding in ruins. Rome was a smoking, reeking, body-strewn Gehenna. The plague descended on her prostrate form, killing friend and foe alike, and the invaders withdrew to the salubrious countryside—to return in the autumn for another massacre. The pope, having raised the first installment of a ransom, was finally allowed to leave, disguised and penniless, for Orvieto. By the time the horror ended, Rome was broken in body and in spirit, its population of 90,000 reduced to 32,000, two out of three houses destroyed.

—————✦————

SAINTS AND RELICS. Saints, saints, saints! A "cloud of witnesses," as St. Paul calls them, surrounds the traveler in Italy. Churches and altars bear their names, their statues decorate façades and piazzas, their feast days crowd the calendar. How many saints are there? The question is just as unanswerable as the old conundrum, "How many angels can dance on the head of a pin?" The "canon," or official roll, to which Rome adds a saint from time to time by "canonizing" him or her, is not all-inclusive. Churchmen say that a total of 12,000 saints is a fair guess, not counting those of whose existence the Church knows nothing and whom it honors on All Saints' Day. The custom of revering some of their dead brethren took root among early Christians in the days of persecution; a Christian killed for his faith was called a martyr ("witness") and the survivors gathered round his tomb, asking the dead to pray for them in heaven. Soon, wherever a Christian died in the "odor of sanctity," a cult sprang up, his tomb became the goal of pilgrims, and local bishops often made the cult official by proclaiming the defunct a "saint." Christendom stands divided on the matter of saints. Protestants do not invoke or venerate them, but they occasionally look at them with friendly feelings. Martin Luther conceded that saints "may pray for us on earth, perhaps in heaven, too," and that we might well "honor, love, and thank them." Nor can non-Catholics abstract them from their culture. Towns and churches perpetuate their memory, legends of their lives have inspired masterpieces by great artists, and boys and girls of every denomination answer to such names as George and James, Catherine and Teresa. For Catholics, *worship* is reserved for Father, Son, and Holy Ghost; but the troubled individual may ask a saint to *intercede* for him or her with God. This time-honored tradition is encouraged and kept up-to-date by Rome. The process, as a rule, starts as a ground swell. Something tells people that a saint has walked among them. Flowers and prayers by the tomb mark the beginnings of a private cult. A group of local stalwarts forms a committee sponsoring the "cause," and the local bishop sends the file to Rome. Only the pope may confer sainthood, and the rules for saint-making form one of the most fascinating aspects of the Vatican's backstage machinery. Laid down by Benedict XIV (1740–58), the "Scholars' Pope," they provide for two distinct phases—Beatification (the candidate is declared "Blessed") and Canonization ("Saint"). No one may be sainted before he is beatified. Each phase requires at least two miracles worked by the candidate *after his death*—a requirement which is occasionally waived. The candidate's entire life is investigated, under a heavy veil of secrecy, by the Vatican's Sacred Congregation for the Causes of the Saints, a board of cardinals whose modern offices face the pope's private quarters across St. Peter's Square. Hundreds of witnesses may be interviewed. The defunct's private correspondence is scrutinized. At present, some 1,250 causes are pending, many of them promoted by religious orders; no more than one in twenty is expected to bear fruit. The most frequent reason for failure is the successful intervention of that potent personage, the promotor general of the faith, better known as the "Devil's Advocate." His job is to disqualify the candidate. A priest himself, he has an overriding interest in seeing a true saint acknowledged—he does his carping, as it were, despite his better self. He may allege that the candidate had an unsaintly temper, or showed himself in other ways unworthy. In the case of Frances Xavier Cabrini (1850–1917), the Devil's Advocate observed that she had had too keen a sense of money, and that her real estate deals betrayed considerable cunning. "You can't fool Mother Cabrini," was the word around Chicago. In 1946, no doubt to the Devil's Advocate's great satisfaction, the immigrant from Italy became the United States' first saint. The canonization, at St. Peter's, is one of the most splendid rituals the Church can offer, with the pope himself officiating at the high altar, flanked by his cardinals in flaming red. In 1969, the Vatican updated its list of saints, reducing "phantom saints" without a proven flesh-and-blood reality behind them to optional or local status—meaning that the observance of their feast days is no longer obligatory throughout the Catholic world. Among those "purged" were some beloved people's saints, including Christopher, protector of travelers; Valentine, the lovers' friend; and Gennaro (Januarius), patron of Naples, whose dried blood, preserved in a glass phial, liquefies several times a year. Survivors of the purge are Nicholas of Bari, our Santa Claus; Cecily, or Cecilia, patroness of music; and Anthony of Padua (1195–1231), whose statue, holding the Infant Jesus, is seen in many churches, and whose aid is invoked in trying to find a lost object. Closely linked with the cult of saints is that of relics. Flourishing in the twilight zone between religious faith and superstition, they draw their magic from the age old concept that something of the power and the grace of the defunct will pass, through them, to the believer. Throughout the Middle Ages, relics helped make the map of Europe, as pilgrimage routes, trodden by thousands, crisscrossed the continent, engendering a noisy world of markets, inns, and fairs. As the Crusaders combed the East for pious souvenirs, skeptics observed that they were turning up enough spines from Jesus' crown of thorns to build a hedgerow. Twelve heads and sixty fingers of St. John the Baptist were at one time revered in various churches. Non-Catholics reject the cult of relics. Calvin, especially, inveighed against it. And the Thirty-nine Articles of the Church of England regard it as "grounded upon no warranty of Scripture, but rather repugnant to the Word of God." The Catholic position is that relics do not touch the doctrine, and that the individual is free to choose between belief and disbelief. True, any new Catholic church still needs the relic of a saint embedded in its altar before it may be consecrated, and the Vatican keeps a supply of relics, many of them tiny bone fragments, for this purpose. Yet, Rome recently disavowed some of its most illustrious mementos. The *Veronica*, a kerchief said to have been offered by a kindly woman to Jesus on his way to Calvary and returned to her with the imprint of his features, is now admitted to be a mere painting. St. Peter's wood-and-ivory bishop's throne, mounted by Bernini in St. Peter's' apse, has been officially declared a work of the ninth century. And the Holy Shroud of Turin, a length of cloth marked with the faint, rust-colored outlines of a crucified man, believed to be the winding sheet of Christ, has come under considerable doubt.

Some Saints Recurring in Italian Art. (Among major sources for their iconography, besides the Bible and the Apocrypha, is Jacopo da Voragine's—c. 1230–c. 1298—*Golden Legend,* one of the most widely read books of the Middle Ages, containing popular versions of the lives of saints.)

Anthony the Abbot—*Antonio Abate*—(c. 251–356), renowned Egyptian hermit and holy man; father of Christian monachism. He is usually presented as a bearded little monk being victimized by the Devil. His *Life* by St. Athanasius, bishop of Alexandria and Doctor of the Church, forty-five years his junior, was translated into many languages and has been called early Christianity's best seller. The son of Christians, Anthony learned to read and write, but had no further education. As a young man, he gave his inheritance to the poor and went into seclusion to devote himself to prayer and austerity. He later retired to an abandoned tomb deep in the desert, where he lived on water, bread, and dates. He was not the first Egyptian hermit; a few Christians had already yielded to the urge to withdraw from the world—a custom practiced from time immemorial in the Far East and India. But while some of these early Christian hermits were ascetical fanatics, given to extreme mortification, Anthony had an admirably balanced mind and impressed all who met him with his urbanity, serenity, and self-possession. A charismatic aura seemed to surround him. The Devil did not like this. Time and again, he assailed Anthony, now taking on the guise of seductive women, now that of monstrous beasts—wolves, lions, bears, serpents, scorpions—threatening and tormenting him. Once, he was beaten senseless by a gang of demons; the man who came to bring him bread took him for dead. "Where wast thou, oh Lord?" Anthony asked in agony when he came to. "I was there, watching," was God's cool answer. "Because you stood your ground, I shall always help you, and make your name known everywhere." Aged thirty-five, Anthony took up what he hoped would be his final abode in some deserted ruins on a mountain top. However, as many pious Christians wished to emulate him and receive his spiritual instruction, he reluctantly heeded their plea and, after nineteen years of solitude, left his retreat and founded a monastery in the plains—probably no more than a scattering of huts. Its only access was across a crocodile-infested canal which the saint often waded. For some years, he roamed the country, founding small monasteries up and down the Nile. (Because these primitive establishments still lacked a written rule and an organized communal life, some scholars view a younger Egyptian, Pachomius [c. 290–c. 346], whose monasteries and nunneries did meet these prerequisites, as the true founder of organized monasticism. Monkdom was brought to Italy by St. Athanasius in 340, while the Egyptian parent institutions withered after the Arab conquest in the seventh century.) Anthony's fame, meanwhile, had spread throughout the Eastern Mediterranean. The emperor Constantine and his two sons wrote him a letter, begging to be remembered in his prayers. In 355, Anthony was persuaded to go to Alexandria, then the Western world's first city after Rome, where he is said to have worked many miracles, and where he preached against the Arian heretics who denied the full divinity of Christ. He frequently debated, through interpreters—since he spoke only Coptic, the Egyptian language—with prominent pagan philosophers. They were pleased with his humble dignity, found his speech "flavored with divine salt," and came away amazed at having encountered such wisdom in a mere *idiotes,* an unlearned fellow. Asked how he could live without books, Anthony answered that all nature was his book. Dismayed by all these time-consuming contacts—"a monk out of his solitude is a fish out of water"—he now forever turned his back on them, retiring to a hut atop a hill near the Red Sea. In his old age, two aides looked after him, keeping unwanted visitors away. He was, to the last, in excellent health, not having lost a single tooth, his eyes undimmed, his mental faculties as keen as ever. He is believed to have died at the age of 105, having embraced all those who had come to bid farewell to him, and leaving his sheepskin to St. Athanasius. The Devil had long since given up.

Catherine of Alexandria. Though she may never have existed, her medieval cult swept the Christian world, and she remains one of the most revered of women saints. (Two Russian empresses changed their Christian names to hers.) Legend presents her as a beautiful, erudite, aristocratic maiden of fourth-century Alexandria, Egypt. Having inveighed against pagan idolatry, she was condemned to martyrdom on a spiked wheel—the "Catherine wheel," her attribute—which broke miraculously at her touch. She was finally beheaded. Her body was carried by angels to the highest mountain top in Sinai, 8,651-foot Mt. Catherine, where a monk found it after a prophetic dream. She was buried in the nearby Greek Orthodox monastery still known as St. Catherine's. She is often shown in paintings receiving a mystical wedding ring from the Infant Christ. (Her namesake, Catherine of Siena [c. 1347–80], a Dominican lay sister, promoted the return of the papacy from Avignon to Rome.)

Jerome, Doctor of the Church (c. 342–420), one of the Four Latin Fathers of the Church, the others being Ambrose, Augustine, and Gregory the Great. He was born near Aquileia, in northeastern Italy or Dalmatia. Although he was brought up a Christian, his love of Latin culture posed a problem for his faith. "Thou art a Ciceronian, not a Christian!" a judging Christ told him in a terrifying vision. Penitent, he spent two to four years in a cave near Chalcis, in the Syrian desert, "among scorpions and wild beasts," praying, meditating, and learning Hebrew. "In that remote and stony desert," he later wrote, "I often thought myself drawn into the pleasures of life in Rome . . . looking at dancing girls as if I were in their midst. In my mortified body, desire was alive." (Even in this remoteness, he had his books with him and managed to write and receive letters.) Later, in Rome, Jerome served as secretary to Pope Damasus (366–84), who commissioned him to translate the Bible into Latin. The task was to take more than twenty years. Besides direct translations from the Hebrew and Greek texts, it also meant revising and coordinating pre-existing Latin renderings, all more or less corrupt. After Damasus's death, Jerome returned to the Middle East followed by a group of pious women whom he had tutored while in Rome. They built a convent and a school in Bethlehem, where Jerome taught Latin and finished his Bible, known since the thirteenth century as the *Vulgate* (from Lat. *vulgus,* "the common people"). Irascible and quarrelsome, Jerome had a peculiar talent for making enemies. He was involved in numerous disputes, both personal and doctrinal. His letters bristle with barbs. He referred to one opponent's book as "vomit" and said of another, who had died, that he had "belched forth" his spirit. Other hermits living near him in the desert, with their matted hair and filthy clothes, were "arrogant hypocrites." His prickly temper notwithstanding, he was the greatest scholar of the early Church. Painters like to portray him seminude in the wilderness, with a skull before him and a stone with which to beat his breast, or, in a richly furnished study, every inch the savant, translating the Good Book. As a figure in a *Sacra Conversazione* ("Sacred Conversation," a type of altarpiece showing the Madonna flanked by saints), he is often presented as a cardinal, a dignity he never held. His attribute is a tame lion, which, legend says, he freed from a thorn caught in his paw—more likely the result of an assimilation of Jerome to Mark.

John the Baptist, the wild man of the desert, last of the Prophets, forerunner of Christ. His mother, Elizabeth, and her kinswoman, the Virgin Mary, were with child at the same time— their "Visitation," or meeting, is the subject of many paintings. Artistic license makes John Jesus' childhood playmate in Madonna paintings. John grew up to be an itinerant preacher, braving the sun and winds of the Palestinian desert, feeding on locusts and wild honey. He may have been a temporary follower of the Essenes, the Jewish sect to which we owe the Dead Sea Scrolls. Haranguing crowds that came to hear him—"O generation of vipers!"—he heralded Him "that cometh from above. . . . the Lamb of God, which taketh away the sin of the world." Asked, "Who art thou?", he replied, "I am the voice of one crying in the wilderness." His baptism of Jesus in the Jordan River is a favorite subject of artists. His bloody end has yielded a variety of compositions ranging from the seductive dance of Salome (King Herod's stepdaughter) at the king's birthday feast, to John's execution on Queen Herodias's prompting in the dungeon beneath the banqueting hall—and to his cutoff head on a silver platter. (Not to be confused with John "the Divine," the young "disciple whom Jesus loved," the presumed author of the fourth gospel and the Apocalypse, who is usually shown "leaning on Jesus' bosom" at the Last Supper. His attribute as one of the Four Evangelists is the eagle.)

Mark. Popular belief identifies the Evangelist with John Mark, who accompanied his cousin Barnabas and Paul, Apostle of the Gentiles (whose attribute is the sword with which he was beheaded), on their first missionary journey, and left them after a quarrel to return to Jerusalem. Scholars believe his Gospel to be the oldest of the four, and some surmise that it is largely based on Peter's eyewitness account of Jesus' ministry and passion. Perhaps because of his vigorous style and his emphasis on action rather than on talk, Mark is often portrayed as a particularly manly figure. According to tradition, he served as bishop of the Christian Church in Alexandria, Egypt, and died a martyr there. In 828, Venetian seafarers stole his remains and brought them to Venice, where a cupolaed Byzantine basilica—since 1807, St. Mark's Cathedral—was built in various stages to enshrine them. Mark is the patron saint of Venice, and his attribute, the lion, is the official emblem of the city.

Mary Magdalene (Mary of Magdala, a village near Capernaum on the Sea of Galilee). Confusion blurs the figure of this saint. The Gospels mention her as a woman whom Christ healed and "out of whom went seven devils." She was present at the Cross, and she came to the empty tomb. Jesus appeared to her after his Resurrection in the guise of a gardener. Beyond that, we are on shifting ground. The Magdalene has been identified with the unnamed woman "which was a sinner," who washed Christ's feet with her tears in Simon's house, wiped them with her hair, and anointed them with the ointment which she carried in an alabaster box; whereupon Christ absolved her of her sins, "for she loved much." To complicate things further, an old tradition also identifies her with Mary, sister of Martha, who anointed Jesus' feet "with a pound of spikenard, very costly," to Judas's dismay. Are we confronted with three women, or merely one? Italian art considers her one person, and she is often represented as the sinner doing tearful penance in a cave; prostrate at the foot of the Cross, her blond hair flowing over her shoulders; or, in the garden by the Sepulchre, being told *noli me tangere* ("touch me not") by the risen Lord. Standing with other saints in a *Sacra Conversazione,* she is usually identified by her ointment jar.

Nicholas, fourth-century Bishop of Myra, a seaport in southern Asia Minor—the modern Demre, Turkey—has long enjoyed wide popularity. Thousands of churches throughout Christendom are dedicated in his name. In order to visit fishing hamlets in his diocese, the bishop had to travel by boat, and he lives on today as the mariners' saint, who can save vessels from shipwreck and bring drowned sailors back to life. Mediterranean fishing crews still parade his picture around the deck in case of danger. But it is mostly as a children's saint that Nicholas is famous. The best-known story about him concerns a man who was too poor to provide dowries for his three pretty daughters, and was faced with the desperate decision to sell them into prostitution. But the good bishop stole up to his house one night and threw three fistfuls of gold coins—or, three clumps of gold—into the girls' bedroom through the window, enough for three rich dowries. Many miracles were attributed to Nicholas after his death. In 1087, some fifty men set out in three ships from the southern Italian port of Bari, which was then trading briskly with the Orient, and took the bishop's bones back to their home port, where they were received with jubilation. A white Romanesque basilica was raised on Bari's waterfront to house the saint, and a popular festival, mobilizing hundreds of gaily decorated boats, is held in that port every ninth of May in memory of his arrival. Gradually, St. Nicholas, via the Dutch *Sinterklaas,* became Santa Claus, or Father Christmas. Nicholas's attribute is three golden balls, and he is often painted in the act of tossing them into the chamber of the sleeping maidens.

Peter Martyr (c. 1205–52). The "Saint of the Inquisition." His parents were Cathars, members of a heretical sect holding the dualistic view that goodness was to be found only in the spiritual realm, and that the visible world was the creation of the Evil Principle. Nevertheless, Peter was sent to a Catholic school. After studying at Bologna university, he joined the young Dominican Order, the scourge of heretics, receiving the black-and-white habit from its founder, St. Dominic (1170–1221), himself. He preached with extraordinary eloquence throughout heresy-infested Lombardy, bringing many Cathars back into the fold. Credited with miraculous powers, he was greeted by expectant crowds wherever he appeared. Pope Gregory IX (1227–41), who instituted the papal Inquisition, appointed him Inquisitor for most of northern Italy. Peter preferred recantation and forgiveness to punishment. However, the inevitable cruelty that went with his office created widespread hatred. (Konrad of Marburg, Inquisitor for Germany, was murdered in 1233. Robert le Bougre, Inquisitor for France, escaped an attempt on his life, and was dismissed for extreme brutality and jailed in 1239.) One April day, as Peter walked with another Dominican through a woods north of Milan, he was set upon by two avenging assassins, one of whom split his skull with a sharp weapon. He is said to have dipped his finger into his own blood and written the words *Credo in Deum* ("I believe in God") on the ground before a second blow finished him. His wounded companion got away, to die a few days later. The murderer fled to safety, repented, and later joined the Dominican Order as a lay brother. Peter was canonized the year after his death by Pope Innocent IV, who authorized the use of the rack on heretics. The ambush in the woods was the subject of a dramatic painting by Titian at Ss. Giovanni e Paolo in Venice, destroyed in a fire in 1867; a copy survives. Peter is usually portrayed with a sword, knife, or hatchet buried in his skull.

Sebastian. Little is known about this Christian martyr so popular with painters of the Renaissance. He is thought to have been born at Narbonne (in Gaul), and raised in Milan, where he was venerated before A.D. 400. According to legend, he joined the army in order to comfort persecuted Christian soldiers and keep them from wavering in their faith, and became an officer in the Imperial guard. When he was found out, the emperor Diocletian (284–305) made him a living target for his Mauretanian archers. Left for dead, Sebastian was nursed back to health by the widow of another martyr, Irene, and went straight to the palace to upbraid the emperor—who had him clubbed to death. He was buried on the Appian Way—the great funerary highway leading southeast from Rome—in the catacombs of the fourth-century basilica that bears his name. He is usually depicted seminude, with arrows lodged in his body.

SAVONAROLA, Fra Girolamo (1452–98). Dominican friar, Catholic reformer, martyr. A native of Ferrara, he developed an early distaste for that city's courtly life, and, at the age of twenty-three, joined the Dominican Order at Bologna. His spreading fame as an ascetic, a thinker, and a preacher, led to his election as prior of the Convent of St. Mark in Florence, giving him a platform for his crusade against the corruption of the clergy and the decay of public morals. He had the face, the strength, and the convictions of the true fanatic. His sermons from the cathedral pulpit drew large crowds and—combined with a gift of prophecy—made him the apostle of the masses. As leader of the party known as the *Piagnoni* ("Weepers"), he drove the Medici from Florence in 1494 and assumed power as the city's dictator. During three years of uncontested rule, he turned gay, art-loving Florence into a puritan City of God where ladies wore drab attire, men gave alms, youths cut their hair and went to church, and taverns closed. Though citizens were encouraged to spy on one another, Florence experienced a fairer government than it had known under the Medici. As Fra Girolamo continued to denounce, with growing vehemence, the immorality and worldliness of the high clergy, he set himself on a collision course with its licentious head, Pope Alexander VI (Borgia). When he attacked the pontiff and his family, Alexander slyly invited him to Rome; Girolamo pleaded sickness. The bewildered Pope then forbade him to preach, ordered him out of Florence, offered him a cardinal's hat. Nothing availed. In 1497, the Florentines made an impressive bonfire of "vanities"—jewelry, perfumes, mirrors, lutes, ladies' hats, and "immoral" books and paintings. The same year saw the first anti-Savonarola riots, and his excommunication by the pope. Behind the local drama lay a larger conflict. France's King Charles VIII, who had invaded Italy in order to claim Naples for the French, was opposed by a league between the pope and Milan that would have been immensely strengthened by the adherence of Florence. As Savonarola refused to get politically entangled, he had to be removed. The pope found willing allies in members of the Florentine upper class, shorn of its influence by Savonarola's party. Calling themselves the *Arrabbiati* (the "Angry Ones"), they gained support from growing discontent. A mob manipulated by aristocrats stormed Savonarola's convent. Officers of the law arrested him, setting in motion the appalling sequence of trials, tortures, "confessions," and his condemnation by two papal commissioners for heresy and sedition. On 23 May 1498, he and two dedicated fellow friars were first hanged, then burned, in Florence's Piazza della Signoria. Unlike Martin Luther twenty years after him, Savonarola did not attack the institution of the papacy itself. He violated no Catholic dogma and, having received papal absolution, died in the Catholic faith. His was, essentially, a medieval mind, the very antithesis of the spirit of the Renaissance, whose pagan overtones he never ceased to censure. "Plato and Aristotle sit in Hell!" Although he could not stop what Italy had launched upon the world, his message permanently blighted many joyous hearts, among them that of Botticelli, whose late paintings reflect the friar's spell. The quest for Fra Girolamo's rehabilitation began almost as soon as his ashes had been thrown into the Arno. "I was misinformed," said Alexander VI; "I would have gladly canonized him," Julius II. Many prominent Catholics, including saints like Philip Neri, revered him as a saint, and he is often called *Beatus* ("Blessed"). A memorial plaque in the piazza hallows the spot where he was put to death.

———————<⟨◆⟩>———————

SCULPTURE BEFORE MICHELANGELO.

Italy docs not deny a rich French heritage in the field of sculpture. But how the impulse that called forth statues and reliefs at Notre Dame in Paris, Chartres, Rheims, Amiens reached Italy remains a mystery. Did teams of French stonemasons journey south and teach Italians how to do it? Did Giovanni Pisano, one of Italy's great thirteenth-century sculptors, travel to France, as some scholars suggest? There is no evidence of such direct transmission. More likely, portable French objects, such as small ivories and illuminated books, were brought to Italy, where they found a receptive artisan class. Under the Holy Roman emperor, Frederick II (1194–1250)—French-Norman on his mother's side—stone sculpture in the round appeared in southern Italy, his favorite domain. Impressive fragments dating from the late 1230s at the museum of Capua, twenty-four miles north of Naples, show the classical serenity of French early Gothic statues. A similar passion for classic forms was the motive force behind the burst of sculptural activity in Pisa, which, starting with Nicola Pisano (c. 1220–c. 1283), made that rich Tuscan city the center of the plastic arts in Italy for over a century. Referred to in some documents as Nicola d'Apulia, the founding father of the Pisan school is thought to have been trained in Frederick's workshops and to have brought with him the seeds of the artistic flowering of the South. He stands at the beginning of the path that leads to Donatello and Michelangelo. His first great work, the hexagonal marble pulpit in the Pisan baptistery, is crowded with finely wrought reliefs illustrating the New Testament. Here, and in his pulpit in the Cathedral of Siena, such disparate currents as Romanesque sculpture, the court art of the South, and French Gothic blend into a new style. Nicola borrowed from antique prototypes which he had close at hand, translating them into a Christian imagery. The Virgin of his Pisan pulpit's *Adoration of the Magi* is the twin of Phaedra on the Roman "Hippolytus" sarcophagus still to be seen in Pisa's *Camposanto* (the old cemetery). His principal collaborators were his son, Giovanni (c. 1250–c. 1315), and Arnolfo di Cambio (c. 1245–1302), who were to spread his art through much of Italy. Giovanni, who infused his figures with a strong individualism, is best known for his design, and sculptural decoration, of the front of Siena cathedral, Italy's first Gothic cathedral façade. His noble statues of Hebrew prophets and Greek thinkers, damaged by long exposure to the elements, have been taken down, and may be studied close-up in the Siena cathedral museum. Arnolfo, active in Florence and Rome, endowed his figures with a monumental simplicity which strongly influenced the young Giotto. Outstanding samples of his art are the portrait statues of Charles I of Anjou (Rome, Capitoline Museum) and of Pope Boniface VIII (Florence, Opera del Duomo), as well as a portion of the latter's tomb in the grottoes of St. Peter's. (As an architect, Arnolfo is credited, somewhat tenuously, with the designs for Florence cathedral and the Palazzo Vecchio.) With Andrea Pisano (c. 1290–c. 1349), apprenticed in Giovanni's workshop, and Andrea's son, Nino, whose sweet Madonnas are in the French taste, the Pisan impetus spent itself. The center of sculptural activity now moved to Florence, fifty miles up the Arno, where a new line of geniuses took over. In 1401, the Calimala, one of Florence's four major guilds, grouping importers and dyers of fine cloth, held a competition for a new set of bronze doors for the Baptistery of S. Giovanni— beloved by Florentines and sung by Dante—to complement the doors in the main entrance made by Andrea Pisano some seventy years earlier. Among the seven sculptors selected from the numerous applicants were Filippo Brunelleschi (1377–1446), and Jacopo della Quercia (1371–1438), who would later create the lovely fountain in the Campo at Siena and the main door of S. Petronio at Bologna. (Vasari to the contrary, Donatello did not compete, being just fifteen years old at the time.) Each candidate was given a year, all expenses paid, to submit a sample relief. The finished panels were exhibited, and the jury's decision was treated as a historic event—which it turned out to be. Young Lorenzo Ghiberti (1378–1455), trained as a goldsmith, was the winner. He was taking on a tricky task. Florentines had little experience with the "lost wax" process of casting bronze, known since antiquity, by which a thin layer of wax is sandwiched between the plaster core, or model, of the sculpture and its enfolding mold; the wax is melted and replaced by the hot molten bronze. Some of Italy's medieval bronze doors were cast in Constantinople, and Andrea Pisano's baptistery doors were cast in Florence by experts from Venice, where the technique was practiced with great skill by bell founders. Ghiberti, who had cast small bronzes in the goldsmith's shop of his stepfather, set up Florence's first bronze foundry, the largest in Italy, which was to remain in use for more than 150 years. Assisted by a hand-picked team which included Donatello, he spent twenty-one years making the two-wing doors consisting of a total of twenty-eight relief panels, twenty of them depicting scenes from the New Testament. So handsome were these doors, their Gothic figures of such grace and beauty, that they brought him instant fame. Among a rash of new commissions was one from Pope Eugene IV for a gold miter adorned with 5.5 pounds of pearls. The cloth merchants now asked him for another, even better, set of baptistery doors (the octagonal building having three entrances). Some twenty-five years later, he presented them with a masterpiece. Illustrating scenes from the Old Testament on ten large panels, the new doors were alive with foreground figures modeled almost in the round, set off by delicate, receding architectural and landscape backgrounds. Though not quite free of Gothic memories, they breathe the air of the young Renaissance. Brunelleschi, Masolino, Filarete (creator of the bronze doors of St. Peter's), Paolo Uccello, Antonio Pollaiuolo took pride in helping with the polishing of the cast panels. Finished in 1452, the doors were placed in the baptistery's main entrance facing the cathedral, while Pisano's doors, by then old-fashioned, were relegated to their present station in the south entrance. Michelangelo later pronounced Ghiberti's second doors worthy of serving as the Gates of Paradise—which is what Florentines still call them. Ghiberti had given some forty-five years of his life to the two sets, forming in the process a whole generation of artists. Himself a Renaissance man, he collected antique sculptures, and wrote a book—the *Commentaries*—containing a history of ancient art and an account of medieval painting in Italy. He was elected a member of the Florence Signoria (the city council) and died, much honored, three years after the installation of the

"Gates of Paradise." Of his pupils, Donato Bardi, known as Donatello (1386–1466), carried the sculptor's art to new heights. Though he, too, was inspired by antiquity (his early trip to Rome with Brunelleschi may be a Vasari fable), he freed himself from its restraining canon, just as he gradually shed the Gothic vestiges still clinging to his early works. Having grown up in the dusty, noisy workshops of the Florence cathedral builders, he remained a man of frugal tastes, caring little about clothes and food. His figures show a reckless freedom and manifest a human dignity, an inner strength, that mark a revolution in the plastic arts. His first great statue, the taller-than-life marble *St. George,* made for the outside of the Florence guild church, Orsanmichele (since replaced by a bronze copy, the original having been moved to the Bargello), stands erect, legs wide apart, ready to take on the world, let alone dragons. The same force flows from the nude bronze *David* (Florence, Bargello), who moodily looks down on Goliath's severed head. An almost frightening expressiveness marks the marble figure of the *Prophet Habakkuk* (Florence, Opera del Duomo) made for the Campanile of Florence cathedral, whose haggard face is the image of prophetic grief: "O Lord, how long shall I cry, and thou wilt not hear!" For contrast, there is, in the same museum, the playful *Cantoria* (Choir Gallery), once in the cathedral, showing frolicking, gamboling putti enacting Dionysiac rites, high on sacred wine. In 1443, Donato moved to Padua—some say, as a result of a quarrel with Brunelleschi—where he created the reliefs and statues for the high altar of the Basilica of S. Antonio (locally, *il Santo* ["the Saint"]), as well as his outstanding work, the equestrian bronze monument of the condottiere, Erasmo da Narni, called *Gattamelata,* commissioned by the warrior's son and widow. It represents the famed commander in a posture of heroic calm, marshaling unseen troops with a wave of his staff. Without it, Verrocchio's *Colleoni* in Venice, some thirty-five years its junior, might not have been attempted. (The copper and tin required for the casting of the *Gattamelata* were shipped to Padua from Venice.) Donato's ten-year stay in Padua decisively affected the artistic fate of northern Italy, replacing its cherished Gothic tradition with the forms and the ideas of the Renaissance. Padua itself became Italy's leading center for small, portable bronzes, turned out by such masters as Andrea Briosco, called "il Riccio" (c. 1470–1532) that have been prized collector's items ever since. It was after his return to Florence that Donato, aged about seventy, fashioned the bronze group of *Judith and Holofernes*—with Judith seemingly aghast at her own deed—which was placed in front of Palazzo Vecchio, and later still, the two pulpits of the Medici family Church of S. Lorenzo, with the intense dramatic power of their bronze reliefs. It was said of Donatello that everything about him was simple, except his art. When his friend and sponsor, Cosimo the Elder de' Medici, sent him a new suit to replace his shabby clothes, he wore it once or twice, then sent it back because it was "too fancy." He kept his money in a basket suspended from the ceiling, allowing friends and pupils to take whatever they needed. As he lay dying, relatives came to see the eighty-three-year-old, asking him to leave his small farm to them—to be told, sternly, that they had never worked it and therefore had no right to it. The land was left to the peasant who had tilled it. Donatello was buried in S. Lorenzo, near the resting place of Cosimo. His tomb has disappeared.

S I E N E S E   A R T , associated with the names of four great painters and scores of lesser ones, went its own way, and that was both its strength and its undoing. Traditional foe of rich and mighty Florence, which it defeated in the bloody battle of Montaperti (1260), sung by Dante, the little Republic of Siena sat amidst its hills, withdrawn and introspective—a crowded brickscape spiky with towers. Its Gothic town hall, Palazzo Pubblico, overlooking the bowl-shaped Campo, scene of the *Palio* horse races to this day; its cliff-like palaces lining dark, narrow streets; and its white-and-dark-green marble cathedral, still make it a unique, stubbornly medieval city. Here, native talent stirred around 1200. A strong Byzantine streak, brought in perhaps by artists fleeing Constantinople—which the Crusaders sacked and occupied in 1204—and reinforcing the old Byzantine foundation common to much Italian art, runs through Sienese painting. Its telltale signs are rigid attitudes, stiff gestures, elongated and boneless hands, and stylized faces with almond eyes. And though the Byzantine eventually yielded to the Gothic, dominant in Italian fourteenth-century painting, and implanted here by such outsiders as Nicola and Giovanni Pisano, it did not altogether disappear. Most of the painting is religious—Siena nurtured innumerable saints. But, side by side with piety, there is a showy aspect to Sienese art, favoring fastidious clothes, decorative detail, and much gold. The leading painters of the Sienese School are Duccio di Buoninsegna (c. 1255–c. 1319), Simone Martini (c. 1283–1344), and the brothers Lorenzetti—Pietro (c. 1280–c. 1348) and Ambrogio (c. 1285–c. 1348). We hear but little about their lives. Of Duccio we know that, of his seven children, four became painters. The record also indicates that he was a troublesome character, often cited for debt; fined for various offenses, such as refusing military service and an oath of allegiance; and even suspected of sorcery. The establishment must have forgiven him. His large (13.5 x 7 ft) *Maestà* (Madonna enthroned among saints and angels) was finished after thirty-two months of work in 1311, and carried in solemn procession from his studio to the cathedral, whose high altar it decorated for the next 194 years. (Now in the cathedral museum.) In this grandiose creation, painted on wood, Duccio combines Byzantine rigor with a new, subtle but pronounced, humanity and with an elegance of line and strength of color that are his very own—revealing an imaginative genius whose hand ennobles all it touches. The Virgin is set apart from the packed crowd of grave-faced celestial figures not only by her size but by her soft expression and by the timid tenderness with which she holds the child. Siena had placed herself under the special protection of the Virgin after Montaperti, and the Madonna was the most painted subject in the embattled city-state. Only four years after the completion of Duccio's altarpiece, Simone Martini, his pupil, and his junior by a quarter-of-a-century, painted another *Maestà*—Siena's first major fresco—for the town hall. The very breath of this enchanting work is Gothic. The figures are more lightly posed, more delicately contoured, less powerfully massed, than Duccio's. Grace takes the place of monumentality. This Queen of Heaven seems a queen of Gothic France, or of a court of love, listening to the song of troubadours. Two kneeling angels offer her baskets of roses and lilies. On the opposite wall of the great hall rides the Sienese captain, *Guidoriccio,* painted by Simone in 1329, the very image of medieval chivalry, reconnoitering the terrain around two rebel fortresses he has just taken. (In fact, the caparisoned horse he is riding had been killed during the fighting.) Simone's third major work—done in collaboration with his brother-in-law, Lippo Memmi—is a golden vision of the *Annunciation* (Florence, Uffizi), whose delicacy of design makes its protagonists, Angel and Virgin, appear translucent and dematerialized. Simone, also the author of a fresco cycle of the life of St. Martin in Assisi's Basilica of St. Francis, spent the last four years of his life at the papal court in Avignon. There he met Petrarch, for whom he painted a (perhaps imaginary) portrait of the poet's adored Laura. From Avignon, his fame spread through Northern Europe. Out of the multitude of Sienese painters of the fourteenth century, the Lorenzetti brothers stand forth as vigorous leaders; their work presents us with a naturalism, a solidity, a sense of action, heretofore unknown in Sienese art. Pietro's tragic *Deposition from the Cross,* at Assisi, is a case in point. His younger brother, Ambrogio, is best known for his frescoes in the Siena town hall, allegories of *Good and Bad Government.* (The latter is largely destroyed.) The most important non-religious picture cycle of the time, the paintings demonstrate, in storybook fashion, what happens under good and bad regimes, as filtered through the master's observing eye. In the "city" portion of *Good Government,* we are looking at a resurrection of old Siena—a crenelated town, where silk-robed maidens dance, workmen and artisans ply their trades, pack animals bring in rich merchandise, while the adjoining "country" scene reflects the same security, the same contentment, of a busy, prosperous peasantry amidst well-cultivated fields, vineyards, and olive groves. (Never before in Italian painting had mere landscape gained such prominence of place.) These scenes of human bliss and toil are watched over by a company of good spirits, among them Justice, Prudence, Temperance, with *Pax* ("Peace") attracting our eye above all others. Dressed in white, crowned with a laurel wreath, this languorous blond woman reclines on a cushion spread over discarded armor. She resembles, in surprising detail, an allegory of *Arcadia* discovered in Pompeii, which

Ambrogio could not possibly have known, but which, in turn, may have descended from a Hellenistic model with which he was familiar. Both Lorenzettis are thought to have died in the Black Death which carried off 27,000 of Siena's 42,000 inhabitants. But was the plague the reason for the decline of Siena's art? Some scholars think it was. After it, Siena, provincial and repetitive, forfeited her renown as an artistic center.

SIGNORELLI, Luca (c. 1445–1523). Painter. Little is known about the artistic training of this master, who was born and died in Cortona (Tuscany), and may have been a pupil of Piero della Francesca. His vivid naturalism and nervous energy, however, point to Antonio Pollaiuolo (1431–98), the Florentine goldsmith, painter, sculptor, whose works he closely studied. One of his finest paintings, the Greek god *Pan,* probably painted for Lorenzo the Magnificent, was destroyed in Berlin during World War II. His frescoes of the Last Judgment in the cathedral of Orvieto, created in 1499–1502 under the spell of Savonarola's apocalyptic sermons, impressed Michelangelo, whose own *Last Judgment* they prefigure. Signorelli follows Dante's vision of the *Inferno,* but adds nightmarish touches of his own when he depicts the end of the world, with fires, earthquakes, tumbling structures; demons, possessed of foul-colored, athletic bodies, viciously torturing the damned; and, above all, a terrifyingly suave Antichrist, bearing Christ's features, working devilish miracles before his fall. Many of Signorelli's nudes, risen or damned, are shown in drastically foreshortened postures, their muscles bulging and their sinews strained, revealing his command of both perspective and anatomy. (When his favorite son died young, he painted him, in dry-eyed sorrow, in the nude.) Signorelli was courteous, soft-spoken, affectionate, a kind teacher, and respected by all those who knew him.

————<◆>————

T A L K I N G   S T A T U E S . Rome is a city of statues, six of which used to "talk." Known as the "Congress of Wits," they served Rome's living wits as silent spokesmen for acrimonious dissent. The elusive marble congress was both a safety valve, allowing citizens to get unorthodox opinions and grievances off their chests, and a sounding board for the vox pop. Gracing nooks and corners in the city center, these ancient Roman monuments were male and female busts and figures, most of them badly mauled by time, and known by such nicknames as *Baboon, Madama Lucrezia, Abbot Luigi.* Anonymous lampoons, many in dialogue form, were affixed to them, and became the talk of Rome. All of the statues are still there, but have long lost their function to graffiti and the press. The club's most celebrated member was *Master Pasquino,* the mutilated torso of a two-man group—perhaps heroes of the *Iliad*—standing at a corner off Piazza Navona. A copy of a work of the third century B.C., it was dug up c. 1500 and soon became the favorite platform for outspoken critics of the ruling popes, who pinned their often humorous lampoons to Pasquino's willing pedestal. The best-remembered Pasquinade—in Latin—was aimed at the baroque Pope, Urban VIII (Barberini), who had removed the valuable bronze supports from under the roof of the Pantheon to cast cannon: *Quod non fecerunt barbari, fecerunt Barberini* ("What the barbarians didn't do, the Barberini did!") The metal left over from the Pope's artillery went into Bernini's Baldachin above the papal altar in St. Peter's.

TIEPOLO, Giambattista (1696–1770). Painter; grand master of the Venetian Baroque. His immortality is based both on the beauty of his easel paintings and on his illusionistic creations, in fresco or on canvas, adorning walls and ceilings in churches, palaces, and villas. He let his compositions extend terrestrial space into infinity, using, for many of his architectural foreshortenings (*quadratura*), the skill of Gerolamo Mengozzi Colonna (c. 1688–1772), an offshoot of the Bibiena school of trompe l'oeil. Tiepolo is known for his short, impulsive brush stroke. Although his art was influenced by such Venetian paintters as Paolo Veronese (1528–88), Sebastiano Ricci (1659–1734), and Giovanni Battista Piazzetta (1683–1754), he soon evolved a highly personal style. His palette, unrivaled for voluptuous color combinations, comprises silvery blues, an apple green, ruby and rose reds, and an inimitable ochre-yellow. His frescoes are alive with multitudes of figures, swarming through space, or grouped in fixed, theatrical arrangements. He makes the most of wind-whipped flags and spread-out angels' wings. Tiepolo's female figures, heavenly or profane, are haughtily provocative. He likes to show a naked leg dangling out of a casually upswept skirt. His character studies of bearded patriarchs betray his respect for Rembrandt (1609–69). The son of a part-owner of a merchant ship, who died soon after his birth, leaving the family well off, Giambattista was independent at the age of twenty-one and rapidly acquired fame. At the age of twenty-three, he married Cecilia, the sister of the painters Gianantonio and Francesco Guardi. They were to have nine children. Like many Venetian ladies, she liked to gamble at the Ridotto, Venice's casino, and is said to have gambled away some of her husband's drawings during a losing streak. Among Tiepolo's early works are the biblical frescoes in the archbishop's palace at Udine, some eighty miles northeast of Venice. Venice itself contains so many of his works that it takes several days to see them.

Outstanding among them are the nine canvases he painted for the ceiling of the Scuola dei Carmini, centered on the scene in which the Virgin bestows the scapular on St. Simon Stock. He decorated the ceiling of the Church of the Gesuati with a vertiginous composition of the *Institution of the Rosary by St. Dominic,* and that of the Church of the Pietà with an aerial *Coronation of the Virgin,* enlivened by a beautiful assortment of musical instruments. Tiepolo's festive scenes of Antony and Cleopatra in Palazzo Labia, with their theatrical costumes, are Venetian stagecraft at its most magnificent. (The greyhound in the embarkation scene belonged to a Venetian lady of Giambattista's acquaintance.) In Milan, Tiepolo decorated the big houses of the local gentry. Some of his most enjoyable frescoes are in the villas of the Venetian mainland, among them Villa Valmarana near Vicenza, with scenes from Homer, Virgil, Tasso, and Ariosto, and the Villa Pisani at Stra, on the Brenta Canal, now property of the Italian state, where he frescoed the ballroom ceiling with the *Apotheosis of the Pisani Family,* an illustrious Venetian line whose first (and only) doge, Alvise, had built the mansion. Contemporary portraits show Giambattista as a short, rotund, slightly stooped figure, with deep-set, prudent eyes, a fine, aquiline nose, and a small, sensuous mouth. He was usually attended by his devoted Moorish servant, probably brought to Italy by pirates, whom he converted from Islam to Christianity. Tiepolo acquired several mainland properties, including a spacious villa at Zianigo, where he went in the autumn with his family, and where he was hoping to spend his old age. Honored in his city and recognized as Europe's leading painter, Tiepolo was in demand throughout the continent. He missed a royal assignment in Stockholm because he asked what the Swedes considered an exorbitant price, and is said to have turned down a call from Saint Petersburg. In 1750, accompanied by two of his sons, the painters Giandomenico and Lorenzo, he went to Würzburg, in southwestern Germany, a city rich in culture and tradition, whose 360-room bishop's palace was built by the great Balthasar Neumann (1687–1753). During his three-year stay in the palace as guest of the reigning prince-archbishop, Karl Philip von Greiffenklau, Tiepolo decorated the ornate Kaisersaal ("Emperor's Hall") with frescoes of the Würzburg wedding of the Holy Roman emperor, Frederick Barbarossa (c. 1123–90), and Beatrice of Burgundy, the bride being escorted by Apollo in a chariot drawn by four white horses. On the ceiling over the main staircase, he painted a bombastic scene, typical of an age that glorified the sovereign ruler, in which the continents of the earth honor his patron, the prince-archbishop. (Another of his graceful greyhounds figures prominently in the fresco.) In these works, the perfect complement to Neumann's splendid architecture, Tiepolo reached the summit of his artistic development. After a nine-year, highly productive, interval in Venice, the master, now in his mid-sixties and tormented by gout, reluctantly accepted an invitation, reinforced by diplomatic pressure, from the Spanish court. Accompanied again by his two sons, he undertook the tedious, two-month journey to Madrid, where he was fated to spend the last eight years of his life. Four of them were taken up with work on the gigantic frescoes, executed at the behest of King Charles III, in the royal palace, among them the *Glory of Spain* (another baroque apotheosis) on the ceiling of the throne room. Made much of in Spain, busy with commissions, he kept sending money and presents to Cecilia in Venice, whom he hoped to rejoin—and whom he was not to see again. (She survived him by nine years.) But the last great Italian painter had outlived his time and, in the end, was overtaken by the neoclassical vogue. Two worlds were clashing, and the star of Anton Raffael Mengs (1728–79), the neoclassical painter who had come to Madrid a year before Tiepolo, was rising at the royal court. Tiepolo's altar paintings for the royal chapel at Aranjuez, near Madrid—perhaps his most spiritual creations—were replaced by insipid works by Mengs. They were Tiepolo's last paintings. He died—too suddenly to receive the last sacraments. His painter sons, being half Guardi and half Tiepolo, did not do badly for themselves. Giandomenico (1727–1804) created the lighthearted frescoes in the Foresteria ("guesthouse") of the Villa Valmarana, the pathetic *Stations of the Cross* at S. Polo in Venice, and a remarkable series of etchings of the *Flight into Egypt*. Lorenzo (1736–76), who remained in Madrid, is known for his fine black-and-white reproductions of his father's works.

———————◄◆►———————

TINTORETTO (Jacopo Robusti, 1518–94). Radical innovator of the Venetian school of painting. His father was a silk dyer, and when the boy first splashed his father's dyes onto the walls of his shop, neighbors called him *il tintoretto* ("the little dyer"). In later life, the artist—brisk, snub-nosed, round-eyed, beetle-browed, bearded—was known for his peppery personality. His speech was rough and straightforward. He was always ready to burst out laughing or fly into a rage. Tradition has it that he was apprenticed at the studio of Titian, but left after a few days. The adolescent watched the artisans painting wedding chests in St. Mark's Square, joined a team of construction workers whose fresh façades he decorated, and exhibited pictures in the Merceria, Venice's bazaar. Living in an age of religious ferment and much soul-searching—the age of the Counter Reformation —he found a new way of saying things. His medium was light— an eerie, sharply focused light that lent his work an other-worldly quality. In order to obtain the effect he desired, he placed wax figurines into a stage-like doll house whose walls were pierced with tiny holes; he darkened the room and lit a candle, which he moved around so that the shaft of light, directed one way or another, made the small phantoms come to life. It was in this ingenious manner that he invented his bold compositions. Before painting his many flying saints and angels, he dangled plaster figures from the ceiling and squinted up at them until he found the proper angle. Tintoretto was just thirty when he burst upon his city's demanding public with a histrionic picture, the *Miracle of the Slave,* commissioned by the Scuola Grande di San Marco, one of Venice's six great "schools," or charitable brotherhoods. Painted in oils on a large canvas (13.5 x 17.5), it illustrates a legend in which St. Mark, the city's patron saint, swoops from the sky to save a slave from torture. The slave, already stripped, lies on the ground, surrounded by an eager crowd, his body shown in sharp foreshortening. The saint, above, is rushing toward him—drawn, in all probability, from one of Jacopo's suspended dummies. So rapid is the action that the entire picture quivers with suspense, making the spectator feel that, if he glanced away for just an instant, all would be changed. The painting, one of his most famous works, stirred up an artistic controversy, then conquered Venice. Over the years, Tintoretto rounded out the story of St. Mark with four more large-sized canvases (four in Venice, Accademia; one in Milan, Brera). Tintoretto grew artistically as long as he lived. "The further you go out to sea," he once said of his art, "the more will the horizon widen." Disdaining the established method of covering the canvas with several smooth layers of thin paint, he used thick paint, laid on with rapid brush strokes. Colleagues called him *furioso* for the creative fury with which he worked. It was said that he "finished a picture before one knew he had started," and that he painted with three brushes—a gold, a silver, and a lead one, the last-named for his potboilers. He often improvised. Some of his canvases are strewn with *pentimenti* ("corrections")—canceled details, such as a foot, or a chin, visible even without X-rays. It was this spontaneity that touched his work with life. Many of his religious paintings were painted gratis. But he demanded high prices for his portraits of distinguished persons. Once, when a German sitter "forgot" to pay him, he asked, "How do you say 'money' in your language?" No price was stipulated for his *Paradise,* one of the largest oil paintings in existence—it measures 74 x 30 ft, contains 1,150 saintly figures, and was executed, in pieces later stitched together, for the Hall of the Grand Council in the doge's palace, where it still is. Tintoretto was then seventy years old. "Your Excellencies, pay me what you wish," he said to the pleased senators. But when the treasurer shelled out the gold coins, Tintoretto stayed his hand well before he had finished. "That is enough." He declined a knighthood offered him by King Henry III of France and a position at the ducal court of Mantua. "Too much to do in Venice." Happily married, he led a homey life in an unfashionable part of Venice and preferred simple clothes to the embroidered silk gowns his wife, Faustina, ordered for him. A talented musician, he invented curious instruments, which only he could play. Of his seven children, one, Domenico, became his chief assistant. The eldest girl, blonde Marietta (*la tintoretta*), who, as a child, dressed as a boy and carried her father's paint and brushes on his rounds, married a goldsmith. Jacopo's circle of close friends included a music master, a physician, and a playwright, Andrea Calmo, whose popular comedies the painter enlivened with fancy costumes. He idolized Michelangelo and sent for replicas of many of his sculptures. "Michelangelo's Design and Titian's Colors!" proclaimed a sign tacked to the wall of his studio, located in the most remote part of his rambling house. Many of his 700 odd surviving works remain in Venice, not a few of them in the churches for which they were originally painted. Some fifty biblical scenes, the result of twenty-four years of labor, grace walls and ceilings of the Scuola Grande di San Rocco, thus turned by him into one of Italy's major art galleries, a monument to his far-ranging genius. It was art for the people, for the poor and sick who drifted into the Scuola asking for alms; Tintoretto's holy personages were paupers, too. A self-portrait done in old age shows him white-bearded and white-haired, full of dignity and ripeness, gazing out on the world with steady, dark, unfathomable eyes (Paris, Louvre). He owned a little farm, a short boat ride from Venice, where he could watch the clouds and cultivate his garden. His painting of the *Last Supper* in S. Giorgio Maggiore (Venice), completed, perhaps, the year in which he died, aged seventy-six, shows a mystical blaze almost dissolving reality. Angels, gliding in through the ceiling (as Christ, in a brilliant halo, breaks bread), turn the scene into a vision of mankind's spiritual union with Divinity. Jacopo is buried in his parish church, Madonna dell'Orto ("of the Garden"), which, in his younger years, he had furnished with some of his most vigorous canvases, and where, in his last years, he had spent many hours of meditation. El Greco, Rembrandt, and the French Impressionists took up the brush he laid aside.

T I T I A N (Tiziano Vecelli, c. 1482–1576). Venetian painter, one of the most imposing figures of the Renaissance. He was born in Pieve di Cadore, in the foothills of the Alps, whose romantic landscapes appear in many of his paintings. His father was an inspector of mines. The boy studied painting in Venice under Giovanni Bellini and probably under Giorgione, whose influence pervades much of his early work. He was urbane, expansive, entertaining, highly intelligent, a fine musician. He shared with most Venetians a well-developed sense of business; he charged high fees, invested in real estate and jewels, and traded in timber from the region of his birth. Upon Giovanni Bellini's death in 1516, Titian, now Venice's unchallenged master artist, inherited his lucrative position as official painter to the republic. With his two intimates, Jacopo Sansovino, sculptor and architect, and Pietro Aretino, pamphleteer extraordinary, he formed an intellectul-artistic triumvirate that was to dominate Venetian taste for thirty years. Among his early paintings, remarkable for their lyric mood and dream-touched figures, are the *Concert champêtre* ("Pastoral Concert"), long attributed to Giorgione (Paris, Louvre), and the *Three Ages of Man* (Edinburgh, National Gallery, duke of Sutherland loan). "A truly Arcadian scene," art historian Johannes Wilde has called the latter. As commissions flowed into his studio from the lords of the land—the Este, della Rovere, Farnese—Titian became part of their circle. His *Sacred and Profane Love* of 1515 (Rome, Borghese) shows that he had absorbed the classical and humanistic standards of the Renaissance. In his thirties, he produced a series of major works, among them two large altarpieces for S. Maria Gloriosa dei Frari in Venice. In one of them, the *Madonna di Cà Pesaro,* he moved the Virgin—one of the loveliest ever painted—from her traditional place in the center to the right, making her the apex of a human pyramid. The earlier *Assunta* ("Assumption of the Virgin"), a stupendous composition in glowing reds, commands, from the apse, the nave of the vast Gothic church whose patroness she is. At roughly the same time, Titian painted three mythological scenes for Alfonso I d'Este of Ferrara. Titian's first meeting with the Holy Roman emperor Charles V in Bologna (1530) opened a new phase in his career. The monarch, then the most powerful man in Europe, took a liking to the artist. He had him paint his portrait in various poses, made him a knight of the Order of the Golden Fleece —intended only for royalty and high nobility—and never again allowed anyone else to paint him. According to legend, when

Titian dropped the wooden stick on which he rested his hand while painting, Charles picked it up, observing that there were plenty of crowned heads, but just one Titian. The master's equestrian portrait of the emperor (Madrid, Prado), riding to his victory at Mühlberg (1547) dressed in the armor he wore that day, is the image of a man who hates what he is doing. (When, in 1557, Charles retired to the Spanish Monastery of San Geronimo de Yuste, he took with him a Titian painting of the Trinity.) A full-length portrait of Charles' only son, King Philip II of Spain (Madrid, Prado), holds up a mirror to a bigoted, inhibited, lonely prince—the purchaser of some of Titian's most voluptuous nudes. Among the finest of his seventy-odd surviving likenesses are that of the doge Andrea Gritti (Washington, D.C., National Gallery); of Pier Luigi Farnese, Paul III's militant son, who sent his armor to the painter's studio for the picture (Naples, Capodimonte); the coldly beautiful *La Bella* (Florence, Pitti); of a man with a blue quilted sleeve (London, National Gallery); of a man with a glove (Paris, Louvre); of a man with a flute (Detroit, Institute of Art). He painted Pope Paul III three times (Naples, Capodimonte). Titian's female nudes, such as his *Danaë* (Madrid, Prado), *Venus and Adonis* and *Venus with the Luteplayer* (both New York, Metropolitan), all dating from his sixties and seventies, established him as one of the most sensual painters of flesh in the history of painting. In his *Rape of Europa* (Boston, Gardner), he barely stays within the bounds of propriety. Yet, in this robust male there dwelt a deeply spiritual force. The *Presentation of the Virgin in the Temple* (Venice, Accademia), perhaps his most beloved painting—"Little Mary" to Venetians—centers upon an almost diaphanous, golden-haloed, small creature in a long blue dress, floating up an enormous flight of stairs. And such somber works as the *Mocking of Christ* (Munich, Alte Pinakothek), which was one of four Titians owned by Tintoretto; the *Entombment* (Paris, Louvre); and the *Pietà* (Venice, Accademia), thought to have been painted for Titian's own tomb, plumb rarely penetrated depths of feeling. According to the painter Palma il Giovane (1544–1628)—who finished the *Pietà*—Titian often composed his figures "in four strokes" on a thick underpainting, then left the canvas, face to wall, for months, while working on some other projects; looking at it, at last, as if it were a "mortal enemy," he'd remove disturbing details "like a surgeon," apply several layers of color, and end up painting with his fingers rather than with the brush. In his old age, Titian—like Michelangelo—evolved an entirely new idiom, freed from Renaissance convention. His *Annunciation* (Venice, San Salvatore) consists of utterly untrammeled smears of gold and brown that bring to mind the ageing Rembrandt; it is signed *fecit fecit*—"made it made it"—after his name, absentmindedly, or to impress the viewer with his astonishing vitality. Before he died, during an outbreak of the plague, Titian was one of Europe's most illustrious personages. By his wife Cecilia—long his mistress—he had two sons, Orazio and Pomponio, and a daughter, Lavinia. Orazio helped him with his work in his last years, as did other pupils in his busy studio. His two surviving self-portraits (Madrid, Prado and West Berlin, Dahlem), show an aristocratic white-beard, with bulging forehead and sunken cheeks.

T R I U M P H . The ceremonial, jubilant, barbaric entry of a victorious general and his legions into Rome—ancient Rome's highest tribute to a victor. Its origins are lost. The Latin word *triumphus* may derive from the Greek *thriambos,* a processional hymn to Dionysos, god of wine. Romulus, first of Rome's seven kings (eighth century B.C.), is said to have celebrated a triumph after personally slaying Acron, king of an enemy tribe. Later, strict requisites were laid down for the granting of a triumph by the Senate. The victory of the returning general had to be decisive, ending a war. At least 5,000 of the enemy had had to be slain in battle. The victor may not enter Rome at once, but must encamp outside the walls with all his army, not an easy thing to do to soldiers longing for home or city life. (Cicero, after his victorious return from Asia Minor, waited for several days, but got no triumph.) The Senate formally debates the matter and, if so inclined, decrees a triumph, defraying the expenses.

A holiday is declared, the streets are decorated, and the procession forms in the Campo Marzio ("Field of Mars"). It is headed by the Senate as a body, followed by a military band leading a string of wagons laden with booty. Particularly precious items, such as looted statues, are carried aloft, interspersed with signboards bearing names and pictures of the conquered cities. Next, led by fluteplayers, come the white bulls with gilded horns that will be sacrificed to Jupiter. Next, priests. Next, arms and banners taken from the enemy, and, perhaps, exotic beasts. Next, captive notables and princes with their families, trembling for their lives, trailed by the common prisoners of war—to be sold as slaves—stumbling along in chains. And now, at last, preceded by a bodyguard of lictors—officers of the law—the *triumphator,* standing in a chariot drawn by four horses abreast. He wears a laurel wreath, a purple tunic, and a gold-embroidered toga. (In early times, his face was daubed with red.) Behind him stands a slave, holding a golden crown over his head, and whispering, *"hominem memento te"* ("remember you are only human!"). The legions, in battle dress and marching order, bring up the rear, singing victory songs or hurling raucous jokes and insults at their chief—part of the game. As the procession turns into the road curving up to the Capitol, the enemy dignitaries are led to the nearby dungeon, to be slaughtered with their families. (One of the few distinguished captives spared was Queen Zenobia of Palmyra, Syria, who, after appearing in the triumph of the emperor Aurelian in 274, was given an estate in Tivoli and married to a Roman senator.) The procession halts at the Temple of Jupiter, where the *triumphator,* after presiding over the sacrifice of bulls, is feted at a banquet, while food, loot, money, and sometimes grants of land are distributed among the soldiers. As night falls, the exhausted hero is piped home by torchlight. Up to the time of Constantine (fourth century), Rome saw some 350 triumphs. Julius Caesar, in 47 B.C.—three years before he was assassinated—held four triumphs in a single month. In the first, in honor of his victory over Gaul (France), forty elephants walked in his pageant, but he nearly fell off his chariot when its axle broke, hardly a good omen. In another, for his lightning victory at Zile (Asia Minor), he displayed the famous inscription, *VENI VIDI VICI* ("CAME SAW WON"). Of uncertain origin, like the triumph itself, is the triumphal arch, perhaps an evolution of the yoke—*jugum,* an arch of spears erected on the battlefield under which the defeated army was made to pass, hence, "subjugate." Of thirty-six triumphal arches built in Rome for the processions to pass through—flimsy improvisations later replaced by solid structures—three still stand: the Arch of Titus, built after 81, showing the seven-armed candlestick taken from the Temple of Jerusalem; the Arch of Septimius Severus, victor over Parthians and Arabs, built in 203; and the Arch of Constantine, built in 315 in honor of his victory ("by the sign of the Cross") over his rival, Emperor Maxentius. All three are tall, marble-clad monuments, adorned with statues and reliefs of triumphs and other martial themes. Triumphs continued throughout the Middle Ages and the Renaissance. The classicizing Holy Roman emperor, Frederick II, was given a triumph in Rome in 1220. The emperor Charles V, after conquering Tunisia, in 1536 held a triumph whose preparations were entrusted to the architect Antonio da Sangallo the Younger (1483–1546), who is said to have pulled down two hundred houses and three churches to clear a road through the untidy city. Triumphs were held in many cities by local princes vying with one another for the most faithful emulation of antiquity. But a new concept of the triumph was emerging. Italian humanism lifted the martial pageant to the realm of pure ideas. Piero della Francesca painted two allegories on the backs of his two Montefeltro portraits in the Uffizi. Duke Federigo and his wife, Battista Sforza, ride separately on triumphal wagons driven by cupids—the armored duke's, drawn by two snow-white chargers; the Duchess's, by unicorns, symbols of chastity. The cardinal and theological Virtues are their fellow travelers. In paintings, tapestries, reliefs, Renaissance art, under the influence of Neoplatonism, blossomed into a profusion of "triumphs"—triumphs of Love, of Fame, of Time, of Chastity. Among the zodiacal allegories painted by Francesco del Cossa (c. 1435–c. 1477) and others for the Hall of the Months in Duke Borso d'Este's Schifanoia Palace at Ferrara is an elaborate *Triumph of Venus,* with the fully-dressed goddess enthroned on a fantastic float drawn over silver-green waves by swans, while a chained knight kneels before her and beautiful young people disport themselves on shore, some making gentle love. Other deities—Apollo and the Muses, Minerva, Mercury—hold triumphs of their own, seated on chariots drawn by strange beasts, such as baboons and griffins. Here is the Renaissance at its most pagan and its most delightful. In contrast to such celebrations stand the surviving late medieval frescoes of the *Triumph of Death,* best seen in Pisa (*Camposanto*) and Palermo (National Gallery). Their exact dates and attributions are debated. Though Petrarch, too, exalted Death Triumphant in his *Triumphs,* these Gothic nightmares, with their rotting corpses and their sporting youths mowed down by a merciless reaper, stem from the mood of anguish and despair that courses through medieval Europe—a mood expressed in the (probably Franciscan) sequence *Dies irae* ("Day of Wrath") still used in Catholic Masses for the Dead; and reinforced by the "Black Death" of 1348. In their sinister beauty, these paintings remind us that, even in Caesar's Rome, the triumph was a ritual of death.

UNIVERSITY. Italy's contribution to the growth of higher education is of venerable date. As early as A.D. 1000, a university-level school of medicine existed at the port of Salerno, southern Italy—known to the modern traveler as the terminal of the Amalfi Drive. It flourished for three centuries. Frequented by students from many countries, it benefited from translations of heretofore unknown Arabic texts. Its graduate physicians were eagerly sought after. Many of them were Jews—among them the Middle Ages' foremost ophthalmologist, Benvenuto Grapheo—whose ability and knowledge established Jewish preeminence in the medical field for centuries to come. (Pope Alexander VI [1492–1503] had a Jewish doctor, Bonet de Lattes, who later also treated Leo X.) Bologna university, in existence before A.D. 1100, was, at first, limited to law. By 1200, medicine and philosophy were added, and, by the time of the Renaissance, its departments comprised theology, rhetoric, logic, Greek, and Hebrew. Starting as a loose aggregation of groups of students, whose professors taught at home or in rented halls, the university soon attained corporate status, and, in 1563, Cardinal (Saint) Charles Borromeo gave it a building of its own. It reached its zenith in the twelfth and thirteenth centuries, when its students—most of them foreigners—numbered 10,000. Dante, Petrarch, and Tasso studied at Bologna. The university's succession of illustrious teachers included many women, among them, in the fourteenth century, Novella d'Andrea, whose great beauty obliged her to lecture behind a screen. One of Bologna's thirteenth-century professors of medicine, Taddeo Alderotti, the leading physician of his age, published a surprisingly advanced textbook on hygiene—*On the Preservation of Health*—recommending plenty of exercise and special care of mouth and teeth. In 1306—the year in which Giotto finished painting his frescoes in Padua's Scrovegni Chapel—Prof. Mondino de Luzzi was the first to dissect, publicly, a human corpse, a practice which the Church had long opposed; he published the first textbook on anatomy. (Dogs, pigs, and monkeys were dissected before that time in order to gain some knowledge of the human body.) Padua university, founded in 1222 and known as *Il Bo,* soon rivaled Bologna's fame. Other early Italian universities are at Rome (founded in 1303), Perugia (1308), and Florence (1349).

VASARI, Giorgio (1511–74). Mannerist painter, Late-Renaissance architect, and chronicler. His *Lives of the Most Excellent Italian Architects, Painters, and Sculptors,* first published in 1550 and in an enlarged edition with *Painters* in the lead in 1568, remains our prime source for Italian medieval and Renaissance art history. Born in Arezzo (Tuscany), Vasari became a protégé of the Medici in Florence (his grandfather had restored Etruscan vases for Lorenzo the Magnificent), where he studied painting and received a broad humanistic education. Inquisitive, hard-working, endowed with a keen sense of values, he was ever ready to admire the creative genius which he considered a reflection of God's own creative power. Vasari carefully recorded the works of art he found in churches, monasteries, palaces, and private houses—there were no museums. He scooped up oral tradition where it was still alive, drawing on people's (sometimes blurred) memories of artists of the past. He had access to the private notes of Raphael and Ghiberti. Michelangelo reminisced for him. Knowing almost everybody in the field of culture, he interviewed collectors and artists up and down the country. He corresponded with observers north of the Alps. There gradually formed in him a concept of Italian art as one continuous crescendo: the visual arts, left fallow by the waning of antiquity, had sprung to life again in the thirteenth century, when artists shed the influence of medieval stereotypes. He states his premise clearly in his *Life of Giotto* (c. 1267–1337) who, he says, "broke with the clumsy Greek [Byzantine] manner, opening the way to modern, good painting, and reintroducing the art of accurately drawing living persons from nature." (Vasari has the distinction of having coined the term "Gothic" to define what he considered a "monstrous and barbarous style.") He looked upon Giotto, Brunelleschi, Masaccio, Leonardo da Vinci, as landmarks of increasing stature. Michelangelo is the only living artist and the last *Life* included in his first edition. The second edition adds many sixteenth-century figures, several of whom he personally knew, to end with a modest autobiography. It also erases the boundaries of his Florentine patriotism, admitting the Venetians and other strangers to his hall of fame. The pattern used attempts to list, describe, and evaluate the artist's works, while giving the reader an impression of his character and life, with precious background glimpses of the customs and history of the time. He dwells, with gusto, on eccentricities. Being no scientific biographer in the modern sense, and working with inadequate tools, Vasari is not always accurate. Some of his dates and attributions are wrong, and his zest for anecdote occasionally runs away with him at the expense of truth. Nor does his judgment always correspond to our own. Piero della Francesca leaves him indifferent—a lacuna that may be the cause of Piero's long neglect by art historians. Still, far more often than not, his appraisal of individual artists stands up remarkably well in the light of modern criticism, as does his view of the evolution of Italian art over a period of four centuries. He frequently warms to his subject, and many *Lives* of his contemporaries show intimacy and affection. Some of his anecdotes—may they be fact or fiction—are unforgettable. Here's Cimabue (c. 1240–c. 1302), journeying through Tuscany and stopping by the wayside to watch a shepherd boy named Giotto sketch one of his sheep with a sharp stone on a smooth rock with such extraordinary skill that he asks the little fellow's father for permission—gladly granted—to take him to his Florence workshop and make a painter out of him. There's Donatello (c. 1386–1466), proudly showing his close friend Brunelleschi the wooden crucifix he has made (Florence; S. Croce), only to be told that it's a yokel he has crucified, not Jesus—the most perfect of all men. "Well, take a piece of wood and make a crucifix yourself!" says Donatello; whereupon Brunelleschi carves the superb crucifix now in S. Maria Novella. When Titian came to Rome, Vasari took time off to be his cicerone. Later, he visited the ageing master—"still painting busily"—in his Venetian palace, and "had great pleasure looking at his works and conversing with him." Vasari had made friends with Michelangelo, thirty-six years his senior, as a young man in Florence, and was, perhaps, the first to see in him not merely the best artist of his age, but one of superhuman measure—"the rarest and most divine of men." Michelangelo seems to have allowed him, willingly, to invade his solitude. The master's human side comes through in—possibly invented—episodes like the one in which he gives the final touches to his giant *David,* with Pier Soderini, gonfalonier (head of state) of Florence, looking on and criticizing the statue's nose. Obligingly, the sculptor climbs the scaffold, chisel in hand, and, making a tapping sound, lets some marble powder dribble down. "Better?" he asks. "Much better," says the pompous official. "You've given it life!" Particularly moving is the vignette of Michelangelo's old age, when he works late at night on the marble *Pietà* now in Florence's Opera del Duomo. Recognizing Vasari's knock, he comes to open the door holding a lantern. But, noting that his visitor is looking at the botched left leg of Christ (Michelangelo later removed it), he drops the light, plunging the studio into darkness, and gently leads his friend back to the door. When Vasari sent him a copy of the first edition of his work, Michelangelo acknowledged it with a gracious sonnet, predicting eternal fame for the author who had rekindled long-extinguished memories. After Michelangelo's death, Vasari designed his tomb in S. Croce. Vasari's private art collection, begun when he was seventeen, comprised numerous drawings by Michelangelo, given him by the master throughout the years of their long friendship, along with works by Giotto, Piero di Cosimo, Giorgione, and others. His own Mannerist frescoes may be seen in Florence's Palazzo Vecchio and his Arezzo house, which he bought in 1540. His best known architectural achievement is the Uffizi Palace, built to house the offices (*uffizi*) of the Medici administration, with the famous Corridor, borne aloft over Ponte Veechio to link the Uffizi with the Palazzo Pitti on the left bank of the Arno River. But it is through his *Lives* that he affects, in an infinity of ways, our understanding of the Renaissance.

VENETIAN ART. Venice seems made of light. Light, filtered through moist air, shines from its limpid skies, to be reflected by the waters of lagoon and Grand Canal, and spend itself in ripples on the gilded ceilings of its palaces. The city's history sets it apart from the rest of Italy. Ever since the fifth century, when mainlanders threatened by barbaric hordes took refuge on the swampy islands of the northern Adriatic, Venetians have shown distinctive characteristics. For many centuries, their city-state was a republic run by a plutocracy, which chose a doge who reigned with the aid of a grand council. Its many bell towers, and two of Europe's proudest structures—the Church of St. Mark's and the doge's palace (Ruskin called the latter, "the central building of the world")—gave it an aspect of splendor that astonished visitors. Its arsenal, or shipyard, described by Dante (*Inferno XXI*), was among the world's most famous. Its fleet carved out a Mediterranean empire whose outposts dotted Asia Minor. Its mercenaries conquered sprawling territories in northern Italy. Its golden sequins (from *zecca*, "mint"), first struck in the thirteenth century, circulated throughout Christendom. Its narrow lanes and its Rialto bridge were crowded with small shops. And the patrician merchants, in their palaces, accumulated Aladdinian treasure. Such is the background of Venetian art which was as much part of the city's fabric as its commerce. Though architects and sculptors lived and worked in Venice—Jacopo Sansovino (1486–1570); Andrea Palladio (1508–80); Vincenzo Scamozzi (1552–1616); Baldassare Longhena (1598–1682), and others—painting remains the undisputed, enchanting mistress of Venetian art. Among its sires were two non-Venetians—Piero della Francesca and Antonello da Messina (c. 1430–79). The latter, a Sicilian, had studied Flemish painting, especially the carefully-finished creations of Jan van Eyck (c. 1390–1441); his own style couples a stern realism—particularly in his masterful small portraits—with subtle luminosity. During his stay in Venice, 1475/6, his presence helped local art break out of its Byzantine-Gothic shell. He is said to have introduced oil painting to Venice. Venetian art asserted its peculiar vigor in a succession of illustrious names, from Giovanni Bellini (c. 1432–1516) to Giambattista Tiepolo (1696–1770). Its chief ingredients were a rendering of reality that made flesh look like flesh, velvet like velvet; a new feeling for nature, expressing itself in beguiling landscape backgrounds; a range of eye-delighting colors; and the inimitable light of Venice, caressing every object, every figure. The Bellini workshop, headed by three members of the family, with an aggregate lifespan of more than one hundred years, was basic to the evolution of this art. Jacopo (c. 1400–c. 1470) had worked in Florence, and his two surviving sketchbooks (Paris, Louvre, and London, British Museum) prove him an accomplished draftsman and meticulous observer. His two sons, Gentile (c. 1430–1507) and Giovanni, followed in his footsteps. His daughter, Nicolosia, married Andrea Mantegna. Gentile, official painter to the republic—a post in which he was succeeded, first by his brother, then by Titian—excelled at large views of Venice, with stately ceremonies and processions. He had the distinction of being sent to Constantinople, where he painted a portrait of Sultan Mahomet II (London, National Gallery). But it is in the works of Giovanni that the power of Venetian art unfolds. His mastery of composition, his ever-fresh inventiveness, his gift for evoking a poetic mood, make him one of Italy's sublime painters. Among his masterpieces are a *St. Francis* (Frick, New York); a *Feast of the Gods* (Washington, D.C., National Gallery); a *Transfiguration* (Naples, Capodimonte); a *Sacred Allegory*, whose meaning has been lost, depicting a group of serene personages in a subliminal landscape (Florence, Uffizi); many portraits; and a multitude of large and small Madonnas. His long, active life, and his distinguished pupils—Titian, Palma il Vecchio, Giorgione—give him the stature of a father of the Venetian Renaissance. Such masters as Cima da Conegliano (c. 1460–c. 1517), Vittore Carpaccio (c. 1460–c. 1526), and Lorenzo Lotto (c. 1480–1556) are heavily indebted to him. Albrecht Dürer (1471–1528) called him "the best." Giovanni is said to have visited the German painter during the latter's stay in Venice to inspect his paint brushes, which, he thought, must be extraordinarily fine to create works like Dürer's. (They weren't.) We know regrettably little about Giorgione (Giorgio da Castelfranco, c. 1447–1510), who died, presumably of the plague, in the spring of his life. He had a reputation as a musician, and his known paintings seem pervaded with elusive music. Much of his output is lost, and only a handful of the works attributed to him can be termed authentic, among them the Madonna altarpiece in the parish church of Castelfranco near Venice; the *Tempest* (Venice, Accademia), whose protagonists—the half-nude woman with a baby, and the soldier—have puzzled generations of beholders; the *Three Philosophers* (Vienna, Kunsthistorisches Museum); and, probably, the *Adoration of the Shepherds* (Washington, D.C., National Gallery). Giorgione deeply marked the art of both Titian and Sebastiano del Piombo (c. 1485–1547). The latter moved to Rome, where Michelangelo provided drawings for some of his paintings, including the dramatic *Raising of Lazarus* (London, National Gallery). Venetian art reached a new pinnacle with Paolo Veronese (Paolo Caliari, 1528–88), a man of inexhaustible imagination and an expert at illusionistic perspective, who was commissioned to decorate part of the doge's palace, both before and after the fires of 1574 and 1577. Among his works are the magnificent illustrations of the story of Esther on the ceiling of the Church of St. Sebastian in Venice, and the frescoes of Palladio's Villa Maser on the Venetian mainland, which deceive the visitor with their trompe-l'oeil open doors and windows. Paolo painted festive entertainment scenes on a large scale, showing ladies and gentlemen, many of them portraits, in the rich costumes of the period. (In the Louvre's *Marriage at Cana* he presents himself, his brother Benedetto, Titian, and Tintoretto as a musical quartet.) His propensity for mixing the sacred and the profane alerted the Inquisition, which asked him why he had introduced décolleté ladies, a Negro waiter, dwarfs, dogs, and German soldiers into his *Last Supper*. An artist, Veronese answered, painted as he pleased, citing Michelangelo's nudes in the Sistine Chapel. He got away with making a few "decent" alterations and changing the objectionable picture's title. As the *Feast in the House of Levi,* the outsized canvas (42 x 18 ft.) is now in Venice's Accademia. The pageant of Venetian painting came to an end with the *Vedutisti,* painters of portable *vedute,* views of Venice—precursors of the picture postcard—turned out by the hundreds for foreigners on whose Grand Tour of Europe Venice was a must. Foremost among this gifted and commercial-minded tribe are Giovanni Antonio Canal (1697–1768), "Il Canaletto," who spent nearly ten years in London, and the more original, but less successful, Francesco Guardi (1712–93), whose impulsive brush-stroke anticipates the dash of the Impressionists. His figures, flitting gracefully across the canvas, are the contemporaries of Casanova and Goldoni, who were just then carrying the fame of Venice into the non-pictorial sphere. The old republic expired in 1797 as a result of the Napoleonic wars and came under the rule of Austria.

VESPUCCI, Simonetta née Cattaneo or Cattani (c. 1455–76). Blond mascot of the Renaissance, hailed for her grace and beauty. Born in "harsh Liguria"—either in Genoa or Portovenere, the "Port of Venus," source of amorous allusions to her beauty—she married the Florentine merchant Marco Vespucci, a distant relative of Amerigo, in 1472. Her Ligurian origin gave her an exotic aura, and she became the toast of Florence. Among her lovers—probably platonic—was Giuliano de' Medici, the handsome younger brother of Lorenzo the Magnificent. In an open-air tournament held in January 1475, at which she officiated as "Queen of Beauty," he displayed extraordinary valor and came out victorious. Politian (1454–94), protégé of the Medici, celebrated the event in a chivalresque poem, in which Giuliano discovers Simonetta in a fragrant forest and addresses her as "nymph or goddess," to which she modestly replies that she is "not divine." And Botticelli (c. 1444–1510) used Politian's sylvan verses, with their vivid imagery of Zephyr blowing upon Flora, whose footsteps make the flowers bloom, as the main theme of his mysterious *Spring*. Simonetta is thought to be present in the painting, either as Flora-Spring, or Venus, while Mercury, likely as not, portrays Giuliano. Thus, the young lady fixes a climactic moment in the Medicean springtide. Barely out of her teens, she died on 28 April 1476 and, beautiful even in death, was borne through the streets of mourning Florence. Just two years later, on 26 April 1478, Giuliano lay bleeding to death from twenty-nine dagger wounds in the cathedral. As for Marco Vespucci, he remarried, and died aged forty-four. Piero di Cosimo, who may have glimpsed Simonetta when he was a small boy, painted her portrait (Musée Condé at Chantilly, near Paris) some ten years after her death. It shows her barebreasted, her pallid, almost childlike face in profile, seen against lowering clouds. Pearls shimmer in her carefully coiffed hair. A snake curling around her lovely neck stretches its head toward its tail but does not touch it—a symbol of the uncompleted cycle of her life. (This picture, although inscribed with Simonetta's name, was long thought to represent Cleopatra, and there remains some doubt about the lady's true identity.)

VILLA AND GARDEN. Much of Italy's hidden charm lies in her villas. The term—dim. of Lat. *vicus,* "village" —signifies both a country house and its garden, often with a farm attached. The garden, like its aristocratic tenants, rose and lily, is an import from the East. Toward the end of the Republic, the urge to own and tame a piece of nature took hold of Roman townsmen. Cicero maintained, at one time, seven villas. Pliny the Younger (A.D. 62–c. 114) has left us an affectionate description of his seaside villa, with its cool vine arbor where it was pleasant to go barefoot, and its garden thick with mulberry and fig trees. Many discriminating Romans built villas on the Bay of Naples, near the cone of Mt. Vesuvius. Lucullus—soldier, intellectual, gourmet—owned a large, leafy garden in Rome itself. And Nero, besides his Vatican Hill property, had a vast landscaped park, enlivened by all kinds of wild and domestic animals, around his "Golden House" in downtown Rome. Antiquity's most celebrated country place is Hadrian's Villa near the modern Tivoli—a well-watered estate originally comprising about 750 acres, which the sophisticated emperor and art collector (A.D. 117–138) transformed into his own Forbidden City, complete with palaces, baths, colonnades, dark woods, and marble statues mirrored in sheets of water. Though ruined and despoiled, it remains one of the wonders of the Roman countryside. Its heart is a circular, arcaded pavilion surrounded by a moat, enclosing in its center a miniature garden with a fountain —the emperor's personal retreat. Here, then, we are already faced with that romantic twinning of art and nature that makes the spell of the Italian garden. Renaissance architects studied Hadrian's pleasure grounds, which thus became the model for villas built by princes, popes, and scholars. The great new burst of villa building, beginning with the new interest in classical antiquity, was to last some 300 years, leaving a legacy of villa gardens reaching from Sicily to the Alps. Much theorizing went into their layout, and major artists were employed in their creation. Leon Battista Alberti (1404–72), in his book on building, *De re aedificatoria,* gave useful directions to the villa-builder, advising him to select hillsides "overlooking the sea, or a great plain, and familiar hills." There are clusters of fine villas within reach of many cities. Frascati, in the Alban Hills, boasts half-a-dozen famous villas, among them the baroque Villa Aldobrandini, built for a papal nephew, and set in a terraced park affording views of the rich plain and distant Rome. Two splendid sixteenth-century villas adorn the landscape north of Rome: Villa Lante, with its glistening water stairway, and Caprarola, a massive pentagon with a lower and an upper park and a view of Mt. Soracte, heaving out of the plain, says Byron, "like a long-swept wave about to break." Favorite sites were inclines cooled by summer breezes, warmed by the winter sun, where terracing furnished the background for pergolas and statuary, topiaries, and alfresco eating. Water, gift of the gods in a hot country, was the garden's soul. It rose from fountains, tumbled down in silver cascades, trickled over the mossy sides of rustic grottoes. Venetians were partial to mazes and water games; the unsuspecting guests might rest on a marble bench or amble along shady paths, to be doused of a sudden by cold jets from hidden pipes. On the mainland, where Venice's merchant princes built some of Italy's finest villas, reigns the genius of Andrea Palladio (1508–80), designer of churches—Venice's Redentore and San Giorgio Maggiore—palaces, and public buildings. Adapting Roman temple architecture to private dwellings, he originated a style whose distinction lies in its classical proportions. His showpieces are the moody Villa "Malcontenta" on the Brenta Canal; the quiet Villa Maser, at Asolo, wondrously frescoed by Paolo Veronese; and Villa Capra ("La Rotonda") at Vicenza, a square, cupolaed, two-story structure, with an Ionic portico on each of its four sides, and a circular hall occupying much of the inner space—a most perfect building. Palladio's classic style has left a trail of stately homes all over the world. Inigo Jones (1573–1652) transplanted it to England. Thomas Jefferson's Monticello, near Charlottesville, Virginia, and many other porticoed patrician mansions in America's Old South, leave little doubt about their Palladian ancestry.

VIOLIN. Among Italy's gifts to mankind, the fiddle is a favorite. A bowed string instrument weighing some thirteen ounces, just small enough to fit between the player's chin and hand, it is the mainstay of the modern orchestra, plays the dominant role in chamber music, and gives off fireworks when sounded by a virtuoso. Meticulously put together from choice woods, it consists of more than seventy separate parts; even a slight modification of almost any one of them will change its timbre. Taken as a piece of wooden sculpture, it is nice to look at, having been perfected, curve by curve, by generations of masters who, being Italian, followed their native bent for visual beauty. Its similarity to the human torso is much in evidence—it has a "back," a "belly," "ribs," a "waist." Descending from a noble family of Asian instruments—the music of *The Arabian Nights*—which were known in Europe by the tenth century, it is a cousin of viola, cello, double bass. Its elder sister is the—less flexible and sonorous—*lira da braccio* (*braccio*, "arm"), played by those solemn little angels in Renaissance Madonna paintings; Raphael gave his Apollo in the Vatican Stanze a graceful *lira da braccio,* instead of the traditional plucked lyre. The violin was born, about 1530, in northern Italy. Both Brescia and Cremona were early centers of violin making, but it was at Cremona, a handsome old cathedral city on the north bank of the Po, that the instrument achieved maturity. Here, three families of craftsmen—Amati, Guarneri, Stradivari—made the world's finest violins from the sixteenth to the eighteenth centuries. Many of their lovingly handwrought instruments, unsurpassed to this day, are still in use. Andrea Amati, the founding father of Cremona's workshop industry, imparted to his instruments a sweet, soft voice that seemed to echo the whole range of human feelings. He made a set of twenty-four string instruments, among them several violins, for King Charles IX of France in 1566. His two sons, Antonio and Girolamo, continued his trade. It was his grandson, Niccolò (1596–1684), the great Amati, who taught both Andrea Guarneri and Antonio Stradivari how to make violins. Guarneri, his son Pietro, and in particular his nephew, Giuseppe (1687–c. 1744), called *del Gesù* ("of Jesus"), turned out a line of specimens noted for their bold contours and their robust tone. Cremona's most perfect instruments were made by the immortal Stradivari (c. 1643–1737). Having put his name to violins in Amati's workshop since his early twenties, he married a widow, bought a house in 1680, and, for more than half a century, created masterpieces, many of them commissioned by the ruling princes of his time. He was a tall, thin man, always wore a white cap and a white leather apron, and, thanks to his modest way of life, saved so much money that "rich as Stradivari" was a local saying. Given to experiments, he often varied curvature and thickness, selected different kinds of wood for their fine grain, and concentrated, for a while, on longer models. He paid attention to minuscule details. His soft, transparent varnish—protecting the wood from atmospheric changes, keeping it elastic, enhancing the instrument's sound, and giving it a glossy, reddish skin—is said to have been mixed and laid on by Antonio according to a secret formula. No two Stradivaris are alike. During his heyday—1700–1725—he produced violins whose sound was powerful, and tender. At least 500 of his violins survive, many bearing the names of famous owners. Of his eleven children, two sons, Francesco and Omobono, carried on their father's art but did not match his genius.

VIVALDI, Antonio (1678–1741). One of Italy's leading composers and violinists, he provides the accompaniment to the visual splendors of eighteenth-century Venice. Long forgotten, he was rediscovered early in the twentieth century. His violin concertos are among the most popular program numbers performed by soloists and orchestras throughout the world. (*Concerto:* a composition for several instruments.) He was born into a Venice rich in musical tradition. His father, Giovanni Battista, played the violin in the republic's orchestra at St. Mark's, and the promising boy no doubt received the best professional training available, though details of his education are not known. In his mid-twenties, he took Holy Orders. But, to his grief, his Masses were cut short by chronic asthma, aggravated by incense and the smoke of candles. The story that he interrupted Mass on one occasion and rushed to the sacristy in order to jot down a musical idea, then calmly returned to the altar, and that the Inquisition thereupon forbade him to say Mass, is probably legend. After three uncompleted services he was, at his request, exempted from his

priestly duties—which did not stop Venetians from calling him
il Prete Rosso ("the Red Priest") because of his red hair. A
contemporary engraving shows him wearing a modish wig over
a lively face with a remarkably high forehead, large eyes topped
by sharply-drawn eyebrows, and lips curled in an enigmatic
smile. Henceforth, his life was music. Venice, at the time, had
no fewer than seven opera houses. Music resounded from its
churches. And its large *Ospedale della Pietà,* a charitable institution caring for girl foundlings, functioned as a musical academy
and concert hall. Many of the girls might have been thrown
into a canal at birth had it not been for this venerable fourteenth-
century foundation, which instructed them, among other things,
in every branch of music, and discharged them with a dowry.
Vivaldi joined the Pietà as choir master. He held the post, with
major interruptions, for more than thirty years, during which
he directed the forty-piece orchestra as well as the choir, feeding
them his own compositions and constantly improving their quality. Under his guidance, the Pietà evolved into an experimental
workshop for some of the finest vocal and instrumental music
to be heard in Italy. Performing behind screens in the Ospedale's
chapel facing the Riva degli Schiavoni, the girls gave concerts
every Saturday night, and on Sundays after Mass; oratorios were
presented during Lent, when places of entertainment were closed.
(The Church of the Pietà, or of the Visitation, which now stands
on the spot, was built shortly after Vivaldi's death.) The doge
himself attended the annual Palm Sunday concert. And foreign
tourists simply hadn't been to Venice if they had not taken in a
Pietà performance. Vivaldi was under considerable pressure to
keep pace with this grueling schedule—audiences wanted to hear
something new—and it was said that he composed music more
rapidly than copyists could transcribe it. No wonder that, for all
his mastery, some of his works show signs of haste. He is credited
with about 580 orchestral compositions—concertos, oratorios,
and sonatas—plus forty-nine operas, twenty-seven of which were
first produced in Venice under his direction. Without the freedom
he bestowed on the violin, Niccolò Paganini's catlike antics on
that instrument, a century later, would have been inconceivable.
His concertos, with their alternation of ensembles and solos, made
musical history. Johann Sebastian Bach (1685–1750) adapted
several of them for harpsichord and organ. Recognized as a mas-

terly violinist and a uniquely sensitive orchestra director, Vivaldi was besieged by invitations and journeyed throughout Europe. He spent three years as music master at the court of Mantua, where the Gonzaga dukes had left a legacy of musical culture. At home, a member of the inner circle of intellectuals and artists, he was on friendly terms with Goldoni and the young Piranesi. Knowing few details of his life, we see him largely through his works, which combine grace with strength—the charm of Guardi and the rich palette of Tiepolo. Many of them address themselves to our sense of poetry. Vivaldi was, in fact, a gifted poet. Each of the four concertos known as the *Four Seasons*—perhaps his best loved work—is prefaced by a sonnet of his own. Listening to this famous cycle, we follow a poet's changing moods through the revolving year, from the elation of the first clear spring day, summer's ripe heat, autumn's feasting, to the crackling ice of winter. The Red Priest, who had earned large sums in his productive years, died poor in Vienna, and was buried in an unmarked grave.

Suggestions for Further Reading

———◆———

Ackerman, James S. *The Architecture of Michelangolo*. 2nd Edition, Revised. New York: Viking Press, 1966.
———. *Palladio*. Revised Edition. Baltimore: Penguin, 1977.
Acton, Harold. *The Last Medici*. Revised Edition. New York: Barnes & Noble Books, 1973.
Antal, Frederick. *Florentine Painting and Its Social Background*. New York: Harper & Row, 1975.
Athenaeus. *Deipnosophists*. 7 vols. (Loeb Classical Library). Cambridge, Mass.: Harvard University Press, nd.
Baldinucci, Filippo. *The Life of Bernini;* translated by Catherine Enggass. University Park, Pa.: Pennsylvania State University Press, 1966.
Barzini, Luigi. *The Italians*. New York: Atheneum, 1964.
Berenson, Bernard. *Italian Painters of the Renaissance*. (Landmarks in Art History Series). Ithaca, N.Y.: Cornell University Press, 1980.
Boccaccio, Giovanni. *The Decameron;* translated by G. H. Mc-William. Baltimore: Penguin, 1972, and other editions.
Boswell, James. *Boswell on the Grand Tour: Italy, Corsica, and France, 1765–1766;* edited by Frank Brady and Frederick A. Pottle. New York: McGraw-Hill, 1955.
Buonarroti, Michel Angelo. *The Sonnets of Michael Angelo Buonarroti;* translated by John Addington Symonds. New York: G. P. Putnam's Sons, 1902, and other editions.
Burckhardt, Jacob. *Civilization of the Renaissance in Italy*. 2 vols. New York: Harper & Row, nd., and other editions.
Casanova, Giacomo. *History of My Life;* translated by Willard R. Trask. 6 vols. New York: Harcourt Brace Jovanovich, 1967–1971.
Castiglione, Baldassare, conte. *The Book of the Courtier;* translated by George Bull. Baltimore: Penguin, 1976.
Cellini, Benvenuto. *Life of Benvenuto Cellini*. New York: E. P. Dutton, 1979.

Cicero, Marcus Tullius. *Works.* (Loeb Classical Library). Cambridge, Mass.: Harvard University Press, nd.

Clark, Kenneth. *Leonardo Da Vinci: An Account of His Development as an Artist.* Baltimore: Penguin, 1976.

————. *The Nude: A Study in Ideal Form.* Garden City, N.Y.: Doubleday, nd.

Clemens, Samuel Langhorne (Mark Twain). *The Innocents Abroad.* New York: New American Library, nd., and other editions.

Conant, Kenneth John. *Carolingian and Romanesque Architecture.* (Pelican History of Art Series). 4th Revised Edition, New York: Penguin, 1978.

Dante Alighieri. *The Divine Comedy;* translated by Dorothy L. Sayers. 3 vols. Baltimore: Penguin, 1950, 1955, 1962, and other editions.

D'Arms, John H. *Romans on the Bay of Naples: A Social and Cultural Study of the Villas and Their Owners from 150 B.C. to A.D. 400.* Cambridge, Mass.: Harvard University Press, 1970.

Decker, Heinrich. *Romanesque Art in Italy;* translated by James Cleugh. London: Thames & Hudson, 1958.

Dennis, George. *The Cities and Cemeteries of Etruria.* 2 vols. New York: E. P. Dutton, 1907.

de Tolnay, Charles. *Michelangelo.* 6 vols., including Vol. 1—The Youth of Michelangelo; Vol. 2—The Sistine Ceiling; Vol. 3—The Medici Chapel; Vol. 4—Tomb of Julius II; Vol. 5—The Final Period; Vol. 6—Michelangelo, Architect. Princeton, N.J.: Princeton University Press, 1969–1970. Also available in a one-volume condensation titled *Michelangelo: Sculptor—Painter—Architect.*

Douglas, Norman. *Old Calabria.* New York: Dodd, Mead, 1927.

Francis, of Assisi, Saint. *The Little Flowers of St. Francis,* being a translation of *I Fioretti di S. Francesco* by Thomas Okey. New York: E. P. Dutton, 1919, and other editions.

Freedberg, S. J. *Painting in Italy: 1500 to 1600.* (Pelican History of Art Series). New York: Viking Press, 1978.

Frontinus, Sextus J. *Stratagems and Aqueducts.* (Loeb Classical Library). Cambridge, Mass.: Harvard University Press, nd.

Goethe, Johann Wolfgang von. *Italian Journey, 1786–1788;* translated by W. H. Auden and Elizabeth Mayer. New York: Pantheon, 1962.

Gregorovius, Ferdinand. *Rome and Medieval Culture: Selections from History of the City of Rome in the Middle Ages;* edited by K. F. Morrison. (Classic European Historians Series). 1894; Reprint. Chicago: University of Chicago Press, 1971.

Hale, John Rigby. *Machiavelli and Renaissance Italy.* London: English Universities Press, 1961.

Hare, Augustus J. C. *Walks in Rome.* 8th American Edition. New York: G. Routledge & Sons, 1882.

Haskell, Francis. *Patrons and Painters: A Study of the Relations between Italian Art and Society in the Age of the Baroque.* Revised Edition. New Haven, Ct.: Yale University Press, 1980.

Haskell, Francis, and Penny, Nicholas. *Taste and the Antique: The Lure of Classical Sculpture 1500–1900.* New Haven and London: Yale University Press, 1981.

Honour, Hugh. *Neo Classicism.* New York: Penguin, 1978.

Italian Renaissance Studies; A Tribute to the Late Cecilia M. Ady, edited by E. F. Jacob. London: Faber & Faber, 1960.

Jerome, Saint. *Select Letters.* (Loeb Classical Library). Cambridge, Mass.: Harvard University Press, nd.

Krautheimer, Richard. *Early Christian and Byzantine Architecture.* (Pelican History of Art Series). New York: Penguin, 1979.

———. *Studies in Early Christian, Medieval and Renaissance Art.* New York: New York University Press, 1969.

———. *Rome: Profile of a City, 312–1308.* Princeton, N.J.: Princeton University Press, 1980.

Lavin, Irving. *Bernini and the Unity of the Visual Arts.* Oxford: Oxford University Press, nd.

Lavin, Marilyn Aronberg. *Piero della Francesca: The Flagellation.* New York: Viking Press, 1972.

Leppmann, Wolfgang. *Winckelmann.* New York: Knopf, 1970.

McCarthy, Mary. *The Stones of Florence.* New York: Harcourt Brace Jovanovich, 1963.

———. *Venice Observed.* New York: Harcourt Brace Jovanovich, 1963.

Machiavelli, Niccolò. *The Prince.* New York: New American Library, 1952, and other editions.

Mack Smith, Denis. *Medieval Sicily (800–1713).* New York: Viking Press, 1968.

Mainstone, Rowland J. *Developments in Structural Form.* Cambridge, Mass.: M.I.T. Press, 1975.

Mantegna, Andrea. *Mantegna: Paintings, Drawings, Engravings;* Complete Edition by Erica Tietze-Conrat. London: Phaidon Press, 1955.

Massingham, Hugh and Pauline Massingham (Editors). *The Englishman Abroad.* London: Phoenix House, 1962.

Masson, Georgina. *The Companion Guide to Rome.* London: Collins, 1965.

————. *Italian Gardens.* New York: Abrams, 1961.

Meiss, Millard. *The Great Age of Fresco: Discoveries, Recoveries, and Survivals.* New York: G. Braziller, in association with the Metropolitan Museum of Art, 1970.

————. *The Painter's Choice: Problems in the Interpretation of Renaissance Art.* New York: Harper & Row, 1977.

————. *Painting in Florence and Siena after the Black Death: The Arts, Religion and Society in the Mid-14th Century.* Princeton, N.J.: Princeton University Press, 1951.

Millon, Henry A. *Baroque and Rococo Architecture.* (Great Ages of World Architecture Series). New York: G. Braziller, 1961.

————. *Key Monuments of the History of Architecture.* Englewood Cliffs, N.J.: Prentice-Hall, 1964.

Norwich, John Julius. *The Kingdom in the Sun, 1130–1194.* London: Faber & Faber, 1977; Distributed in the U.S. by Merrimack Book Service.

————. *The Other Conquest.* New York: Harper & Row, 1967. Published in Great Britain as: *The Normans in the South, 1016–1130.*

Origo, Iris, marchesa. *The Merchant of Prato, Francesco di Marco Datini, 1335–1410.* New York: Knopf, 1957.

Panofsky, Erwin. *Meaning in the Visual Arts.* Garden City, N.Y.: Doubleday, 1974.

————. *Problems in Titian, Mostly Iconographic.* New York: New York University Press, 1969.

————. *Renaissance and Renascences in Western Art.* New York: Harper & Row, 1972.

————. *Studies in Iconology: Humanistic Themes in the Art of the Renaissance.* New York: Harper & Row, 1972.

Partner, Peter. *Renaissance Rome: A Portrait of a Society, 1500–1559.* Berkeley, Calif.: University of California Press, 1977.

Pater, Walter. *The Renaissance: Studies in Art and Poetry;* edited by Donald L. Hill. Berkeley, Calif.: University of California Press, 1980.

Petronius Arbiter. *Satyricon.* Bound with *Apocolocyntosis* of Seneca. (Loeb Classical Library). Cambridge, Mass.: Harvard University Press, nd.

Pius II, pope. *Memoirs of a Renaissance Pope; the Commentaries of Pius II,* an abridgment; translated by Florence A. Gragg, edited by Leona C. Gabel. New York: G. P. Putnam's Sons, 1959.

Pliny the Elder. *Natural History;* edited by E. H. Warmington. 10

vols. (Loeb Classical Library). Cambridge, Mass.: Harvard University Press, nd.

Pliny the Younger. *Letters*. 2 vols. (Loeb Classical Library). Cambridge, Mass.: Harvard University Press, nd.

Plutarch. *The Parallel Lives*. 11 vols. (Loeb Classical Library). Cambridge, Mass.: Harvard University Press, nd.

Polo, Marco. *The Travels of Marco Polo*. Revised from Marsden's translation and edited with an Introduction by Manuel Komroff. New York: The Modern Library, 1931, and other editions.

Prager, Frank D. and Gustina Scaglia. *Brunelleschi: Studies of His Technology and Inventions*. Cambridge, Mass.: M.I.T. Press, 1970.

Redig de Campos, Deoclecio. *Wanderings among Vatican Paintings*. Rome: L. del Turco, 1961.

Ridolfi, Roberto. *The Life of Niccolò Machiavelli;* translated by Cecil Grayson. Chicago: University of Chicago Press, 1963.

Ruskin, John. *The Stones of Venice*. New York: E. P. Dutton, 1907, and other editions.

Schevill, Ferdinand. *The Medici*. New York: Harper & Row, nd.

Shearman, John K. G. *Mannerism*. New York: Penguin, 1978.

———. *Raphael's Cartoons in the Collection of Her Majesty the Queen, and the Tapestries for the Sistine Chapel*. London & New York: Phaidon Press, 1972.

Sitwell, Sacheverell. *Southern Baroque Art; A Study of Painting, Architecture and Music in Italy and Spain of the 17th and 18th Centuries*. London: G. Richards Ltd., 1924.

Suetonius. Lives of the Caesars. 2 vols. (Loeb Classical Library). Cambridge, Mass.: Harvard University Press, nd.

Symonds, John Addington. *Renaissance in Italy: The Age of the Despots*. New York: Charles Scribner's Sons, 1918. This forms volume one of the author's series *Renaissance in Italy* and was published in Great Britain as *The Age of the Despots*.

Taylor, Francis Henry. *The Taste of Angels, a History of Art Collecting from Ramses to Napoleon*. Boston: Little, Brown, 1948.

Trevelyan, Janet Penrose (Ward). *A Short History of the Italian People from the Barbarian Invasions to the Attainment of Unity*. Revised Edition. New York: G. P. Putnam's Sons, 1926.

Van Cleve, Thomas Curtis. *The Emperor Frederick II of Hohenstaufen, Immutator Mundi*. New York: Oxford University Press, 1972.

Vasari, Giorgio. *The Lives of the Painters, Sculptors and Architects*. 4 vols. (Everyman's Library). London: J. M. Dent & Sons Ltd., 1927, and other editions.

SUGGESTIONS FOR FURTHER READING

Virgil. *Eclogues, Georgics, Aeneid, Minor Poems.* 2 vols. (Loeb Classical Library). Cambridge, Mass.: Harvard University Press, nd.

Weiss, Roberto. *The Renaissance Discovery of Classical Antiquity.* Atlantic Highlands, N.J.: Humanities Press, 1969.

White, John. *The Birth and Rebirth of Pictorial Space.* 2nd Edition. London: Faber & Faber, 1967.

Wilde, Johannes. *Venetian Art from Bellini to Titian.* (Oxford Studies in the History of Art and Architecture Series). New York: Oxford University Press, 1974.

Wilton-Ely, John. *The Mind and Art of Giovanni Battista Piranesi.* London: Thames & Hudson, 1978.

Wind, Edgar. *Bellini's Feast of the Gods, a Study in Venetian Humanism.* Cambridge, Mass.: Published for the Harvard College Library by Harvard University Press, 1948.

—————. *Giorgione's Tempesta, with Comments on Giorgione's Poetic Allegories.* New York: Oxford University Press, 1969.

—————. *Michelangelo's Prophets and Sibyls.* Oxford: Oxford University Press, 1965.

—————. *Pagan Mysteries in the Renaissance.* 2nd Edition. New York: W. W. Norton, 1969.

Wittkower, Rudolf. *Art and Architecture in Italy, 1600 to 1750.* 2nd Revised Edition. (Pelican History of Art Series). Baltimore: Penguin, 1965.

—————. *Gian Lorenzo Bernini, the Sculptor of the Roman Baroque.* 2nd Edition. London: Phaidon Press, 1966.

INDEX

INDEX

INDEX

INDEX

INDEX